First NeuralGen Workshop: Methods for Optimizing and Evaluating Neural Language Generation

Minneapolis, Minnesota, USA
6 June 2019

ISBN: 978-1-5108-8777-0

NAACL HLT 2019

**NeuralGen Workshop: Methods for Optimizing and
Evaluating Neural Language Generation**

Proceedings of the First Workshop

June 6, 2019
Minneapolis, Minnesota

Introduction

NeuralGen is the first workshop on Methods for Optimizing and Evaluating Neural Language Generation, being held at NAACL 2019 in Minneapolis, Minnesota. The goal of this workshop is to discuss new frontiers for language generation that address some of the recurring problems in existing techniques (eg. bland, repetitive language). More specifically, this workshop is aimed at sharing novel modeling techniques that go beyond maximum likelihood training, new techniques for robust evaluation and interpretation of model output, and strategies for generalization of generation systems.

We are pleased to have received 42 submissions, covering a wide range of topics related to modeling, evaluation and analysis of novel generation systems. 17 of the submissions have been accepted into the final program (approximately 40% acceptance rate). The workshop schedule includes 11 archival papers and 17 poster presentations. We are also thankful to have seven invited speakers: Kyunghyun Cho, He He, Graham Neubig, Yejin Choi, Alexander Rush, Tatsunori Hashimoto, and Hal Daumé III. The workshop also includes a panel discussion from the speakers and spotlight talks for a selection of accepted papers.

We would like to thank our invited speakers, authors, and reviewers for contributing to our program. Additionally, we would like to express gratitude to our sponsors, who have been generous in supporting the workshop.

Antoine Bosselut, Asli Celikyilmaz, Srinivasan Iyer, Marjan Ghazvininejad, Urvashi Khandelwal, Hannah Rashkin, Thomas Wolf

Organizers:

Antoine Bosselut, University of Washington
Asli Celikyilmaz, Microsoft Research
Srinivasan Iyer, University of Washington
Marjan Ghazvininejad, Facebook AI Research
Urvashi Khandelwal, Stanford University
Hannah Rashkin, University of Washington
Thomas Wolf, HuggingFace

Steering Committee:

Yejin Choi, University of Washington and Allen Institute for AI
Dilek Hakkani-Tür, Amazon Research
Dan Jurafsky, Stanford University
Alexander Rush, Harvard University

Program Committee:

Adji Dieng, Columbia University
Matthew Peters, Allen Institute for AI
Alexander Rush, Harvard University
Maxwell Forbes, University of Washington
Andrew Hoang, University of Washington
Mohit Iyyer, University of Massachusetts, Amherst
Angela Fan, Facebook AI Research
Nelson Liu, University of Washington
Ari Holtzman, University of Washington
Ofir Press, University of Washington
Arun Chaganty, Eloquent Labs
Ondrej Dusek, Heriot-Watt University
Caiming Xiong, Salesforce Research
Po-Sen Huang, Deepmind
Chandra Bhagavatula, Allen Institute for AI
Ramakanth Pasunuru, University of North Carolina
Dallas Card, Carnegie Mellon University
Rik Koncel-Kedziorski, University of Washington
Daniel Fried, University of California, Berkeley
Roee Aharoni, Bar-Ilan University
Dinghan Shen, Duke University
Ronan Le Bras, Allen Institute for AI
Elizabeth Clark, University of Washington
Saadia Gabriel, University of Washington
Gabi Stanovsky, Allen Institute for AI
Sachin Mehta, University of Washington
He He, New York University
Sam Wiseman, Toyota Technological Institute at Chicago

Ioannis Konstas, Heriot-Watt University
Sebastian Gerhmann, Harvard University
Jan Buys, University of Washington
Siva Reddy, Stanford University
Jesse Dodge, Carnegie Mellon University
Spandana Gella, Amazon AI
John Wieting, Carnegie Mellon University
Tatsunori Hashimoto, Stanford University
Keisuke Sakaguchi, Allen Institute for AI
Terra Blevins, University of Washington
Lianhui Qin, University of Washington
Vered Shwartz, Bar-Ilan University
Lifu Huang, Rensselaer Polytechnic Institute
Verena Rieser, Heriot-Watt University
Maarten Sap, University of Washington
Yangfeng Ji, University of Virginia

Invited Speakers:

Kyunghyun Cho, New York University and Facebook AI Research
Yejin Choi, University of Washington and Allen Institute for AI
Hal Daumé III, University of Maryland and Microsoft Research
Tatsunori Hashimoto, Stanford University
He He, New York University and Amazon Web Services
Graham Neubig, Carnegie Mellon University
Alexander Rush, Harvard University

Table of Contents

Conference Program

Thursday, June 6, 2019

9:00–9:10   *Opening Remarks*

9:10–9:45   **Invited Talk: Kyunghyun Cho**

9:45–10:20   **Invited Talk: He He**

10:20–10:35   *Coffee Break*

10:35–11:10   **Invited Talk: Graham Neubig**

11:10–11:45   **Invited Talk: Yejin Choi**

11:45–13:15   *Lunch*

13:15–13:50   **Invited Talk: Alexander Rush**

13:50–14:15   **Spotlight Talks**

14:15–15:45   **Poster Session**

An Adversarial Learning Framework For A Persona-Based Multi-Turn Dialogue Model
Oluwatobi Olabiyi, Anish Khazane, Alan Salimov and Erik Mueller

DAL: Dual Adversarial Learning for Dialogue Generation
Shaobo Cui, Rongzhong Lian, Di Jiang, Yuanfeng Song, Siqi Bao and Yong Jiang

Towards Coherent and Engaging Spoken Dialog Response Generation Using Automatic Conversation Evaluators
Sanghyun Yi, Rahul Goel, Chandra Khatri, Tagyoung Chung, Behnam Hedayatnia, Anu Venkatesh, Raefer Gabriel and Dilek Hakkani-Tur

Jointly Measuring Diversity and Quality in Text Generation Models
Danial Alihosseini, Ehsan Montahaei and Mahdieh Soleymani Baghshah

15:45–16:20   Invited Talk: Tatsunori Hashimoto

16:20–16:55   Invited Talk: Hal Daumé III

16:55–17:55   Panel

17:55–18:00   *Closing Remarks*

An Adversarial Learning Framework For A Persona-Based Multi-Turn Dialogue Model

Oluwatobi Olabiyi
Capital One Conversation Research
Vienna VA
oluwatobi.olabiyi@capitalone.com

Anish Khazane
Capital One Conversation Research
San Fransisco CA
anish.khazane@capitalone.com

Alan Salimov
Capital One Conversation Research
San Fransisco CA
alan.salimov@capitalone.com

Erik T. Mueller
Capital One Conversation Research
Vienna VA
erik.mueller@capitalone.com

Abstract

In this paper, we extend the persona-based sequence-to-sequence (Seq2Seq) neural network conversation model to a multi-turn dialogue scenario by modifying the state-of-the-art hredGAN architecture to simultaneously capture utterance attributes such as speaker identity, dialogue topic, speaker sentiments and so on. The proposed system, phredGAN has a persona-based HRED generator (PHRED) and a conditional discriminator. We also explore two approaches to accomplish the conditional discriminator: (1) $phredGAN_a$, a system that passes the attribute representation as an additional input into a traditional adversarial discriminator, and (2) $phredGAN_d$, a dual discriminator system which in addition to the adversarial discriminator, collaboratively predicts the attribute(s) that generated the input utterance. To demonstrate the superior performance of phredGAN over the persona Seq2Seq model, we experiment with two conversational datasets, the Ubuntu Dialogue Corpus (UDC) and TV series transcripts from the Big Bang Theory and Friends. Performance comparison is made with respect to a variety of quantitative measures as well as crowd-sourced human evaluation. We also explore the trade-offs from using either variant of $phredGAN$ on datasets with many but weak attribute modalities (such as with Big Bang Theory and Friends) and ones with few but strong attribute modalities (customer-agent interactions in Ubuntu dataset).

1 Introduction

Recent advances in machine learning especially with deep neural networks has lead to tremendous progress in natural language processing and dialogue modeling research (Sutskever et al., 2014; Vinyals and Le, 2015; Serban et al., 2016). Nevertheless, developing a good conversation model capable of fluent interaction between a human and a machine is still in its infancy stage. Most existing work relies on limited dialogue history to produce response with the assumption that the model parameters will capture all the modalities within a dataset. However, this is not true as dialogue corpora tend to be strongly multi-modal and practical neural network models find it difficult to disambiguate characteristics such as speaker personality, location and sub-topic in the data.

Most work in this domain has primarily focused on optimizing dialogue consistency. For example, Serban et al. (2016, 2017b,a) and Xing et al. (2017) introduced a Hierarchical Recurrent Encoder-Decoder (HRED) network architecture that combines a series of recurrent neural networks to capture long-term context state within a dialogue. However, the HRED system suffers from lack of diversity and does not have any guarantee on the generator output since the output conditional probability is not calibrated. Olabiyi et al. (2018) tackles these problems by training a modified HRED generator alongside an adversarial discriminator in order to increase diversity and provide a strong and calibrated guarantee to the generator's output. While the hredGAN system improves upon response quality, it does not capture speaker and other attributes modality within a dataset and fails to generate persona specific responses in datasets with multiple modalities.

On the other hand, there has been some recent work on introducing persona into dialogue models. For example, Li et al. (2016b) integrates attribute embeddings into a single turn (Seq2Seq) generative dialogue model. In this work, Li et al. consider persona models, one with Speaker-only representation and the other with Speaker and Addressee representations (Speaker-Addressee model), both of which capture certain

Proceedings of the Workshop on Methods for Optimizing and Evaluating Neural Language Generation (NeuralGen), pages 1–10
Minneapolis, Minnesota, USA, June 6, 2019. ©2019 Association for Computational Linguistics

speaker identity and interactions. Nguyen et al. (2018) continue along the same line of thought by considering a Seq2Seq dialogue model with Responder-only representation. In both of these cases, the attribute representation is learned during the system training. Zhang et al. (2018) proposed a slightly different approach. Here, the attributes are a set of sentences describing the profile of the speaker. In this case, the attributes representation is not learned. The system however learns how to attend to different parts of the attributes during training. Still, the above persona-based models have limited dialogue history (single turn); suffer from exposure bias worsening the trade-off between personalization and conversation quality and cannot generate multiple responses given a dialogue context. This is evident in the relatively short and generic responses produced by these systems, even though they generally capture the persona of the speaker.

In order to overcome these limitations, we propose two variants of an adversarially trained persona conversational generative system, $phredGAN$, namely $phredGAN_a$ and $phredGAN_d$. Both systems aim to maintain the response quality of $hredGAN$ and still capture speaker and other attribute modalities within the conversation. In fact, both systems use the same generator architecture (PHRED generator), i.e., an $hredGAN$ generator (Olabiyi et al., 2018) with additional utterance attribute representation at its encoder and decoder inputs as depicted in Figure 1. Conditioning on external attributes can be seen as another input modality as is the utterance into the underlying system. The attribute representation is an embedding that is learned together with the rest of model parameters similar to Li et al. (2016b). Injecting attributes into a multi-turn dialogue system allows the model to generate responses conditioned on particular attribute(s) across conversation turns. Since the attributes are discrete, it also allows for exploring different what-if scenarios of model responses. The difference between the two systems is in the discriminator architecture based on how the attribute is treated.

We train and sample both variants of $phredGAN$ similar to the procedure for $hredGAN$ (Olabiyi et al., 2018). To demonstrate model capability, we train on a customer service related data such as the Ubuntu Dialogue Corpus (UDC) that is strongly bimodal between question poser and answerer, and transcripts from a multi-modal TV series *The Big Bang Theory* and *Friends* with quantitative and qualitative analysis. We examine the trade-offs between using either system in bi-modal or multi-modal datasets, and demonstrate system superiority over state-of-the-art persona conversational models in terms of human evaluation of dialogue response quality as well as automatic evaluations with perplexity, BLEU, ROUGE and distinct n-gram scores.

2 Model Architecture

In this section, we briefly introduce the state-of-the-art $hredGAN$ model and subsequently show how we derive the two persona versions by combining it with the distributed representation of the dialogue speaker and utterance attributes, or with an attribute discrimination layer at the end of the model pipeline.

2.1 $hredGAN$: Adversarial Learning Framework

Problem Formulation: The $hredGAN$ (Olabiyi et al., 2018) formulates multi-turn dialogue response generation as: given a dialogue history of sequence of utterances, $\boldsymbol{x_i} = \left(x_1, x_2, \cdots, x_i\right)$, where each utterance $x_i = \left(x_i^1, x_i^2, \cdots, x_i^{M_i}\right)$ contains a variable-length sequence of M_i word tokens such that $x_i{}^j \in V$ for vocabulary V, the dialogue model produces an output $y_i = \left(y_i^1, y_i^2, \cdots, y_i^{T_i}\right)$, where T_i is the number of generated tokens. The framework uses conditional GAN structure to learn a mapping from an observed dialogue history to a sequence of output tokens. The generator, G, is trained to produce sequences that cannot be distinguished from the ground truth by an adversarially trained discriminator, D akin to a two-player min-max optimization problem. The generator is also trained to minimize the cross-entropy loss $\mathcal{L}_{MLE}(G)$ between the ground truth x_{i+1}, and the generator output y_i. The following objective summarizes both goals:

$$G^*, D^* = \arg \min_G \max_D \left(\lambda_G \mathcal{L}_{cGAN}(G, D) + \lambda_M \mathcal{L}_{MLE}(G)\right). \tag{1}$$

where λ_G and λ_M are training hyperparamters and $\mathcal{L}_{cGAN}(G, D)$ and $\mathcal{L}_{MLE}(G)$ are defined in Eqs.

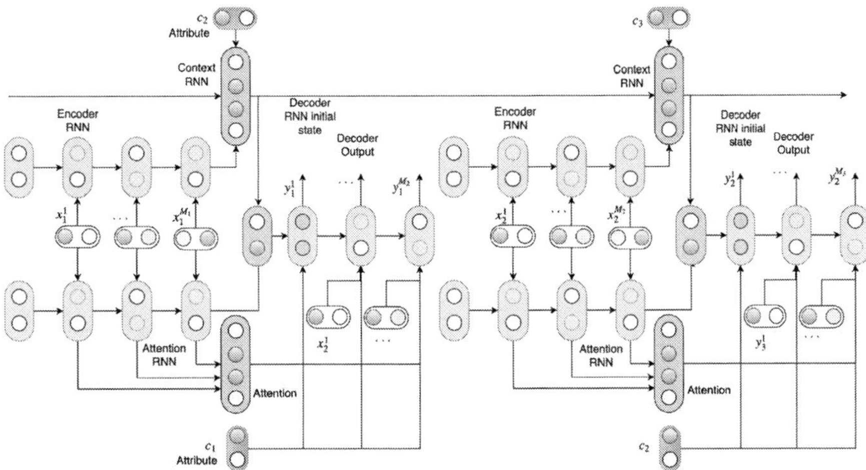

Figure 1: **The PHRED generator with local attention** - The attributes c, allows the generator to condition its response on the utterance attributes such as speaker identity, subtopics and so on.

(5) and (7) of Olabiyi et al. (2018) respectively. Please note that the generator G and discriminator D share the same encoder and embedding representation of the word tokens.

2.2 $phredGAN$: Persona Adversarial Learning Framework

The proposed architecture of $phredGAN$ is very similar to that of $hredGAN$ (Olabiyi et al., 2018). The only difference is that the dialogue history is now $\boldsymbol{x_i} = \big((x_1, c_1), (x_2, c_2), \cdots, (x_i, c_i)\big)$ where c_i is additional input that represents the speaker and/or utterance attributes. Please note that c_i can either be a sequence of tokens or single token such that $c_i{}^j \in Vc$ for vocabulary Vc. Also, at the ith turn, c_i and c_{i+1} are the source/input attribute and target/output attribute to the generator respectively. The embedding for attribute tokens is also learned similar to that of word tokens.

Both versions of $phredGAN$ shares the same generator architecture (PHRED) but different discriminators. Below is the highlight of how they are derived from the $hredGAN$ architecture.

Encoder: The context RNN, $cRNN$ takes the source attribute c_i as an additional input by concatenating its representation with the output of $eRNN$ as in Figure 1. If the attribute c_i is a sequence of tokens, then an attention (using the output of $eRNN$) over the source attribute representations is concatenated with the output of $eRNN$. This output is used by the generator to create a context state for a turn i.

Generator: The generator decoder RNN, $dRNN$ takes the target attribute c_{i+1} as an additional input as in Fig. 1. If the attribute c_{i+1} is a sequence of tokens, then an attention (using the output of $dRNN$) over the attribute representations is concatenated with the rest of the decoder inputs. This forces the generator to draw a connection between the generated responses and the utterance attributes such as speaker identity.

Noise Injection: As in Olabiyi et al. (2018), we also explore different noise injection methods.

Objective: For $phredGAN$, the optimization objective in eq. (1) can be updated as:

$$G^*, D^*_{adv}, D^*_{att} = arg \min_{G} \Big($$
$$\max_{D_{adv}} \lambda_{G_{adv}} \mathcal{L}^{adv}_{cGAN}(G, D_{adv})$$
$$+ \min_{D_{att}} \lambda_{G_{att}} \mathcal{L}^{att}_{c}(G, D_{att})$$
$$+ \lambda_M \mathcal{L}_{MLE}(G)\Big). \tag{2}$$

where $\mathcal{L}^{adv}_{cGAN}(G, D_{adv})$ and $\mathcal{L}^{att}_{c}(G, D_{att})$ are the traditional adversarial and attribute prediction loss respectively and dependent on the architectural variation. It is worth to point out that while the former is adversarial, the later is collaborative in nature. The MLE loss is common and can be expressed as:

$$\mathcal{L}_{MLE}(G) = \mathbb{E}_{x_{i+1}}[-log\, P_G\big(x_{i+1}|\boldsymbol{x_i}, c_{i+1}, z_i\big)]. \tag{3}$$

where z_i the noise sample and depends on the choice of either utterance-level or word-level noise input into the generator (Olabiyi et al., 2018).

2.3 $phredGAN_a$: Attributes as a Discriminator Input

$phredGAN_a$ shares the same discriminator architecture as the $hredGAN$ but with additional input, c_{i+1}. Since it does not use attribute prediction, $\lambda_{G_{att}} = 0$.

The adversarial loss, $\mathcal{L}_{cGAN}^{adv}(G, D)$ can then be expressed as:

$$\mathcal{L}_{cGAN}^{adv}(G, D_{adv}) =$$
$$\mathbb{E}_{\boldsymbol{x_i}, c_{i+1}, x_{i+1}}[\log D_{adv}(\boldsymbol{x_i}, c_{i+1}, x_{i+1})] +$$
$$\mathbb{E}_{\boldsymbol{x_i}, c_{i+1}, z_i}[1 - \log D_{adv}(\boldsymbol{x_i}, c_{i+1}, G(\boldsymbol{x_i}, c_{i+1}, z_i))]$$
$$(4)$$

The addition of speaker or utterance attributes allows the dialogue model to exhibit personality traits given consistent responses across style, gender, location, and so on.

2.4 $phredGAN_d$: Attributes as a Discriminator Target

$phredGAN_d$ does not take the attribute representation at its input but rather uses the attributes as the target of an additional discriminator D_{att}. The adversarial and the attribute prediction losses can be respectively expressed as:

$$\mathcal{L}_{cGAN}^{adv}(G, D_{adv}) = \mathbb{E}_{\boldsymbol{x_i}, x_{i+1}}[\log D_{adv}(\boldsymbol{x_i}, x_{i+1})]$$
$$+\mathbb{E}_{\boldsymbol{x_i}, z_i}[1 - \log D_{adv}(\boldsymbol{x_i}, G(\boldsymbol{x_i}, c_{i+1}, z_i))]$$
$$(5)$$

$$\mathcal{L}_c^{att}(G, D_{att}) = \mathbb{E}_{c_{i+1}}[-\log D_{att}(c_{i+1}|\boldsymbol{x_i}, x_{i+1})]$$
$$+\mathbb{E}_{c_{i+1}}[-\log D_{att}(c_{i+1}|\boldsymbol{x_i}, G(\boldsymbol{x_i}, c_{i+1}, z_i))]$$
$$(6)$$

Attribute Discriminator: In addition to the existing word-level adversarial discriminator D_{adv} from $hredGAN$, we add an attribute discriminator, D_{att}, that discriminates on an utterance level to capture attribute modalities since attributes are assigned at utterance level. The discriminator uses a unidirectional RNN (D_{attRNN}) that maps the input utterance to the particular attribute(s) that generated it. The attributes can be seen as hidden states that inform or shape the generator outputs. The attribute discriminator can be expressed as:

$$D_{att}(c_{i+1}|\boldsymbol{x_i}, \chi) = D_{attRNN}(\boldsymbol{h_i}, E(\chi)) \quad (7)$$

where $E(.)$ is the word embedding lookup (Olabiyi et al., 2018), $\chi = x_{i+1}$ for groundtruth and $\chi = y_i$ for the generator output.

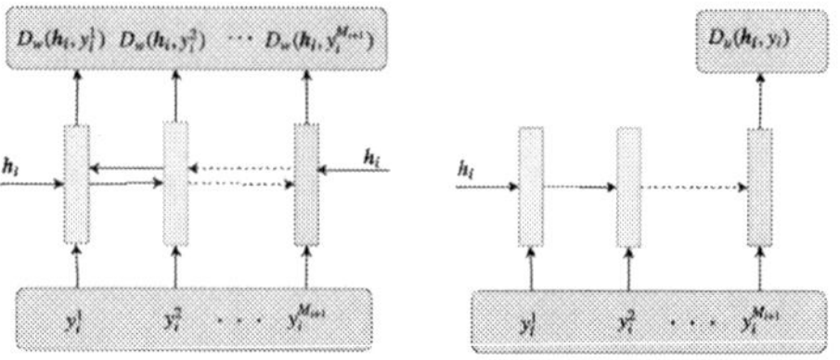

Figure 2: **The $phredGAN_d$ dual discriminator - Left:** D_{adv} is a word-level discriminator used by both $phredGAN_a$ and $phredGAN_d$ to judge normal dialogue coherency as in $hredGAN$. **Right:** D_{att}, an utterance-level attribute discriminator is used only in $phredGAN_d$ to predict the likelihood a given utterance was generated from a particular attribute.

3 Model Training and Inference

3.1 Model Training

We train both the generator and the discriminator (with shared encoder) of both variants of $phredGAN$ using the training procedure in Algorithm 1 (Olabiyi et al., 2018). For both variants, $\lambda_{G_{adv}} = \lambda_M = 1$, and for $phredGAN_a$ and $phredGAN_d$, $\lambda_{G_{att}} = 0$ and $\lambda_{G_{att}} = 1$ respectively. Since the encoder, word embedding and attribute embedding are shared, we are able to train the system end-to-end with back-propagation.

Encoder: The encoder RNN, $eRNN$, is bidirectional while $cRRN$ is unidirectional. All RNN units are 3-layer GRU cell with hidden state size of 512. We use word vocabulary size, $V = 50,000$ with word embedding size of 512. The number of attributes, Vc is dataset dependent but we use an attribute embedding size of 512. In this study, we only use one attribute per utterance so there is no need to use an attention mechanism to combine the attribute embeddings.

Generator: The generator decoder RNN, $dRNN$ is also a 3-layer GRU cell with hidden state size of 512. The $aRNN$ outputs are connected to the $dRNN$ input using an additive attention mechanism (Bahdanau et al., 2015).

Adversarial Discriminator: The word-level discriminator RNN, D_{RNN} is a bidirectional RNN, each 3-layer GRU cell with hidden state size of 512. The output of both the forward and the backward cells for each word are concatenated and passed to a fully-connected layer with binary output. The output is the probability that the word is from the ground truth given the past and future words of the sequence, and in the case of $phredGAN_a$, the responding speaker's embed-

Algorithm 1 Adversarial Learning of phredGAN

Require: A generator G with parameters θ_G.
Require: An adversarial discriminator D_{adv} with parameters $\theta_{D_{adv}}$.
Require: An attribute discriminator D_{att} with parameters $\theta_{D_{att}}$.
Require: Training hyperparameters, $isTarget$, $\lambda_{G_{att}}$, $\lambda_{G_{adv}}$, and λ_M.

  for number of training iterations **do**
    Initialize $cRNN$ to zero_state, h_0
    Sample a mini-batch of conversations, $x = \{x_i, c_i\}_{i=1}^{N}$, $x_i = ((x_1, c_1), (x_2, c_2), \cdots, (x_i, c_i))$ with N utterances. Each utterance mini batch i contains M_i word tokens.
    for $i = 1$ **to** $N - 1$ **do**
      Update the context state.
$$h_i = cRNN(eRNN(E(x_i)), h_{i-1}, c_i)$$
      Compute the generator output similar to Eq. (11) in (Olabiyi et al., 2018).
$$P_{\theta_G}\left(y_i|, z_i, x_i, c_{i+1}\right) = \left\{ P_{\theta_G}\left(y_i^j | x_{i+1}^{1:j-1}, z_i^j, x_i, c_{i+1}\right) \right\}_{j=1}^{M_{i+1}}$$
      Sample a corresponding mini batch of utterance y_i.
$$y_i \sim P_{\theta_G}\left(y_i|, z_i, x_i, c_{i+1}\right)$$
    end for
    Compute the adversarial discriminator accuracy D_{adv}^{acc} over $N - 1$ utterances $\{y_i\}_{i=1}^{N-1}$ and $\{x_{i+1}\}_{i=1}^{N-1}$
    if $D_{adv}^{acc} < acc_{D_{adv}^{th}}$ **then**
      if $isTarget$ **then**
        Update $phredGAN_d$'s $\theta_{D_{adv}}$ and $\theta_{D_{att}}$.
$$\sum_i [\nabla_{\theta_{D_{adv}}} \log D_{adv}(h_i, x_{i+1}) + \nabla_{\theta_{D_{adv}}} \log(1 - D_{adv}(h_i, y_i)) + \nabla_{\theta_{D_{att}}} - \log D_{att}(c_{i+1}|h_i, x_{i+1})]$$
      else
        Update $phredGAN_a$'s $\theta_{D_{adv}}$ with gradient of the discriminator loss.
$$\sum_i [\nabla_{\theta_{D_{adv}}} \log D_{adv}(h_i, c_{i+1}, x_{i+1}) + \nabla_{\theta_{D_{adv}}} \log(1 - D_{adv}(h_i, c_{i+1}, y_i))]$$
      end if
    end if
    if $D_{adv}^{acc} < acc_{G_{th}}$ **then**
      Update θ_G with the generator's MLE loss only.
$$\sum_i [\nabla_{\theta_G} - \log P_{\theta_G}\left(y_i|, z_i, x_i, c_{i+1}\right)]$$
    else
      Update θ_G with attribute, adversarial and MLE losses.
$$\sum_i [\lambda_{G_{att}} \nabla_{\theta_G} - \log D_{att}(c_{i+1}|h_i, y_i) + \lambda_{G_{adv}} \nabla_{\theta_G} \log D_{adv}(h_i, c_{i+1}, y_i) + \lambda_M \nabla_{\theta_G} - \log P_{\theta_G}\left(y_i|, z_i, x_i, c_{i+1}\right)]$$
    end if
  end for

---

gradient descent algorithm. Finally, the model is implemented, trained, and evaluated using the TensorFlow deep learning framework.

3.2 Model Inference

We use an inference strategy similar to the approach in Olabiyi et al. (2018).

For the modified noise sample, we perform a linear search for α with sample size $L = 1$ based on the average word-level discriminator loss, $-log D_{adv}(G(.))$ (Olabiyi et al., 2018) using trained models run in autoregressive mode to reflect performance in actual deployment. The optimum α value is then used for all inferences and evaluations. During inference, we condition the dialogue response generation on the encoder outputs, noise samples, word embedding and the attribute embedding of the intended responder. With multiple noise samples, $L = 64$, we rank the generator outputs by the discriminator which is also conditioned on encoder outputs, and the intended responder's attribute embedding. The final response is the response ranked highest by the discriminator. For $phredGAN_d$, we average the confidences produced by D_{adv} and D_{att}.

4 Experiments and Results

In this section, we explore the performance of PHRED, $phredGAN_a$ and $phredGAN_d$ on two conversational datasets and compare their performances to non-adversarial persona Seq2seq models (Li et al., 2016b) as well as to the adversarial $hredGAN$ (Olabiyi et al., 2018) with no explicit persona.

4.1 Datasets

TV Series Transcripts dataset (Serban et al., 2016). We train all models on transcripts from two popular TV drama series, Big Bang Theory and Friends. Following a similar preprocessing setup in Li et al. (2016b), we collect utterances from the top 12 speakers from both series to construct a corpus of 5,008 lines of multi-turn dialogue. We split the corpus into training, development, and test set with a 94%, 3%, and 3% proportions, respectively, and pair each set with a corresponding attribute file that maps speaker IDs to utterances in the combined dataset.

Due to the small size of the combined transcripts dataset, we first train the models on the larger Movie Triplets Corpus (MTC) by Banchs

ding.

Attribute Discriminator: The attribute discriminator RNN, $D_{att RNN}$ is a unidirectional RNN with a 3-layer GRU cell, each of hidden state size 512. A softmax layer is then applied to project the final hidden state to a prespecified number of attributes, V_c. The output is the probability distribution over the attributes.

Others: All parameters are initialized with Xavier uniform random initialization (Glorot and Bengio, 2010). Due to the large word vocabulary size, we use sampled softmax loss (Jean et al., 2015) for MLE loss to expedite the training process. However, we use full softmax for model evaluation. For both systems, parameters updates are conditioned on the word-level discriminator accuracy performance as in Olabiyi et al. (2018) with $acc_{D_{adv}^{th}} = 0.99$ and $acc_{G_{th}} = 0.75$. The model is trained end-to-end using the stochastic

(2012) which consists of 240,000 dialogue triples. We pre-train the models on this dataset to initialize the model parameters to avoid overfitting on a relatively small persona TV series dataset. After pre-training on MTC, we reinitialize the attribute embeddings in the generator from a uniform distribution following a Xavier initialization (Glorot and Bengio, 2010) for training on the combined person TV series dataset.

Ubuntu Dialogue Corpus (UDC) dataset (Serban et al., 2017b). We train the models on 1.85 million conversations of multi-turn dialogue from the Ubuntu community hub, with an average of 5 utterances per conversation. We assign two types of speaker IDs to utterances in this dataset: questioner and helper. We follow a similar training, development, and test split as the UDC dataset in Olabiyi et al. (2018), with 90%, 5%, and 5% proportions, respectively, and pair each set with a corresponding attribute file that maps speaker IDs to utterances in the combined dataset

While the overwhelming majority of utterances in UDC follow two speaker types, the dataset does include utterances that do not classify under either a questioner or helper speaker type. In order to remain consistent, we assume that there are only two speaker types within this dataset and that the first utterance of every dialogue is from a questioner. This simplifying assumption does introduce a degree of noise into each persona model's ability to construct attribute embeddings. However, our experiment results demonstrate that both $phredGAN_a$ and $phredGAN_d$ are still able to differentiate between the larger two speaker types in the dataset.

4.2 Evaluation Metrics

We use similar evaluation metrics as in Olabiyi et al. (2018) including perplexity, BLEU (Papineni et al., 2002), ROUGE (Lin, 2014), distinct n-gram (Li et al., 2016a) and normalized average sequence length (NASL) scores. For human evaluation, we follow a similar setup as Li et al. (2016a), employing crowd-sourced judges to evaluate a random selection of 200 samples. We present both the multi-turn context and the generated responses from the models to 3 judges and asked them to rank the general response quality in terms of relevance, informativeness, and persona. For N models, the model with the lowest quality is assigned a score 0 and the highest is assigned a score N-

1. Ties are not allowed. The scores are normalized between 0 and 1 and averaged over the total number of samples and judges. For each model, we also estimate the per sample score variance between judges and then average over the number of samples, i.e., sum of variances divided by the square of number of samples (assuming sample independence). The square root of result is reported as the standard error of the human judgement for the model.

4.3 Baseline

We compare the non-adversarial persona HRED model, PHRED with the adversarially trained ones, i.e. $hredGAN$, $phredGAN_a$ and $phredGAN_d$, to demonstrate the impact of adversarial training. Please note that no noise was added to the PHRED model.

We also compare the persona models to Li et al.'s work (Li et al., 2016b) which uses a Seq2Seq framework in conjunction with learnable persona embeddings. Their work explores two persona models in order to incorporate vector representations of speaker interaction and speaker attributes into the decoder of their Seq2Seq models i.e., Speaker model (SM) and Speaker-Addressee model (SAM). All reported results are based on our implementation of their models in Li et al. (2016b).

4.4 Hyperparameter Search

For both $phredGAN_a$ and $phredGAN_d$, we determine the noise injection method and the optimum noise variance α that allows for the best performance on both datasets. We find that $phredGAN_d$ performs optimally with word-level noise injection on both Ubuntu and TV transcripts, while $phredGAN_a$ performs the best with utterance-level noise injection on TV transcripts and word-level injection on UDC. For all $phredGAN$ models, we perform a linear search for optimal noise variance values between 1 and 30 at an increment of 1, with a sample size of $L = 1$. For $phredGAN_d$, we obtain an optimal α of 4 and 6 for the UDC and TV Transcripts respectively. For $phredGAN_a$, we obtain an optimal value of 2 and 5 for the combined TV series dataset and the much larger UDC respectively.

4.5 Results

We will now present our assessment of performance comparisons of $phredGAN$ against the

Table 1: $phredGAN$ vs. Li et al. (2016b) on BBT Friends TV Transcripts.

Model	Teacher Forcing	Autoregression				Human
	Perplexity	BLEU	ROUGE-2	DISTINCT-1/2	NASL	Evaluation
TV Series						
SM	**22.13**	1.76 %	22.4 %	2.50%/18.95%	0.786	0.5566 ± 0.0328
SAM	23.06	1.86 %	20.52 %	2.56%/18.91%	0.689	0.5375 ± 0.0464
$hredGAN$	28.15	2.14 %	6.81 %	1.85 %/6.93 %	1.135	0.5078 ± 0.0382
$phred$	30.94	2.41 %	14.03 %	0.66 %/2.54 %	1.216	0.3663 ± 0.0883
$phredGAN_a$	25.10	**3.07 %**	**30.47 %**	**2.19 %/19.02 %**	**1.218**	$\mathbf{0.6127 \pm 0.0498}$
$phredGAN_d$	28.19	2.76 %	14.68 %	0.70 %/4.76 %	1.163	0.4284 ± 0.0337

Table 2: $phredGAN$ vs. Li et al. (2016b) on UDC.

Model	Teacher Forcing	Autoregression				Human
	Perplexity	BLEU-2/4	ROUGE-2	DISTINCT-1/2	NASL	Evaluation
UDC						
SM	28.32	0.437%/$\sim$ 0%	9.19 %	1.61%/5.79%	0.506	0.4170 ± 0.0396
SAM	**26.12**	0.490%/$\sim$ 0%	10.23 %	1.85%/6.85%	0.512	0.4629 ± 0.0171
$hredGAN$	48.18	**2.16%**/$\sim$ 0%	11.68 %	**5.16%/18.21%**	1.098	$\mathbf{0.5876 \pm 0.0532}$
$phred$	34.67	0.16%/$\sim$ 0%	7.41%	0.56%/1.44%	0.397	0.4399 ± 0.0445
$phredGAN_a$	31.25	1.94%/$\sim$ 0%	**19.15%**	1.05%/5.28%	**1.520**	0.4920 ± 0.0167
$phredGAN_d$	28.74	2.02%/**0.10%**	16.82%	1.38%/5.77%	1.387	$\mathbf{0.5817 \pm 0.0615}$

baselines, PHRED, $hredGAN$ and Li et al.'s persona Seq2Seq models.

4.6 Quantitative Analysis

We first report the performance on TV series transcripts in table 1. The performance of both SM and SAM models in Li et al. (2016b) compared to the hredGAN shows a strong baseline and indicates that the effect of persona is more important than that of multi-turn and adversarial training for datasets with weak multiple persona. However, once the persona information is added to the $hredGAN$, the resulting $phredGAN$ shows a significant improvement over the SM and SAM baselines with $phredGAN_a$ performing best. We also observe that PHRED performs worse than the baseline S(A)M models on a number of metrics but we attribute this to the effect of persona on a limited dataset that results into less informative responses. This behavior was also reported in Li et al. (2016b) where the persona models produce less informative responses than the non-personal Seq2seq models but it seems to be even worse in multi-turn context. However, unlike the Speaker-Addressee and PHRED models that suffer from lower response quality due to persona conditioning, we note that conditioning the generator and discriminator of $phredGAN$ on speaker embeddings does not compromise the systems ability to produce diverse responses. This problem might have been alleviated by the adversarial training that encourages the generator model to produce longer, more informative, and diverse responses that have high persona relevance even with a limited dataset.

We also compare the models performances on the UDC. The evaluation result is summarized in table 2. While the deleterious effect of persona conditioning on response diversity is still worse with PHRED than with S(A)M models, we note that $hredGAN$ performs much better than the S(A)M models. This is because, the external persona only provides just a little more information than is already available from the UDC utterances. Therefore, performance on UDC is mostly driven by longer dialogue context and adversarial training. We also note an improvement of $phredGAN$ variants over the $hredGAN$ in a variety of evaluation metrics including perplexity, ROUGE with the exception of distinct n-grams. This is expected as $phredGAN$ should be generally less diverse than $hredGAN$ since each persona attribute of $phredGAN$ covers only a limited region of the data distribution. This, however, leads to better response quality with persona, something not achievable with $hredGAN$. Also, the much better ROUGE(F1) score indicates that $phredGAN$ is able to strike a better balance between diversity and precision while still capturing the characteristics of the speaker attribute modality in the UDC dataset. Within the $phredGAN$ variants, $phredGAN_d$ seems to perform better. This is not surprising as speaker classification is much easier on UDC than on TV series. The attribute discriminator, D_{att} is able to provide more informative feedback on UDC than on TV series where it is more difficult to accurately predict the speaker. Therefore, we recommend $phredGAN_a$ for datasets with weak attribute distinction and $phredGAN_d$ for strong attribute distinction.

4.7 Qualitative Analysis[1]

In addition to the quantitative analysis above, we report the results of the human evaluation in the last column of Tables 1 and 2 for the TV Series and UDC datasets respectively. The human evaluation scores largely agrees with the automatic evaluations on the TV Series with $phredGAN_a$ clearly giving the best performance. However, on the UDC, both $hredGAN$ and $phredGAN_d$ performs similarly which indicates that there is a trade off between diversity and persona by each model. We believe this is due to the strong persona information that already exists in the UDC utterances.

An additional qualitative assessment of these results are in Table 3 with responses from several characters in the TV series dataset and the two characters in UDC.

We see that for TV drama series, $phredGAN$ responses are comparatively more informative than that of the Speaker-Addressee model of Li et al. (2016b). For example, all the characters in the TV series respond the same to the dialogue context. Similar behavior is reported in Li et al. (2016b) where for the Speaker-Addressee model, nearly all the characters in the TV series respond with "Of course I love you." to the dialogue context, "Do you love me?" despite the fact that some of the responders sometimes have unfriendly relationship with the addressee. Many of the novel situations explored by $phredGAN$ are unachievable with the Speaker-Addressee model due to lack of informative responses. For example, by conditioning as Sheldon from The Big Bang Theory and asking "Do you like me?", our model responds with annoyance if conditioned as Penny ("No, you don't understand. You're an idiot"), brevity with

Leonard ("Yes?") and sarcasm with Raj ("Well , you know , we could be a little more than my friend's friends.") The wide range of responses indicate our model's ability to construct distinct attribute embeddings for each character even from a limited dataset. The other interesting responses in Table 3 indicate $phredGAN$'s ability to infer not only the context of the conversation but important character information about the addressee.

We also see similar results with our model's output on UDC in Table 4. We demonstrate that by conditioning as either a helper or questioner from the UDC dataset, $phredGAN$ models are able to respond differently to input utterances as well as stay close to the context of the conversation. For the purpose of completeness, we also show some samples from PHRED generator on both UDC and TV series dataset in Table 5.

5 Conclusion and Future Work

In this paper, we improve upon state-of-the-art persona-based response generation models by exploring two persona conversational models: $phredGAN_a$ which passes the attribute representation as an additional input into a traditional adversarial discriminator, and $phredGAN_d$ a dual discriminator system which in addition to the adversarial discriminator from $hredGAN$, collaboratively predicts the attribute(s) that are intrinsic to the input utterance. Both systems demonstrate quantitative improvements upon state-of-the-art persona conversational systems such as the work from Li et al. (2016b) with respect to both quantitative automatic and qualitative human measures.

Our analysis also demonstrates how both variants of $phredGAN$ perform differently on datasets with weak and strong modality. One of our future direction is to take advantage of $phredGAN_d$'s ability to predict utterance attribute such as speaker identity from just the utterance. We believe its performance can be improved even with weak modality by further conditioning adversarial updates on both the attribute and adversarial discriminator accuracies. Overall, this paper demonstrates clear benefits from adversarial training of persona generative dialogue system and leaves the door open for more interesting work in this domain.

---

[1]Tables 3, 4 and 5 referenced in this section are in the appendix.

References

D. Bahdanau, K. Cho, and Y. Bengio. 2015. Neural machine translation by jointly learning to align and translate. In *Proceedings of International Conference of Learning Representation (ICLR 2015)*.

R. E. Banchs. 2012. Movie-dic: A movie dialogue corpus for research and development. In *Proceedings of the 50th Annual Meeting of the Association for Computational Linguistics*, pages 203–207.

X. Glorot and Y. Bengio. 2010. Understanding the difficulty of training deep feedforward neural networks. In *International conference on artificial intelligence and statistics*.

S. Jean, K. Cho, R. Memisevic, and Y. Bengio. 2015. On using very large target vocabulary for neural machine translation. In *arXiv preprint arXiv:1412.2007*.

J. Li, M. Galley, C. Brockett, J. Gao, and B. Dolan. 2016a. A diversity-promoting objective function for neural conversation models. In *Proceedings of NAACL-HLT*.

J. Li, M. Galley, C. Brockett, G. Spithourakis, J. Gao, and B. Dolan. 2016b. A persona-based neural conversation model. In *Proceedings of the 54th Annual Meeting of the Association for Computational Linguistics*, pages 994–1003.

C. Y. Lin. 2014. Rouge: a package for automatic evaluation of summaries. In *Proceedings of the Workshop on Text Summarization Branches Out*.

H. Nguyen, D. Morales, and T. Chin. 2018. A neural chatbot with personality. In *Stanford NLP Course website: https://web.stanford.edu/class/cs224n/ reports/2761115.pdf*.

O. Olabiyi, A. Salimov, A. Khazane, and E. Mueller. 2018. Multi-turn dialogue response generation in an adversarial learning framework. In *arXiv preprint arXiv:1805.11752*.

K. Papineni, S. Roukos, T. Ward, and W. Zhu. 2002. Bleu: A method for automatic evalution of machine translation. In *Proceedings of the 40th Annual Meeting of the Association for Computational Linguistics*, pages 311–318.

I. Serban, A. Sordoni, Y. Bengio, A. Courville, and J. Pineau. 2016. Building end-to-end dialogue systems using generative hierarchical neural network models. In *Proceedings of The Thirtieth AAAI Conference on Artificial Intelligence (AAAI 2016)*, pages 3776–3784.

I. V. Serban, T. Klinger, G. Tesauro, K. Talamadupula, B. Zhou, Y. Bengio, and A. Courville. 2017a. Multiresolution recurrent neural networks: An application to dialogue response generation. In *Proceedings of The Thirty-first AAAI Conference on Artificial Intelligence (AAAI 2017)*.

I. V. Serban, A. Sordoni, R. Lowe, L. Charlin, J. Pineau, A. Courville, and Y. Bengio. 2017b. A hierarchical latent variable encoder-decoder model for generating dialogue. In *Proceedings of The Thirty-first AAAI Conference on Artificial Intelligence (AAAI 2017)*.

I. Sutskever, O. Vinyals, and Q. Le. 2014. Sequence to sequence learning with neural networks. In *Proceedings of Advances in Neural Information Processing Systems (NIPS)*, pages 3104–3112.

O. Vinyals and Q. Le. 2015. A neural conversational model. In *Proceedings of ICML Deep Learning Workshop*.

C. Xing, W. Wu, Y. Wu, M. Zhou, Y. Huang, and W. Ma. 2017. Hierarchical recurrent attention network for response generation. In *arXiv preprint arXiv:1701.07149*.

S. Zhang, E. Dinan, J. Urbanek, A. Szlam, D. Kiela, and J. Weston. 2018. Personalizing dialogue agents: I have a dog, do you have pets too? In *arXiv preprint arXiv:1801.07243v3*.

A   Appendix

Table 3: $hredGAN$ vs $phredGAN$ vs Li et al. (2016b) on TV Transcripts

Model	Speaker	Response
Big Bang Theory TV Series		
Context_0	Sheldon	Do you like me?
$phredGAN_a$	Leonard	Yes ?
$phredGAN_d$	Leonard	You can ' t do that ? !
$phredGAN_a$	Penny	No , you don ' t understand . You ' re an idiot .
$phredGAN_d$	Penny	You ' re right . . .
$phredGAN_a$	Howard	Well , I don ' t know what to say . This is the part I ' ve ever seen .
$phredGAN_d$	Howard	You ' re right , you ' re just gonna go with this guy .
$phredGAN_a$	Raj	Well , you know , we could be a little more than my friends ' s friends .
$phredGAN_d$	Raj	You know . I can ' t can ' t do I can ' go , I can ' t do that . . .
SM	L/P/H/R[2]	Yeah , I ' m sure . Oh , but I can ' t believe it . I ' m not gonna be in here
SAM	L/P/H/R	I ' m not going to be a good time .
$hredGAN$	NA	Okay , I ' m gonna go see my friend .
Context_0	Howard	We can't go home.
Context_1	Leonard	Alright, I'll be right back.
$phredGAN_a$	Howard	Okay , well , before you and Penny get out and get married with Penny just get married.
$phredGAN_d$	Howard	You ' ll see , I ' ll just go .
SM	Howard	Okay .
SAM	Howard	Okay , well , you ' re really good at this .
$hredGAN$	NA	Okay , I ' m gonna go see my old .
Context_0	Amy	Spent a lot of my childhood throwing coins into wishing wells hoping for friends.
Context_1	Penny	Whoa, whoa, give me a second to catch up here. Hold on.
Context_2	Amy	That'd be my boyfriend. Happier playing his dopey Star Trek game with his friends than hanging out with me.
$phredGAN_a$	Penny	You know , when you ' re being so nice about Sheldon and I want to take him to like his own girlfriend
$phredGAN_d$	Penny	You , I ' m sorry , I didn ' t have it . d be back in the bathroom . .
SM	Penny	I ' m sorry , I ' m sorry . I ' m just saying that you ' re going to have to answer to
SAM	Penny	It ' s not gonna happen .
$hredGAN$	NA	Okay , I ' m gonna go see my new .
Context_0	Sheldon	I recently read that during World War Two, Joseph Stalin had a research program to create supersoldiers by having women impregnated by gorillas.
$phredGAN_a$	Howard	You ' re right . I don ' t know what you ' re talking about , Sheldon .
$phredGAN_d$	Howard	You ' re kidding . .
SM	Howard	Well , my last was a little . I was just trying to be a good time .
SAM	Howard	That would be great .
$hredGAN$	NA	Okay , I ' m gonna go see my new friend , and then we ' ll go .
Friends TV Series		
Context_0	Rachel	Do you like me?
$phredGAN_a$	Joey	Yeah .
$phredGAN_d$	Joey	You ' re right . . . .
$phredGAN_a$	Ross	Well , no , no , no . I mean . I just , I don ' t know . . . .
$phredGAN_d$	Ross	You ' want to know sex . .
$phredGAN_a$	Monica	Well , I do . And I ' m not gonna tell you another guy .
$phredGAN_d$	Monica	You ' re a , you ' re really good . . . .
$phredGAN_a$	Chandler	No , I do not . You are a mean little man . .
$phredGAN_d$	Chandler	You ' re right , I can ' t do that .
SM	J/R/M/C[3]	Yeah , I ' m sure . Oh , but I can ' t believe it . I ' m not gonna be in here
SAM	J/R/M/C	I ' m not going to be a good time .
$hredGAN$	NA	Okay , I ' m gonna go see my friend .

Table 4: $hredGAN$ vs $phredGAN$ vs Li et al. (2016b) on UDC

Model	Speaker	Response
UDC		
Context_0	asker	all i need some quick amarok help. i cant hear my music
Context_1	helper	is amarok muted?
Context_2	asker	no
$phredGAN_a$	helper	use the UNK drivers , and then run the UNK command to get the UNK
$phredGAN_d$	helper	ok , so you re not using the right driver for the network card , you re using the UNK ?
$phred$	helper	you can try to install the _UNK package
SM	helper	ok , thanks
SAM	helper	ok , thanks
$hredGAN$	helper	I have no idea why it would be a bit of a bit.
Context_0	asker	anyone had problems with the kernel update from today? giving me a kernel panic
Context_1	helper	you can select previous kernels at the bootloader (grub) menu on booth.
$phredGAN_a$	asker	it says that it is not installed . . .
$phredGAN_d$	asker	ok , so i ll have to reinstall the new kernel , i ll try that.
$phred$	asker	you can try to install the drivers from the live cd
SM	asker	I ' m not sure what you mean . . .
SAM	asker	I ' m not sure how to do that . . .
$hredGAN$	asker	I ' m not sure how to do that , but I can ' t boot from a CD . . .
Context_0	asker	how do I install Ubuntu?
$phredGAN_a$	helper	use the alternate cd , it should be in the repos , its a good place to get the source of the kernel
$phredGAN_d$	helper	ok , so you have to reinstall the kernel from the CD , and you can t install the iso to the CD
$phred$	helper	yes
SM	helper	you can use the command line
SAM	helper	what is your question ?
$hredGAN$	helper	you can use the _UNK to install the _UNK

Table 5: Sample of PHRED outputs on UDC and TV Series

Source	Speaker	Utterance
Big Bang Theory and Friends TV Series		
Context_0	Howard	Okay, you have to understand something, we're in a hospital right now.
Response_0	Penny	Oh , I ' m sorry . I was just trying to be a girl .
Context_0	Sheldon	Did I? Well, that can't be right. No one's ever done that before. Except me, because I just did it. Sheldon and his brain, yeah
Response_0	Leonard	I ' m sorry . I just don ' t want to be a man who ' s going to be my girlfriend .
Context_0	Leonard	She's gotten really hooked on Age of Conan, she's playing non-stop.
Response_0	Raj	Oh , I ' m sorry . I ' m sorry . I ' m sorry . I ' m sorry . I ' m
UDC		
Context_0	asker	all i need some quick amarok help. i cant hear my music
Context_1	helper	is amarok muted?
Context_2	asker	no
Response_0	helper	you can try to install the _UNK package
Context_0	asker	anyone had problems with the kernel update from today? giving me a kernel panic
Context_1	helper	you can select previous kernels at the bootloader (grub) menu on booth.
Response_0	asker	you can try to install the drivers from the live cd
Context_0	asker	how do I install Ubuntu?
Response_0	helper	yes

---

[2]Actors: Leonard/Penny/Howard/Raj

[3]Actors: Joey/Ross/Monica/Chandler

DAL: Dual Adversarial Learning for Dialogue Generation

Shaobo Cui [1], Rongzhong Lian [2], Di Jiang [2], Yuanfeng Song [2], Siqi Bao [2], Yong Jiang [1]

[1] Tsinghua University, China

[2] Baidu Inc., China

cuishaobo16@mails.tsinghua.edu.cn

{lianrongzhong, jiangdi, songyuanfeng, baosiqi}@baidu.com

jiangy@sz.tsinghua.edu.cn

Abstract

In open-domain dialogue systems, generative approaches have attracted much attention for response[1] generation. However, existing methods are heavily plagued by generating safe responses and unnatural responses. To alleviate these two problems, we propose a novel framework named Dual Adversarial Learning (DAL) for high-quality response generation. DAL innovatively utilizes the duality between query generation and response generation to avoid safe responses and increase the diversity of the generated responses. Additionally, DAL uses adversarial learning to mimic human judges and guides the system to generate natural responses. Experimental results demonstrate that DAL effectively improves both diversity and overall quality of the generated responses. DAL outperforms state-of-the-art methods regarding automatic metrics and human evaluations.

1 Introduction

In recent years, open-domain dialogue systems are gaining much attention owing to their great potential in applications such as educational robots, emotional companion, and chitchat. The existing approaches for open-domain dialogue systems can be divided into two categories: retrieval-based approaches (Hu et al., 2014; Ji et al., 2014) and generative approaches (Ritter et al., 2011; Shang et al., 2015). The retrieval-based approaches are based on conventional information retrieval techniques and strongly rely on the underlying corpus (Wang et al., 2013; Lu and Li, 2013). Since the capability of retrieval-based approaches is strongly limited by corpus, generative approaches are attracting more attention in the field of open-domain dialogue research. The *de facto* backbone of generative approaches is the Seq2Seq model (Bahdanau

---

[1] We use *query* and *response* to denote the first and second utterances in a single-turn dialogue.

et al., 2014) , which is essentially an encoder-decoder neural network architecture. Despite their success, Seq2Seq model and its variants (Sordoni et al., 2015; Vinyals and Le, 2015) are heavily plagued by **safe responses** (generic and dull responses such as "I don't know" or "Me too") and **unnatural responses** (such as "I want to go, but I don't want to go").

In this paper, we propose a novel framework named Dual Adversarial Learning (DAL) to alleviate the aforementioned two problems. DAL consists of two generative adversarial networks (GANs): one for query generation and the other for response generation. The response generation model is used to transfer from the query domain $\mathcal{Q}$ to the response domain $\mathcal{R}$, while the query generation model is for transformation from $\mathcal{R}$ to $\mathcal{Q}$. Here we consider the response generation task and the query generation task as **dual** tasks. The generators of these two GANs are connected through the duality constraint. As such, in DAL, there are two kinds of signals that jointly instruct the optimization of generators: (1) the dual signal from the duality constraint between these two generators; (2) the adversarial signal from the discriminators. The dual signal is utilized to model the mutual relation between query generation and response generation. We use an instance to better illustrate this mutual relation: for a given query "Where to have dinner?", compared with a safe response "I dont know", a more diverse and specific response "The Indian cuisine around the corner is great" usually has a higher probability of being transformed back to the given query. DAL takes full advantage of this intuition via dual learning, which avoids generating safe responses and improves the diversity of the generated responses. Additionally, in order to make the generated responses as natural as possible, the adversarial signal in DAL mimics human judges to alle-

Proceedings of the Workshop on Methods for Optimizing and Evaluating Neural Language Generation (NeuralGen), pages 11–20

Minneapolis, Minnesota, USA, June 6, 2019. ©2019 Association for Computational Linguistics

viate unnatural responses. We compare DAL with state-of-the-art methods through extensive experiments, and DAL demonstrates superior performance regarding automatic metrics, human evaluations, and efficiency.

There are **crucial differences** between our dual approach and Maximum Mutual Information (MMI) (Li et al., 2016) though both utilize the reverse dependency to improve the diversity of the generated responses. Due to the challenging mutual information objective, the distribution $p(r|q)$ is same as that in vanilla Seq2Seq in MMI. More specifically, $p(r|q)$ in MMI is trained only by maximum likelihood estimation (MLE) objective at training time (we use $p(r|q)$ to denote the probability distribution of predicting the response r given the query q). The mutual information in MMI is utilized only at inference time, and the inference process is not only time-consuming but also inaccurate in MMI. However, $p(r|q)$ in our dual approach is trained by not only the maximum likelihood estimation objective but also the diversity objective (duality constraint) at training time. Since the dual approach directly incorporates the reverse dependency information at the training time, it can avoid the time-consuming inference plaguing MMI. Additionally, the dual approach does not need to maintain a large size optional response set for the time-consuming reranking strategy in MMI-bidi (one variant of MMI). The dual approach shows its efficiency superiority over MMI in real-life applications, which is shown in our efficiency experiment.

Our dual approach is quite different from the reinforcement learning based structure having two Seq2Seq models in (Zhang et al., 2018) [2]. In (Zhang et al., 2018), G_1, which generates a response $\hat{r}$ given a query q, uses the conditional probability $P_2(q|\hat{r})$ calculated by G_2 as the coherence measure to guide G_1 in the reinforcement learning process. Similarly, G_2, which generates a query $\hat{q}$ given a response r, uses the conditional probability $P_1(r|\hat{q})$ calculated by G_1 as the coherence measure to guide G_2 in the reinforcing learning process. However, in our work, we utilize the joint probability $p(q,r)$ to connect these two Seq2Seq models and thus avoid unstable and time-consuming reinforcement learning in the dual approach. Besides, our DAL framework is

---

²Our dual approach is finished independently with this work in addition to the crucial difference. We did not notice this paper until our work is done.

strongly different from previous structures that are composed of two GANs, such as CycleGAN (Zhu et al., 2017), DiscoGAN (Kim et al., 2017) and DualGAN (Yi et al., 2017). Those works can only be utilized on the image translation task and two generators are connected by *cycle consistency*, i.e., for each image x in domain $\mathcal{X}$, the image translation cycle is supposed to bring x to the original image: $x \rightarrow G_1(x) \rightarrow G_2(G_1(x)) \approx x$. However, *cycle consistency* is difficult to be applied into the text generation task. In our paper, we use the *joint distribution* of query-response pairs rather than *cycle consistency* to enforce the duality between these two dual generators.

The contributions of this paper are as follows:

• To the best of our knowledge, this is the first work that adopts the duality to avoid safe responses for dialogue generation. It sheds light on the utility of query generation in improving the performance of response generation.

• DAL is a novel framework that integrates dual learning and adversarial learning, which complementary and jointly contributes to generating both diverse and natural responses.

The rest of this paper is organized as follows. The related work is firstly reviewed. The DAL framework is introduced in Section 3 and the training of DAL is described in Section 4. Experimental results are shown in Section 5, followed by the conclusion of this paper in Section 6.

2   Related Work

Dual Learning   Many machine learning tasks have emerged in dual forms, such as dual neural machine translation (dual-NMT) (He et al., 2016), image classification and conditional image generation (van den Oord et al., 2016). Dual learning (He et al., 2016) is proposed on the assumption that the dual correlation could be used to improve both the primal task and its dual task: the primal task aims to map from input space $\mathcal{X}$ to output space $\mathcal{Y}$, whereas the dual task takes samples from space $\mathcal{Y}$ and maps to space $\mathcal{X}$. Tang et al. (2017) implemented a dual framework for the question answering system. Their model regards the answer selection (given a question and its several candidate answers, select the most satisfying answer to answer the question) and the question generation as dual tasks, which increases the performance of both.

Adversarial Learning   Adversarial learn-

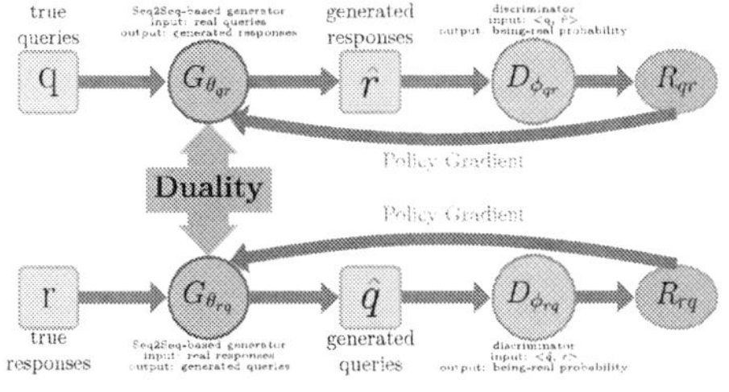

(a) The architecture of DAL.

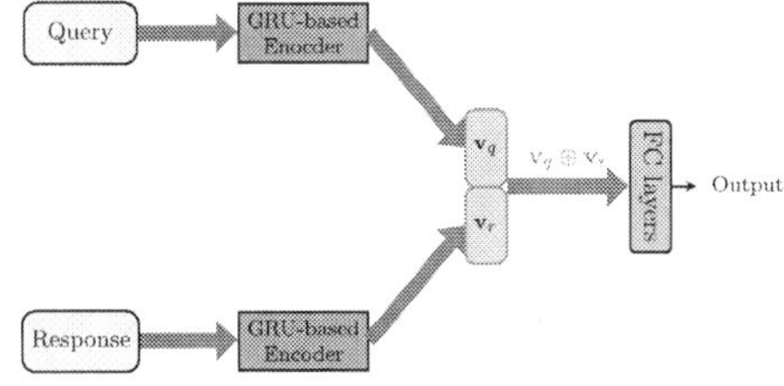

(b) The architecture of the discriminator.

Figure 1: Dual Adversarial Learning.

ing (Goodfellow et al., 2014), or Generative Adversarial Networks (GAN), has proven to be a promising approach for generation task. A GAN usually contains two neural networks: a generator G and a discriminator D. G generates samples while D is trained to distinguish generated samples from true samples. By regarding the sequence generation as an action-taking problem in reinforcement learning, Li et al. (2017) proposed to apply GAN to dialogue generation, in which the output of the discriminator is used as the reward for the generator's optimization.

Work on the Safe Response Problem There is some existing work on the safe response problem. The first kind of approach is to introduce specific keywords (Mou et al., 2016) or topic information (Xing et al., 2017) into the generated responses. These methods help to increase the dialogue coherence (Peng et al., 2019) by keywords introduction. However, these methods shift the difficulty from diverse response generation to keyword or topic prediction, which are also challenging tasks. The second kind of approach takes the reverse dependency (the query generation task given the responses) into consideration. Li et al. (2016) considered the reverse dependency and proposed Maximum Mutual Information (MMI) method, which is empirically plagued by ungrammatical responses (MMI-antiLM) and huge decoding space (MMI-bidi).

3 DAL Framework

In this section, we firstly given an overview of DAL framework and then elaborate the discriminators and the generations. We also present the reason why duality promotes diversity.

3.1 Overview

The architecture of DAL is presented in Figure 1(a). The real query and response are denoted by q and r, whereas the generated query and response are denoted as $\hat{q}$ and $\hat{r}$. DAL consists of two GANs (one for query generation and the other for response generation). Generators are denoted by $G_{\theta_{qr}}$ and $G_{\theta_{rq}}$ and the corresponding discriminators are denoted as $D_{\phi_{qr}}$ and $D_{\phi_{rq}}$. The input of $G_{\theta_{qr}}$ is a real query q and the output is the generated response $\hat{r}$. Similarly, for $G_{\theta_{rq}}$, the input is a real response r and the output is the generated query $\hat{q}$. For $D_{\phi_{qr}}$, the input is the *ficto-facto* query-response pair $\langle q, \hat{r} \rangle$, and the output R_{qr} is estimated probability of the query-response pair being human-generated, which is estimated by $D_{\phi_{qr}}$. Analogously, the input of $D_{\phi_{rq}}$ is the *ficto-facto* pair $\langle \hat{q}, r \rangle$, and the output R_{rq} is the estimated probability of the input pair being human-generated. $G_{\theta_{qr}}$ and $G_{\theta_{rq}}$ are connected by the duality constraint derived from the joint probability $P(q, r)$. The adversarial signal from discriminators, R_{qr}, R_{rq}, are passed to the corresponding generators as the reward through policy gradient.

3.2 Discriminator

The discriminator mimics a human judge and guides the generator to generate natural utterances. The architecture of the discriminator is shown in Figure 1(b). Gated Recurrent Unit (GRU) based (Bahdanau et al., 2014) neural networks are used to obtain the query embedding $\mathbf{v}_q$ and the response embedding $\mathbf{v}_r$. The concatenation vector $\mathbf{v}_q \oplus \mathbf{v}_r$ is used as the abstract representation of the query-response pair. $\mathbf{v}_q \oplus \mathbf{v}_r$ is further passed through two fully-connected layers. The output of the last fully-connected layer is the estimated probability of the query-response pair being human-generated. The objective of the discriminator is formalized as follows:

$$\min_{\phi} - \mathbb{E}_{\langle q,r \rangle \sim p_{data}} \left[\log \left(D_{\phi}(\langle q, r \rangle) \right) \right]$$
$$- \mathbb{E}_{\langle q,r \rangle \sim G_{\theta}} \left[\log \left(1 - D_{\phi}(\langle q, r \rangle) \right) \right] \quad (1)$$

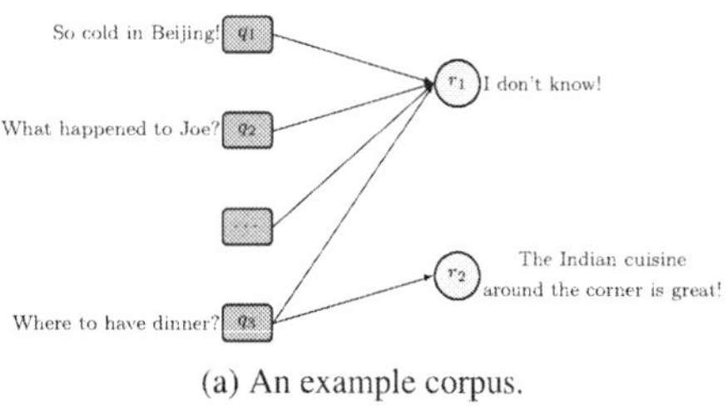

(a) An example corpus.

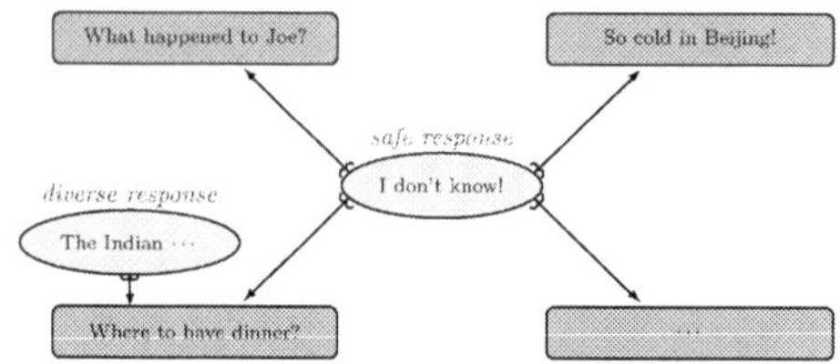

(b) Queries and responses with duality constraint.

Figure 2: An example to illustrate why duality promotes diversity.

where p_{data} denotes the real-world query-response distribution. For the response generation task, D_ϕ is $D_{\phi_{qr}}$ and G_θ is $G_{\theta_{qr}}$, while for the query generation task, D_ϕ is $D_{\phi_{rq}}$ and G_θ is $G_{\theta_{rq}}$.

3.3 Dual Generators

Both generators adopt the Seq2Seq structure, in which GRU is used as the basic unit. The constraint between the dual tasks (query generation and response generation) can be represented with the joint probability $P(q, r)$:

$$P(q, r) = P_q(q)P(r|q; \theta_{qr}) = P_r(r)P(q|r; \theta_{rq}) \quad (2)$$

where $P_q(q)$ and $P_r(r)$ are language models pre-trained on the query corpus and the response corpus. In this paper, we use smoothed bigram language models for both $P_q(q)$ and $P_r(r)$. $P(r|q; \theta_{qr})$ and $P(q|r; \theta_{rq})$ are the dual generators. Both $P(r|q; \theta_{qr})$ and $P(q|r; \theta_{rq})$ can be obtained through the markov chain rule:

$$\begin{cases} P(r|q; \theta_{qr}) = \prod_{t=1}^{|r|} P(r^t|r^{0:t-1}, q; \theta_{qr}) \\ P(q|r; \theta_{rq}) = \prod_{t=1}^{|q|} P(q^t|q^{0:t-1}, r; \theta_{rq}) \end{cases}$$

where $P(r^t|r^{0:t-1}, q; \theta_{qr})$ and $P(q^t|q^{0:t-1}, r; \theta_{rq})$ are formulations of decoders in Seq2Seq models.

3.4 Duality Promotes Diversity

To better illustrate why duality increases the diversity of the generated responses, we show some query-response pair examples in Figure 2(a). In Figure 2(a), each directional arrow starts from a query while ends at its corresponding response. It can be observed that: (1) Safe response r_1 : "I don't know" connects to many queries, i.e., $\{q_1, q_2, q_3, \cdots\}$. (2) More diverse and specific response r_2 : "The Indian cuisine around the corner is great", nevertheless, exactly corresponds to only one query q_3 : "Where to have dinner?". [3]

In the training process of $G_{\theta_{rq}}$, the increase of $\log P(q_3|r_2; \theta_{rq})$, denoted by $\Delta \log P(q_3|r_2; \theta_{rq})$ [4], is much bigger than the increase of $\log P(q_3|r_1; \theta_{rq})$, denoted by $\Delta \log P(q_3|r_1; \theta_{rq})$. Formally,

$$\Delta \log P(q_3|r_2; \theta_{rq}) \gg \Delta \log P(q_3|r_1; \theta_{rq})$$

The reason behind this phenomenon is as follows. The safe response r_1 relates with queries $\{q_1, q_2, q_3, \cdots\}$. When $G_{\theta_{rq}}$ is provided with $\langle q_1, r_1 \rangle$ or $\langle q_2, r_1 \rangle$, $G_{\theta_{rq}}$ is optimized to increase the log conditional probability $\log P(q_1|r_1; \theta_{rq})$ or $\log P(q_2|r_1; \theta_{rq})$, it is inevitable that $\log P(q_3|r_1, \theta_{rq})$ will decrease to a certain extent, since these log conditional probabilities share the same parameters θ_{rq}. The same principle applies to $\log P(q_2|r_1, \theta_{rq})$ when $G_{\theta_{rq}}$ is provided with $\langle q_1, r_1 \rangle$ or $\langle q_3, r_1 \rangle$. However, the diverse response r_2 is uniquely connected to the query q_3, in that case, $G_{\theta_{rq}}$ takes all efforts to increase $\log P(q_3|r_2, \theta_{rq})$.

With the duality constraint in Eq. 2, we obtain:

$$\frac{P(q|r; \theta_{rq})}{P(r|q; \theta_{qr})} = \frac{P_q(q)}{P_r(r)} = k(q, r). \quad (3)$$

Since both $P_q(q)$ and $P_r(r)$ are obtained from the pre-trained language models, both of them are constant for any query-response pair $\langle q, r \rangle$. $k(q, r) = \frac{P_q(q)}{P_r(r)}$ is also constant for any $\langle q, r \rangle$. Take the log formulation of Eq. 3, we can obtain:

$$\log P(q|r; \theta_{rq}) - \log P(r|q; \theta_{qr}) = \log k(q, r).$$

From above equation, we observe that the increase of $\log P(q|r; \theta_{rq})$, denoted as $\Delta \log P(q|r; \theta_{rq})$,

---

[3] There may exist several other queries that can be replied using "The Indian cuisine around the corner is great". But

this number is much smaller than those that can be replied using "I don't know". For simplicity, we only show only one query here for the response "The Indian cuisine around the corner is great". This would not affect the following analysis.

[4] The reason why the probability is in log formulation is that the probability which the maximum likelihood objective optimize is in log formulation rather than origin formulation

14

and the increase of $\log P(r|q;\theta_{qr})$, denoted by $\Delta \log P(r|q;\theta_{qr})$, is supposed to be equal for any query-response pair $\langle q, r \rangle$, since $\log k(q,r)$ is constant during the training process. Therefore,

$$\Delta \log P(q_3|r_2;\theta_{rq}) \gg \Delta \log P(q_3|r_1;\theta_{rq})$$

in turn makes

$$\Delta \log P(r_2|q_3;\theta_{qr}) \gg \Delta \log P(r_1|q_3;\theta_{qr}).$$

When $G_{\theta_{qr}}$ finishes its training process, we obtain $P(r_2|q_3;\theta_{qr}) \gg P(r_1|q_3;\theta_{qr})$. This indicates that it is more likely for $G_{\theta_{qr}}$ to assign higher probability to the diverse response given the query.

We use Figure 2(b) to visually explain this intuition. We suppose that both queries and responses "possess" their own spatial space. The coordinates of the ellipse and the rectangle represent the locations of the query q and the response r in the spatial space. The distance between q and r represents the probability of transforming between q and r, namely $P(q|r)$ and $P(r|q)$. The shorter the distance, the larger the probability. When $G_{\theta_{qr}}$ and $G_{\theta_{rq}}$ are provided with a query-response pair $\langle q, r \rangle$, the training objectives of $G_{\theta_{qr}}$ and $G_{\theta_{rq}}$ are to increase the probability $P(r|q)$ and $P(q|r)$, i.e., to shorten the distance between q and r. Since the safe response r_1 corresponds to $\{q_1, q_2, q_3, \cdots\}$, the position of this safe response is determined by all involved queries. Because each of these involved queries attempts to "drag" r_1 close to itself, the safe response r_1 "chooses" to keep a distance with each of them to balance the involved queries. However, the diverse response r_2 corresponds to exactly one query q_3. r_2 "selects" to stay as close to q_3 as possible. As it can be seen from the figure, the distance between q_3 and r_2 is much shorter than the distance between q_3 and r_1, i.e., $P(r_2|q_3)$ is much larger than $P(r_1|q_3)$. In other words, with the duality constraint, $G_{\theta_{qr}}$ tends to generate diverse responses rather than safe responses.

4 Training of DAL

Duality Constraint for Diversity Direct enforcement of the constraint in Eq. 2 is intractable. The duality constraint in Eq. 2 can be *relaxed* into a regularization term (Tang et al., 2017):

$$\Upsilon = [\log P_r(r) + \log P(q|r;\theta_{rq}) \\ - \log P_q(q) - \log P(r|q;\theta_{qr})]^2. \quad (4)$$

We minimize Υ to enforce the duality constraint in order to generate more diverse responses.

Adversarial Signal for Naturalness The decoding phase in the Seq2Seq model involves sampling discrete words. This discrete sampling makes the optimization of the generator based upon the discriminator's guidance non-differentiable. To circumvent the non-differentiable obstacle, we optimize each generator through reinforcement learning. The policy gradient is applied to pass the discriminator's adversarial signal to the generator. The discriminator D_ϕ gives a score $J(\theta)$ based on its judgment of how likely the generated $\langle q, r \rangle$ is human-generated:

$$J(\theta) = \mathbb{E}_{\langle x,y \rangle \in G_\theta}[D_\phi(\langle x, y \rangle)].$$

For response generation, $J(\theta)$ is $J(\theta_{qr})$, G_θ is $G_{\theta_{qr}}$, D_ϕ is $D_{\phi_{qr}}$, x is the real query and y is the generated response. Analogously, in query generation, $J(\theta)$ is $J(\theta_{rq})$, G_θ is $G_{\theta_{rq}}$, D_ϕ is $D_{\phi_{rq}}$, x is the real response and y is the generated query. $J(\theta)$ is used as the reward for the optimization of G_θ. With the likelihood ration trick (Williams, 1992; Sutton et al., 2000), the gradient of $J(\theta)$ can be approximated as:

$$\nabla_\theta J(\theta) \simeq [D_\phi(\langle x, y \rangle) - b] \cdot \nabla_\theta \log(p(y|x;\theta)),$$

where b is used to reduce the variance of the estimation while keeping the estimation unbiased, and $p(y|x;\theta)$ is the probability distribution defined by the generator G_θ.

Combined Gradient In DAL, the gradient for updating each generator is the weighted combination of $\nabla_\theta J(\theta)$ (for natural responses) and $\nabla_\theta \Upsilon$ (for avoidance of safe responses):

$$\begin{cases} \nabla_{\theta_{qr}} G_{\theta_{qr}} = \nabla_{\theta_{qr}} \Upsilon - \lambda_{qr} \cdot \nabla_{\theta_{qr}} J(\theta_{qr}) \\ \nabla_{\theta_{rq}} G_{\theta_{rq}} = \nabla_{\theta_{rq}} \Upsilon - \lambda_{rq} \cdot \nabla_{\theta_{rq}} J(\theta_{rq}) \end{cases} \quad (5)$$

Teacher Forcing When the generator is trained with only the adversarial signals from the discriminator and the duality constraint, the training process of the generator easily collapses. This is because the discriminator sometimes is remarkably better than the corresponding generator in certain training batches. The discriminator can easily discriminate all the generated utterances from real ones. The generator realizes that it generates low-quality samples but cannot figure out the good standard. To stabilize the training process, after each update with the combined gradient $\nabla_{\theta_{qr}} G_{\theta_{qr}}$ or $\nabla_{\theta_{rq}} G_{\theta_{rq}}$, the generators are provided with real query-response pairs and are strengthened with maximum likelihood training, which is also known as Teacher Forcing (Li et al., 2017; Lamb et al., 2016). The training procedure

---

Algorithm 1 Training of DAL.

Input: Pre-trained language models: $P_q(q)$ on query corpus and $P_r(r)$ on response corpus.
Output: $G_{\theta_{qr}}$ and $G_{\theta_{rq}}$
  1: Randomly initialize $G_{\theta_{qr}}, G_{\theta_{rq}}, D_{\phi_{qr}}, D_{\phi_{rq}}$.
  2: Pre-train $G_{\theta_{qr}}$ and $G_{\theta_{rq}}$ using MLE.
  3: Pre-train $D_{\phi_{qr}}$ and $D_{\phi_{rq}}$ by Eq. 1.
  4: **while** models have not converged **do**
  5:     **for** $i = 1, \cdots, d$ **do**
  6:         Update $D_{\phi_{qr}}$ and $D_{\phi_{rq}}$ by Eq. 1.
  7:     **end for**
  8:     **for** $j = 1, \cdots, g$ **do**
  9:         Sample $\langle q, r \rangle$ from real-world data.
10:         Update $G_{\theta_{qr}}$ by $\nabla_{\theta_{qr}} G_{\theta_{qr}}$ in Eq. 5.
11:         Teacher Forcing: update $G_{\theta_{qr}}$ with $\langle q, r \rangle$
12:         Update $G_{\theta_{rq}}$ by $\nabla_{\theta_{rq}} G_{\theta_{rq}}$ in Eq. 5.
13:         Teacher Forcing: update $G_{\theta_{rq}}$ with $\langle q, r \rangle$
14:     **end for**
15: **end while**

---

of DAL is presented in Algorithm 1. Firstly, we use maximum likelihood estimation to pre-train $G_{\theta_{qr}}$ and $G_{\theta_{rq}}$. Analogously, $D_{\phi_{qr}}$ and $D_{\phi_{rq}}$ are also pre-trained according to Eq. 1. After the pre-training phase, each generator is optimized by both duality constraint and adversarial signal, followed with the regularization of Teacher Forcing. The corresponding discriminators are simultaneously optimized.

5 Experiments

5.1 Experimental Settings

Baselines In order to verify the performance of DAL, we compare the following methods: *Seq2Seq:* the standard Seq2Seq model (Sutskever et al., 2014). *MMI-anti:* the mutual information method (Li et al., 2016), which uses an anti-language model in inference. *MMI-bidi:* the mutual information method (Li et al., 2016), which first generates a N-best response set with $p(r|q)$ and then reranks this response set with $p(q|r)$ in inference. *Adver-REIN:* the adversarial method adopting REINFORCE algorithm (Li et al., 2017). *GAN-AEL:* the adversarial method with an approximate embedding layer to solve the non-differentiable problem (Xu

et al., 2017). *DAL-Dual (ours):* DAL trained only with maximum likelihood (Teacher Forcing) and duality constraint ($\nabla_{\theta_{qr}} \Upsilon$ or $\nabla_{\theta_{rq}} \Upsilon$). *DAL-DuAd (ours):* DAL-Dual with adversarial learning (Algorithm 1).

Both *DAL-Dual* and *DAL-DuAd* are methods proposed by us: the former incorporates the dual signal only, while the later combines the dual signal and the adversarial signal. In *DAL-Dual*, the guidance of each generator can be formulated as

$$\nabla_\theta G_\theta = \nabla_\theta \text{MLE} + \lambda_{dual} \cdot \nabla_\theta \Upsilon,$$

where $\nabla_\theta \text{MLE}$ is the guidance from teacher forcing and $\nabla_\theta \Upsilon$ is the guidance from the duality constraint. In *DAL-DuAd*, the guidance of each generator can be formulated as

$$\nabla_\theta G_\theta = \nabla_\theta \text{MLE} + \lambda_{dual} \cdot \nabla_\theta \Upsilon + \lambda_{gan} \cdot \nabla_\theta J(\theta),$$

where $\nabla_\theta J(\theta)$ is the adversarial signal.
Experimental Settings A Sina Weibo dataset (Zhou et al., 2017) is employed to train the models. We treat each query-response pair as a single-turn conversation. Attention mechanism (Luong et al., 2015) is applied in all the methods to enhance the performance. All the methods are implemented based on the open source tools Pytorch(Paszke et al., 2017) and OpenNMT (Klein et al., 2017). 1,000,565 query-response pairs are employed as the training data, 3,000 pairs as the validation data. The test data is another unique 10,000 query-response pairs. The length of all the dialogue utterances in the training corpus ranges from 5 to 50. Batch size is set to 64. The vocabulary size is set to 50,000. The dimension of word embedding is set to 500. All the methods adopt a beam size of 5 in the decoding phase. The maximum length of the target sequence is set to 50. Gradient clipping strategy is adopted when the norm exceeds a threshold of 5. There are 2 fully-connected layers (1000*500, 500*1) in the discriminator structure of *DAL-DuAd*. The vanilla *Seq2Seq*, *MMI-anti* and *MMI-bidi* use SGD as the optimizer, whose initial learning rate is 1.0. *Adver-REIN*, *GAN-AEL*, *DAL-Dual*, and *DAL-DuAd* use Adam (Kingma and Ba, 2014) as the optimizer, whose initial learning rate is 0.001, $\beta_1 = 0.9$, and $\beta_2 = 0.999$. Both Adam and SGD used in all the methods adopt a decay rate of 0.5 after the 8th epoch. The dropout (Srivastava et al., 2014) probability is set to 0.5. λ_{dual} is set

to 0.025 for both $G_{\theta_{qr}}$ and $G_{\theta_{rq}}$. λ_{dual} is set to 0.025 and λ_{gan} is set to 1 for both $G_{\theta_{qr}}$ and $G_{\theta_{rq}}$. In Algorithm 1, d is set to 1 and g is set to 5. In *MMI-bidi*, the size of the N-best list is set to 5. In *MMI-anti*, γ is set to 0.15 and λ is set to 0.3.

5.2 Experimental Results

We firstly evaluate DAL on the task of generating of diverse responses. Then we resort to human annotators to evaluate the overall quality of the generated responses. Finally, we present several cases generated by all the involved method.

Response Diversity DISTINCT is a well-recognized metric to evaluate the diversity of the generated responses (Li et al., 2016; Xing et al., 2017). In our experiment, we employ DISTINCT-1 and DISTINCT-2, which calculate distinct unigrams and bigrams in the generated responses respectively. Table 1 presents the results of the five methods.

Method	DISTINCT-1	DISTINCT-2
Seq2Seq	0.031	0.137
MMI-anti	0.033	0.141
MMI-bidi	0.034	0.143
Adver-REIN	0.036	0.145
GAN-AEL	0.038	0.149
DAL-Dual (*ours*)	**0.052**	**0.209**
DAL-DuAd (*ours*)	**0.049**	**0.201**

Table 1: Results of diversity evaluation.

From Table 1, we have the following observations: (1) Both *MMI-anti* and *MMI-bidi* slightly improve the performance as compared with *Seq2Seq*. *MMI-bidi* heavily relies on the diversity of the N-best response set generated by $p(r|q)$. When N is not large enough to include some infrequently-occurring responses into the optional set, this set may lack diversity, and thus the ultimate response obtained with the reranking strategy also lacks diversity. However, when N is large, some responses having low coherence with the given query will be included in the optional set, and such responses may be selected as the final response, which hurts the performance of *MMI-bidi*. Therefore, the selection of N is an arduous task. *MMI-anti* also heavily relies on the anti-language model to obtain diverse responses. (2) Compared with *Seq2Seq*, our *DAL-Dual* improves diversity by 67.7% measured by DISTINCT-1 and 52.6% measured by DISTINCT-2, which reveals the effectiveness of the dual approach in improving diversity. (3) As expected, compared with *Adver-Rein* and *GAN-AEL*, our *DAL-DuAd* further im-

proves the diversity of the generated responses. This observation proves our assumption that, with the guidance of discriminators $D_{\phi_{qr}}$ and $D_{\phi_{rq}}$, the generator $G_{\theta_{rq}}$ is able to influence the generator $G_{\theta_{qr}}$ to produce more diverse responses. We do notice that *DAL-Dual* achieves slightly better performance than *DAL-DuAd* on diversity. The reason is that sometimes adversarial methods tend to generate some short but quality responses such as "Let's go!" for given queries such as "We can have dinner together tonight. " or "There is an exhibition at the National Museum.". However, this short but natural response would harm diversity.

Response Quality Since the word overlap-based metrics such as BLEU (Papineni et al., 2002) and embedding-based metrics are inappropriate for response quality evaluation due to their low correlation with human judgment (Liu et al., 2016; Mou et al., 2016), we resort to human annotators to evaluate the overall quality of the generated responses. We employ 3 annotators to evaluate the quality of 200 responses generated from each of the aforementioned methods. **2**: the response is natural, relevant and informative. **1**: the response is appropriate for the given query but may not be very informative. **0**: the response is completely irrelevant, incoherent or contains syntactic errors. The final score for each response is the average of the scores from all the annotators. The human evaluation results are listed in Table 2.

Method	Human rating	Kappa
Seq2Seq	0.470	0.56
MMI-anti	0.568	0.46
MMI-bidi	0.523	0.60
Adver-REIN	0.767	0.49
GAN-AEL	0.758	0.52
DAL-Dual (*ours*)	0.730	0.47
DAL-DuAd (*ours*)	**0.778**	0.50

Table 2: Results of human elevation: response quality.

The agreement among annotators is calculated with Fleiss' kappa (Fleiss, 1971). The agreement ratio is in a range from 0.4 to 0.6, showing moderate agreement. Based on the results, we have the following observations: (1) *DAL-DuAd* achieves the highest quality score, indicating that our *DAL-DuAd* has the ability to produce coherent and informative responses. (2) *Adver-REIN* and *GAN-AEL* also obtain fairly good pointwise scores. This is because the adversarial learning mechanism effectively guides the generated responses to be close to the human-generated responses. (3) Com-

		Chinese	English (translated)
First case	Query	我无聊的把鼠标垫的内容一字不落的看完了	I feel so bored that I read all the words printed on the mouse pad.
	Seq2Seq	不要这样嘛!	Come on!
	MMI-anti	哈哈哈哈哈哈!	Haha Haha Haha!
	MMI-bidi	不错不错!	Good, good!
	Adver-REIN	没事没事!	It's nothing!
	GAN-AEL	哈哈。。。	Haha ...
	DAL-Dual	你太可爱了!	You are so cute!
	DAL-DuAd	我也是这么想的.	I also catch such an idea.
Second case	Query	昨天刚看了《等风来》，想去下尼泊尔，这个神奇的国度.	I watched the movie *Up in the Wind* yesterday. It inspires me to visit Nepal, such an amazing country.
	Seq2Seq	我也想去, 可是没去过.	I want to go, but I haven't.
	MMI-anti	不错啊!	Good!
	MMI-bidi	真的假的???	Seriously???
	Adver-REIN	我也想去, 可是没去过.	I want to go, but I haven't.
	GAN-AEL	也我就怕语言问题.	Also I am concern about the language.
	DAL-Dual	真的很神奇!	It's really amazing!
	DAL-DuAd	好神奇的国度!	What an amazing country!

Figure 3: Case study.

pared with *Seq2Seq*, *MMI-anti* and *MMI-bidi*, our *DAL-Dual* obtains relatively satisfactory performance on overall quality. It shows that the dual signal can also improve the overall quality.

Case Study We present several cases in Figure 3. For the first case involving *the content on the mouse pad*, most of the baselines generate generic responses such as"Come on!", "Haha!" or "It's nothing!". On the contrary, our *DAL-Dual* and *DAL-DuAd* method produce much more diverse and informative responses, such as "You are so cute!" and "I also catch such an idea.". These two entertaining responses are also topically coherent and logically consistent with the given query. In the second cases, our methods are also capable of capturing the topic *amazing country* shown in the query, and well generate the diverse and coherent responses following the topic of the query, such as "What an amazing country!" or "It is really amazing!". In contrast, the baselines still tend to provide safe responses lacking diversity to different queries.

5.3 Comparison of Efficiency

Efficiency is a crucial factor for real-life applications such as online chatbots. We conduct an experiment to evaluate the efficiency of all the methods under study. The efficiency experiment is conducted ten times on one Tesla K40m GPU whose memory is 11471M. The average time consumed by each method to generate the responses for 1000 queries is reported in Figure 4. *MMI-bidi-5*, *MMI-bidi-10* and *MMI-bidi-20* denote the *MMI-bidi* method with the N-best size of 5, 10 and 20 respectively. We can see that *MMI-anti* and *GAN-AEL* are the most time-consuming in all the baselines. Besides, we note that *MMI-bidi* method with the reranking strategy, even with a relatively small N-best size of 5, consumes much

longer time than our methods, which severely limits *MMI-bidi*'s application in practice. However, *Seq2Seq*, *Adver-REIN*, *DAL-Dual* and *DAL-DuAd* have very similar efficiency performance. Compared with *Seq2Seq* and *Adver-REIN*, *DAL-Dual* and *DAL-DuAd* achieve much better performance on diversity and overall quality. Therefore, DAL is more suitable for real-life applications.

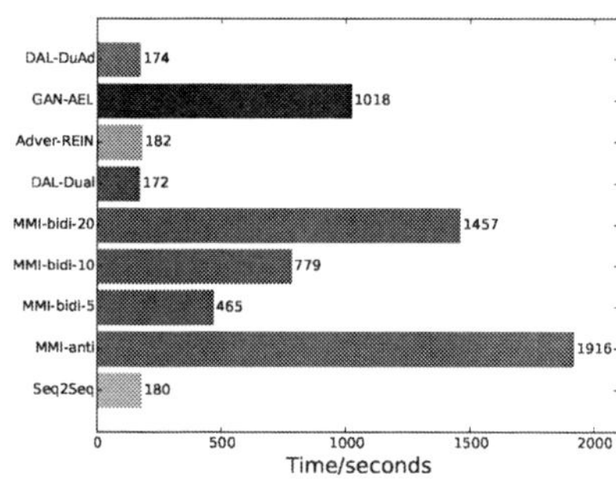

Figure 4: Time consumed by different methods.

6 Conclusion

We propose a novel framework named DAL to alleviate two prominent problems (safe responses and unnatural responses) plaguing dialogue generation. The dual learning proposed in this paper is the first effort to utilize the reverse dependency between queries and responses to reduce the probability of safe response generation and improve the diversity of the generated responses. Adversarial learning makes the generated responses as natural to human-generated ones as possible. DAL seamlessly integrates dual learning and adversarial learning, which are complementary to each other. Experimental results show that DAL achieves better performance than the state-of-the-art methods in terms of diversity, overall quality and efficiency.

References

Dzmitry Bahdanau, Kyunghyun Cho, and Yoshua Bengio. 2014. Neural machine translation by jointly learning to align and translate. *arXiv preprint arXiv:1409.0473*.

Joseph L Fleiss. 1971. Measuring nominal scale agreement among many raters. *Psychological bulletin*, 76(5):378.

Ian Goodfellow, Jean Pouget-Abadie, Mehdi Mirza, Bing Xu, David Warde-Farley, Sherjil Ozair, Aaron Courville, and Yoshua Bengio. 2014. Generative adversarial nets. In *NIPS*, pages 2672–2680.

Di He, Yingce Xia, Tao Qin, Liwei Wang, Nenghai Yu, Tieyan Liu, and Wei-Ying Ma. 2016. Dual learning for machine translation. In *NIPS*, pages 820–828.

Baotian Hu, Zhengdong Lu, Hang Li, and Qingcai Chen. 2014. Convolutional neural network architectures for matching natural language sentences. In *NIPS*, pages 2042–2050.

Zongcheng Ji, Zhengdong Lu, and Hang Li. 2014. An information retrieval approach to short text conversation. *arXiv preprint arXiv:1408.6988*.

Taeksoo Kim, Moonsu Cha, Hyunsoo Kim, Jung Kwon Lee, and Jiwon Kim. 2017. Learning to discover cross-domain relations with generative adversarial networks. In *ICML*, pages 1857–1865.

Diederik P Kingma and Jimmy Ba. 2014. Adam: A method for stochastic optimization. *arXiv preprint arXiv:1412.6980*.

Guillaume Klein, Yoon Kim, Yuntian Deng, Jean Senellart, and Alexander Rush. 2017. Opennmt: Open-source toolkit for neural machine translation. *Proceedings of ACL 2017, System Demonstrations*, pages 67–72.

Alex M Lamb, Anirudh Goyal ALIAS PARTH GOYAL, Ying Zhang, Saizheng Zhang, Aaron C Courville, and Yoshua Bengio. 2016. Professor forcing: A new algorithm for training recurrent networks. In *NIPS*, pages 4601–4609.

Jiwei Li, Michel Galley, Chris Brockett, Jianfeng Gao, and Bill Dolan. 2016. A diversity-promoting objective function for neural conversation models. In *NAACL-HLT*, pages 110–119.

Jiwei Li, Will Monroe, Tianlin Shi, Sébastien Jean, Alan Ritter, and Dan Jurafsky. 2017. Adversarial learning for neural dialogue generation. In *EMNLP*, pages 2157–2169.

Chia-Wei Liu, Ryan Lowe, Iulian Serban, Mike Noseworthy, Laurent Charlin, and Joelle Pineau. 2016. How not to evaluate your dialogue system: An empirical study of unsupervised evaluation metrics for dialogue response generation. In *EMNLP*, pages 2122–2132.

Zhengdong Lu and Hang Li. 2013. A deep architecture for matching short texts. In *NIPS*, pages 1367–1375.

Thang Luong, Hieu Pham, and Christopher D Manning. 2015. Effective approaches to attention-based neural machine translation. In *EMNLP*, pages 1412–1421.

Lili Mou, Yiping Song, Rui Yan, Ge Li, Lu Zhang, and Zhi Jin. 2016. Sequence to backward and forward sequences: A content-introducing approach to generative short-text conversation. In *COLING*, pages 3349–3358.

Aaron van den Oord, Nal Kalchbrenner, Lasse Espeholt, Oriol Vinyals, Alex Graves, et al. 2016. Conditional image generation with pixelcnn decoders. In *NIPS*, pages 4790–4798.

Kishore Papineni, Salim Roukos, Todd Ward, and Wei-Jing Zhu. 2002. Bleu: a method for automatic evaluation of machine translation. In *ACL*, pages 311–318.

Adam Paszke, Sam Gross, Soumith Chintala, Gregory Chanan, Edward Yang, Zachary DeVito, Zeming Lin, Alban Desmaison, Luca Antiga, and Adam Lerer. 2017. Automatic differentiation in pytorch. In *NIPS-W*.

Jinhua Peng, Zongyang Ma, Di Jiang, and Hua Wu. 2019. Integrating bayesian and neural networks for discourse coherence. In *Companion Proceedings of the 2019 World Wide Web Conference*. International World Wide Web Conferences Steering Committee.

Alan Ritter, Colin Cherry, and William B Dolan. 2011. Data-driven response generation in social media. In *EMNLP*, pages 583–593.

Lifeng Shang, Zhengdong Lu, and Hang Li. 2015. Neural responding machine for short-text conversation. In *ACL*, volume 1, pages 1577–1586.

Alessandro Sordoni, Michel Galley, Michael Auli, Chris Brockett, Yangfeng Ji, Margaret Mitchell, Jian-Yun Nie, Jianfeng Gao, and Bill Dolan. 2015. A neural network approach to context-sensitive generation of conversational responses. In *NAACL-HLT*, pages 196–205.

Nitish Srivastava, Geoffrey Hinton, Alex Krizhevsky, Ilya Sutskever, and Ruslan Salakhutdinov. 2014. Dropout: a simple way to prevent neural networks from overfitting. *The Journal of Machine Learning Research*, 15(1):1929–1958.

Ilya Sutskever, Oriol Vinyals, and Quoc V Le. 2014. Sequence to sequence learning with neural networks. In *NIPS*, pages 3104–3112.

Richard S Sutton, David A McAllester, Satinder P Singh, and Yishay Mansour. 2000. Policy gradient methods for reinforcement learning with function approximation. In *NIPS*, pages 1057–1063.

Duyu Tang, Nan Duan, Tao Qin, and Ming Zhou. 2017. Question answering and question generation as dual tasks. *arXiv preprint arXiv:1706.02027*.

Oriol Vinyals and Quoc Le. 2015. A neural conversational model. *arXiv preprint arXiv:1506.05869*.

Hao Wang, Zhengdong Lu, Hang Li, and Enhong Chen. 2013. A dataset for research on short-text conversations. In *EMNLP*, pages 935–945.

Ronald J Williams. 1992. Simple statistical gradient-following algorithms for connectionist reinforcement learning. *Machine learning*, 8(3-4):229–256.

Chen Xing, Wei Wu, Yu Wu, Jie Liu, Yalou Huang, Ming Zhou, and Wei-Ying Ma. 2017. Topic aware neural response generation. In *AAAI*, pages 3351–3357.

Zhen Xu, Bingquan Liu, Baoxun Wang, SUN Chengjie, Xiaolong Wang, Zhuoran Wang, and Chao Qi. 2017. Neural response generation via gan with an approximate embedding layer. In *EMNLP*, pages 617–626.

Zili Yi, Hao Zhang, Ping Tan, and Minglun Gong. 2017. Dualgan: Unsupervised dual learning for image-to-image translation. In *ICCV*, pages 2868–2876. IEEE.

Hainan Zhang, Yanyan Lan, Jiafeng Guo, Jun Xu, and Xueqi Cheng. 2018. Reinforcing coherence for sequence to sequence model in dialogue generation. In *IJCAI*, pages 4567–4573.

Hao Zhou, Minlie Huang, Tianyang Zhang, Xiaoyan Zhu, and Bing Liu. 2017. Emotional chatting machine: Emotional conversation generation with internal and external memory. *arXiv preprint arXiv:1704.01074*.

Jun-Yan Zhu, Taesung Park, Phillip Isola, and Alexei A Efros. 2017. Unpaired image-to-image translation using cycle-consistent adversarial networks. In *ICCV*, pages 2242–2251. IEEE.

How to Compare Summarizers without Target Length? Pitfalls, Solutions and Re-Examination of the Neural Summarization Literature

Simeng Sun[1]   Ori Shapira[2]   Ido Dagan[2]   Ani Nenkova[1]

[1]Department of Computer and Information Science, University of Pennsylvania
[2]Computer Science Department, Bar-Ilan University, Ramat-Gan, Israel
{simsun, nenkova}@seas.upenn.edu
obspp18@gmail.com, dagan@cs.biu.ac.il

Abstract

Until recently, summarization evaluations compared systems that produce summaries of the same target length. Neural approaches to summarization however have done away with length requirements. Here we present detailed experiments demonstrating that summaries of different length produced by the same system have a clear non-linear pattern of quality as measured by ROUGE F1 scores: initially steeply improving with summary length, then starting to gradually decline. Neural models produce summaries of different length, possibly confounding improvements of summarization techniques with potentially spurious learning of optimal summary length. We propose a new evaluation method where ROUGE scores are normalized by those of a random system producing summaries of the same length. We reanalyze a number of recently reported results and show that some negative results are in fact reports of system improvement once differences in length are taken into account. Finally, we present a small-scale human evaluation showing a similar trend of perceived quality increase with summary length, calling for the need of similar normalization in reporting human scores.

1   Introduction

Algorithms for text summarization of news developed between 2000 and 2015, were evaluated with a requirement to produce a summary of a pre-specified length.[1] This practice likely followed the DUC shared task, which called for summaries of length fixed in words or bytes (Over

et al., 2007) or influential work advocating for fixed summary length around 85-90 words (Goldstein et al., 1999).

With the advent of neural methods, however, the practice of fixing required summary length was summarily abandoned. There are some exceptions (Ma and Nakagawa, 2013; Kikuchi et al., 2016; Liu et al., 2018), but starting with (Rush et al., 2015), systems produce summaries of variable length. This trend is not necessarily bad. Prior work has shown that people prefer summaries of different length depending on the information they search for (Kaisser et al., 2008) and that variable length summaries were more effective in task-based evaluations (Mani et al., 1999).

There are, at the same time, reasons for concern. The confounding effect of output length has been widely acknowledged for example in earlier work on sentence compression (McDonald, 2006; Clarke and Lapata, 2007); for this task a meaningful evaluation should explicitly take output length into account (Napoles et al., 2011). For summarization in general, prior to 2015, researchers reported ROUGE *recall* as standard evaluation. Best practices for using ROUGE call for truncating the summaries to the desired length (Hong et al., 2014)[2]. (Nallapati et al., 2016) suggested using ROUGE F1 instead of recall, with the following justification "*full-length recall favors longer summaries, so it may not be fair to use this metric to compare two systems that differ in summary lengths. Full-length F1 solves this problem since it can penalize longer summaries.*". The rest of the neural summarization literature adopted F1 evaluation without further discussion.

In this paper we study how ROUGE F1 scores

---

[1]Here is a list of the most cited 'summarization' papers of that period according to Google Scholar (Erkan and Radev, 2004; Radev et al., 2004; Gong and Liu, 2001; Conroy and O'leary, 2001; Lin and Hovy, 2000; Mihalcea, 2004; Goldstein et al., 2000). All of them present evaluations in which alternative systems produce summaries of the same length, with two of the papers fixing the number of sentences rather than number of words.

[2]As a matter of fact, the established practice was to require human references of different lengths in order to evaluate system outputs of the respective length, a practice that has recently been shown unnecessary (Shapira et al., 2018).

Proceedings of the Workshop on Methods for Optimizing and Evaluating Neural Language Generation (NeuralGen), pages 21–29
Minneapolis, Minnesota, USA, June 6, 2019. ©2019 Association for Computational Linguistics

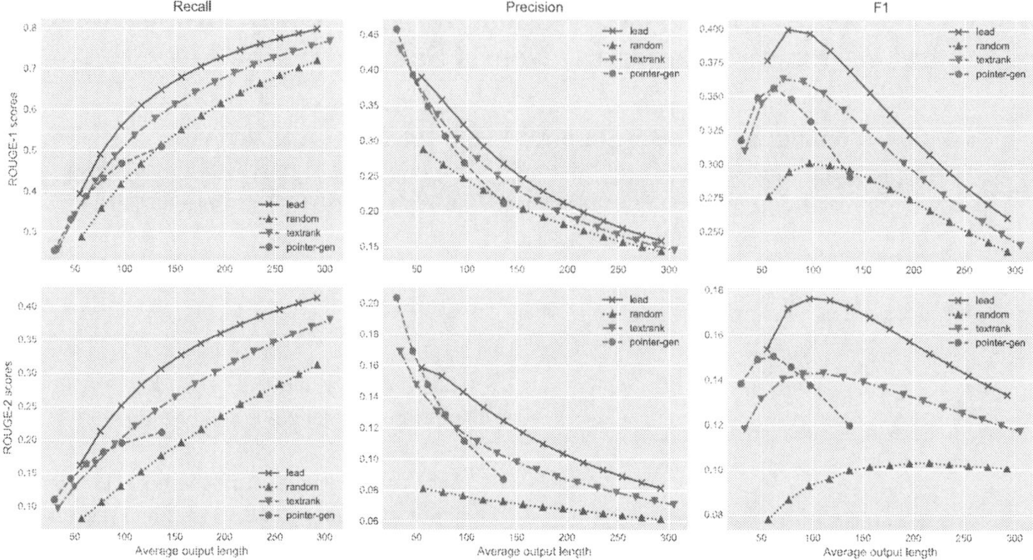

Figure 1: ROUGE recall, precision and F1 scores for lead, random, textrank and Pointer-Generator on the CNN/DailyMail test set.

change with summary length, finding that in the ranges of typical lengths for neural systems it in fact does not penalize longer summaries. We propose an alternative evaluation that appropriately normalizes ROUGE scores and reinterpret several recent results to show that not taking into account differences in length may have favored misleading conclusions. We also present a pilot analysis of summary length in human evaluation.

2 ROUGE and Summary Length

First we examine the behavior of four systems and their respective ROUGE-1 scores (overlap of unigrams between the summary and the reference), on the CNN/DailyMail test set (Nallapati et al., 2016). ROUGE F1 scores have a non-linear pattern with respect to summary length. The graphs for ROUGE-2 (bigram) have the same shape as can be seen from the second row of graphs. Of the four systems, three non-neural baselines are evaluated for lengths between 50 and 300, with a step of 20. Both sentence and word tokenization are performed using nltk (Bird et al., 2009) and words are lowercased. The four systems are as follows:

Lead Extracts full sentences from the beginning of the article with a total number of tokens no more than the desired length. Many papers on neural abstractive methods produce summaries with ROUGE scores worse than this baseline, usually comparing with the version of extracting the first three sentences of the article.

Random Randomly and non-repetitively selects full sentences with a total number of tokens that is no more than the desired length.

TextRank Sentences are scored by their centrality in the graph with sentences as the nodes (Erkan and Radev, 2004; Mihalcea, 2004). We use the Gensim.summarization package (Barrios et al., 2016) to produce these summaries.

Pointer-gen: We use the pre-trained Pointer-Generator model of (See et al., 2017) to get outputs with varying lengths by restricting both minimum and maximum decoding steps.[3] The largest values for min and max decoding step are set to 130 and 150 respectively due to limited computing resources.

Figure 1 shows that ROUGE recall keeps increasing as the summary becomes longer, while precision decreases. For recall, it is clear that even the random system produces better scoring summaries if it is allowed longer length. For all four systems, ROUGE F1 curves first rise steeply, then decline gradually. For summaries longer than 100 words, none of the systems produces a better score than corresponding system with shorter

---

[3] https://github.com/abisee/pointer-generator, we used the Tensorflow 1.0 version pre-trained pointer-generator model. The pre-trained model performs slightly worse than what was reported in their paper.

summaries. For the range of less than 100 words however, where most of the current systems fall as we will soon see, the trend is unclear since curves overlap and cross. In that range, differences in length may be responsible for differences in ROUGE scores.

It is possible that such behavior is related to the fact that ROUGE uses *word overlap* for comparison. Given the current trends of using text representations and similarity, we also check the shape of curves when representing the lead baseline and reference summary in *semantic space* using different methods. A higher cosine similarity between the two representations indicates a better baseline summary.

We represent summary and reference in embedding space using five methods: (1,2) two universal sentence encoders (Cer et al., 2018); (3) the Infersent (Conneau et al., 2017) model; (4) average and (5) max over each dimension of every word in the input with word2vec word embeddings (Mikolov et al., 2013).

Figure 2 shows the change in similarity between the lead baseline and the reference summary. For all representations, for summary lengths below 100 words, the similarity increases with length. After 100 words, the similarities plateau or slightly decrease for one representation. This indicates that when the number of words is not explicitly tracked, length is still a confounding factor and may affect the evaluations that are based on embedding similarities.

3 Normalizing ROUGE

In the data we saw so far, it is clear that difference in length may account for difference in system performance, while in some pairs of system, one is better than the other irrespective of the length of their summaries, as with the lead and random systems. Therefore, it is of interest to adopt a method that normalizes ROUGE scores for summary length and then re-examine prior literature to see if any of the conclusions change once summary length is taken into account. [4]

Simply dividing by summary length is unwarranted given the non-linear shape of the F1 curve. Instead, we choose to normalize the F1 score of a

---

[4] We could penalize summaries that are shorter or longer than the reference, similar to the brevity penalty in BLEU (Papineni et al., 2002). Such an approach however assumes that the reference summary length is ideal and deviations from that are clearly undesirable, a fairly strong assumption.

system by that of a random system which produces same average output length. The output length of a random baseline is easily controllable and any system is expected to be at least as good in content selection as the random baseline.

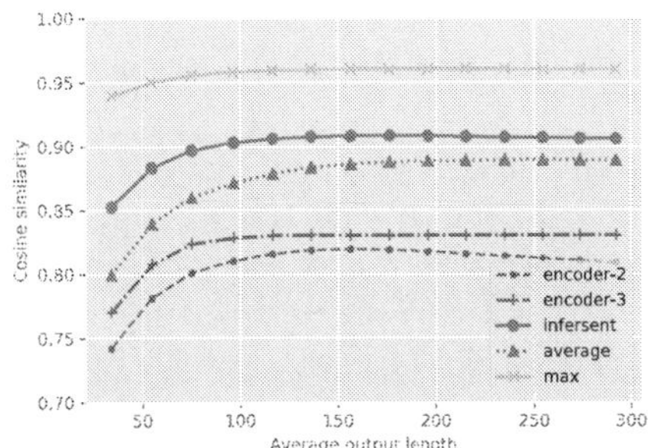

Figure 2: Cosine similarities between summaries generated by lead systems and reference in embedding space on the CNN/DailyMail test set.

The new score also has a useful intuitive interpretation. The score minus one is the percentage of a system improving upon a random system which has same average summary length. In general, it is easier for a system that produces shorter summaries to improve a lot upon a random baseline which has equally short summaries , and more difficult for systems that produce long summaries. The normalized ROUGE score can thus distinguish a poor system which achieves higher ROUGE scores because of generating longer texts from a system which has good summarization techniques but tends to generate shorter summaries. In addition, the random system is independent of the systems to be evaluated, thus the normalizing values can be computed beforehand.

4 Evaluation on CNN/DailyMail Test Set

We re-test 16 systems on the CNN/DailyMail test set:
(1) Pointer-Generator (See et al., 2017) and its variants: a baseline sequence-to-sequence attentional model (*baseline*), a Pointer-Generator model with soft switch between generating from vocabulary and copying from input (*pointer-gen*) and the same Pointer-Generator with coverage loss (*pointer-cov*) for preventing repetitive generation. There are three other content-selection variants proposed in (Gehrmann et al., 2018) which are also based on Pointer-Generator: (i) aligning ref-

erence with source article (*mask-hi*, *mask-lo*) (ii) training tagger and summarizer at the same time (*multitask*), and (iii) a differentiable model with a soft mask predicted by selection probabilities (*DiffMask*).

(2) Abstractive system with bottom-up attention (*bottom-up*) (Gehrmann et al., 2018) and the same model using Transformer (*BU_trans*) (Vaswani et al., 2017).

(3) Neural latent extractive model (*latent_ext*) and the same model with compression over the extracted sentences (*latent_cmpr*) (Zhang et al., 2018). This setting is important to study, because compression naturally produces a shorter summary and a meaningful analysis of the effect is needed.

(4) TextRank system used in previous section, with maximum summary length set to 50 and 70.

(5) Lead-3 related systems: the first 3 sentences of each article (*lead3*); compressed first 3 sentences of each article which has length of corresponding *pointer-gen* (*lead-pointer*) and *pointer-cov* (*lead-cov*) output, similar to (3). The compression model we used is a Pointer-Generator trained on 1160401 aligned sentence/reference pairs extracted from CNN/DailyMail training data and Annotated Gigaword (AGIGA) (Napoles et al., 2012). We extract the pairs from CNN/DailyMail when every token from the summary sentence can be found in the article sentence. The pairs are extracted from AGIGA when over 70% tokens of a lead sentence are also in the headline. The minimum and maximum decoding step are set to be equal so that the output lengths are fixed. Specifically, let c_i be the length of a summary produced by *pointer-gen*, l_i be the length of lead 3 sentences for the same article and $l_i^{(j)}$ be the length of jth sentence ($j \leq 3$). The jth lead sentence is forced to have output length of $l_i^{(j)} c_i / l_i$ tokens. The average number of tokens are not exactly the same since the size after scaling may be off by at most 1 token.

The random scores are the average over n activations of random systems introduced in §2 ($n = 10$ in our setting). The instability of random systems can be mitigated by setting n to be large enough. Besides, the average over large amounts of test articles can also weaken this issue since we focus on system-level comparison instead of input-level. Given a system output length, we use linear interpolation of the two closest points to

System	Len.	Sys. F1	Rand. F1	Norm.
latent_cmpr	43	$0.362_{[+2]}$	$0.245_{[+0]}$	$1.473_{[+13]}$
baseline	48	$0.311_{[-1]}$	$0.257_{[+0]}$	$1.209_{[-1]}$
textrank_50	50	$0.345_{[-1]}$	$0.259_{[+0]}$	$1.331_{[+1]}$
mask_lo	51	$0.371_{[+2]}$	$0.263_{[+0]}$	$1.410_{[+9]}$
BU_trans	53	$0.410_{[+10]}$	$0.266_{[+0]}$	$\mathbf{1.541}_{[+11]}$
bottom_up	55	$\mathbf{0.412}_{[+10]}$	$0.272_{[+0]}$	$1.517_{[+9]}$
pointer-gen	56	$0.362_{[-3]}$	$0.273_{[+0]}$	$1.327_{[-4]}$
lead-pointer	56	$0.377_{[+0]}$	$0.273_{[+0]}$	$1.381_{[+2]}$
mask_hi	58	$0.377_{[+0]}$	$0.276_{[+0]}$	$1.366_{[-2]}$
DiffMask	58	$0.380_{[+0]}$	$0.277_{[+0]}$	$1.373_{[-1]}$
lead-cov	61	$0.383_{[+0]}$	$0.279_{[+0]}$	$1.369_{[-3]}$
pointer-cov	62	$0.392_{[+0]}$	$0.280_{[+0]}$	$1.403_{[+0]}$
multitask	63	$0.376_{[-6]}$	$0.281_{[+0]}$	$1.341_{[-8]}$
textrank_70	71	$0.363_{[-9]}$	$0.288_{[+0]}$	$1.259_{[-12]}$
latent_ext	82	$0.409_{[-1]}$	$\mathbf{0.296}_{[+0]}$	$1.384_{[-4]}$
lead3	**85**	$0.401_{[-3]}$	$\mathbf{0.296}_{[+0]}$	$1.351_{[-10]}$
Rank change	-	48	0	90
Spearman	-	0.500	1.000	0.205
Pearson	-	0.491	0.949	0.194

Table 1: System performance on the CNN/DailyMail test set, including average summary length, system ROUGE-1 F1 score, ROUGE-1 F1 for the random system with same average length. Systems are ordered by length. Values in the last three columns are subscripted by the difference in rank when sorted by corresponding item as compared to when sorted by length. In the bottom of the table, we show the sum of absolute rank change, Spearman and Pearson correlation between corresponding values and length.

estimate the ROUGE score of a random system which has the same average output length.[5]

Table 1 shows the average length of summaries produced by each system, the system ROUGE-1 F1 score, the corresponding ROUGE-1 F1 score of a random system with the same average summary length, and the proposed normalized ROUGE-1 evaluation score. The bottom of the table gives the sum of absolute system rank change with respect to the ordering by summary length and correlations between corresponding values with summary length.

All systems produce summaries in the 43–85 word range, where we already established that ROUGE F1 increases steeply with summary length. Another important observation is that the scores of random systems follow exactly the ordering by length; here summary length alone is responsible for the over 5 ROUGE point improvement. Next to notice is that the normalization

---

[5] We also explored another kind of random baseline where the last sentence is truncated to get a summary of fixed length. The effect of that normalization is the same as to that presented here. Detailed results can be found in our supplementary material.

24

leads to about double the difference in rank change with respect to length than regular ROUGE F1. Hence, these scores give information about summary quality that is less related to summary length.

Now we get to revisit some of the conclusions drawn solely from ROUGE scores, without taking summary length into account. Many of the neural abstractive systems produce outputs with scores worse than the lead3 baseline. However this baseline results in the longest summaries. Moreover, after normalization, it becomes clear that *lead3* is in fact considerably worse than *pointer-cov*. As presented in Fig. 1, the TextRank system with summary length of 70 has better ROUGE scores than the same system with summary length of 50. Once these are normalized, however, the system with shorter summaries appears to be more effective (6 points better in normalized score). Finally, we compare the two pairs of extractive systems as well as their versions in which the extracted sentences are compressed. The compressed summaries are about 40 words shorter for the systems in **(3)** and 30 words shorter in **(5)**. Plain ROUGE scores decidedly indicate that compression worsens system performance. When normalized however, *latent_cmpr* emerges as the third most effective system, immediately follow the bottom-up systems (Gehrmann et al., 2018). This is not the case for the simplistic compression variant in *lead3*, which produces shorter summaries but barely changes its rank in the normalized score ranking.

Finally, we compare the systems that reported outperforming the *lead3* baseline. The *latent_ext* system results in summaries very similar in length to *lead3*. Given previous analysis, one might think the ROUGE improvement is due to summary length. However, the normalized score shows that this is not the case and that the *latent_ext* is indeed better than *lead3*. Even more impressive is the analysis of the bottom-up system, which has better ROUGE scores than lead even though it produces shorter summaries. It keeps its first place position even after normalization.

Overall, the analyses we present provide compelling evidence for the importance of summary length on system evaluation. Relying only on ROUGE would at times confound improvement in content selection with the learned ability to generate longer summaries.

Dim.	Question
IN	How well does the summary capture the key points of the article?
RL	Are the details provided by the summary consistent with details in the article?
VE	How efficient do you think the summary conveys the main point of the article?
UC	How much unnecessary content do you think the summary contains?
SR	To what degree do you think the summary is a perfect surrogate of the article?
CN	How much additional informative information can a reader find from the article after reading the summary?

Table 2: Prompts presented to Amazon Mechanical Turk workers

System	CN	IN	RL	SR	UC	VE	LE
frag	4.58	2.96	3.79	2.88	3.46	3.59	31.32
lead3	4.32	3.36	4.11	3.27	3.39	3.72	78.80
ptr_c	4.43	3.22	3.98	3.05	3.33	3.95	71.37
ptr_n	4.40	3.10	4.00	3.11	3.49	3.69	41.50
ptr_s	4.37	3.28	3.96	3.26	3.47	3.89	68.42
textrank	4.51	3.16	4.18	3.18	3.54	3.68	49.13

Table 3: Human ratings for each system. LE stands for summary length. The rest dimensions are described in table 2.

	CN	IN	RL	SR	UC	VE	LE
CN	1.00*	-	-	-	-	-	-
IN	-0.87*	1.00*	-	-	-	-	-
RL	-0.40	0.59	1.00*	-	-	-	-
SR	-0.81	0.88*	0.74	1.00*	-	-	-
UC	-0.36	0.42	-0.16	-0.06	1.00*	-	-
VE	-0.52	0.61	0.08	0.36	0.60	1.00*	-
LE	-0.79	0.96*	0.44	0.71	0.64	0.73	1.00*

Table 4: Correlation among the six human rating dimensions defined in Table 2 and summary length **LE**. Each dimension is the same as in Table 3. Entries with p-value smaller than 0.05 are marked with *.

5 Human Evaluation on Newsroom

We also conduct a pilot human evaluation experiment using the same data as in (Grusky et al., 2018). The human evaluation data are 60 articles from the Newsroom test set and summaries generated by seven systems. These are (1) extractive systems: first three sentences of the article (*lead3*), textrank with word limit of 50 (*textrank*) and the 'fragments' system (*frag*) representing the best performance an extractive system can achieve. (2) an abstractive system (Rush et al., 2015) (*abstractive*) trained on Newsroom data and (3) systems with mixed strategies: Pointer-Generator trained

Max Len.	Informativeness	Verbosity
50	4.13	4.58
70	4.55	4.35
90	4.94	4.42
110	5.22	4.32

Table 5: Average informativeness and verbosity rating for lead system with max length of 50, 70, 90 and 110.

System	CN	IN	RL	SR	UC	VE
frag	1.16	0.75	0.96	0.73	0.88	0.86
lede3	0.86	0.67	0.82	0.65	0.68	0.66
ptr_c	0.91	0.66	0.82	0.63	0.68	0.63
ptr_n	1.04	0.73	0.95	0.74	0.83	0.78
ptr_s	0.91	0.68	0.82	0.68	0.72	0.64
textrank	1.02	0.71	0.94	0.72	0.80	0.75

Table 6: Human ratings normalized by interpolated informativeness rating in table 5.

on CNN/DailyMail data set (*ptr_c*), on subset of Newsroom training set (*ptr_s*) and a subset of Newsroom training data (*ptr_n*). After examining the outputs of each system, the *abstractive* system was excluded because the model was not properly trained. Human evaluation results for each system are shown in Table 3.

We ask annotators to rate six aspects of summary content quality informativeness (*IN*), relevance (*RL*), verbosity (*VE*), unnecessary content (*UC*), making people want to continue reading the original article after reading the summary (*CN*) and being a sufficient substitute for the original article (*SR*) and compute the correlation among these dimensions as well as with summary length. Instead of rating in the range of 1 to 5 as in the original article, we ask the workers to rate in a range of 1 to 7, with higher value corresponds to summary is informative and relevant to the source article, not verbose, has no unnecessary content, much information to be attained after reading summary and can serve as a perfect surrogate to the article. The correlation among six aspects and with summary length are shown in table 4.

Some of the newly introduced questions, such as unnecessary content and verbosity, were intended to capture aspects of the summary which may favor shorter summaries. Relevance is the score introduced in the original (Grusky et al., 2018) study and measures to faithfulness of content, as neural systems tend to include summary content that is not supported by the original article being summarized.

We find that in general people favor systems that produce longer summaries. However, similar to our initial experiment with ROUGE, there is no way to know if the improvement is due simply to the longer length, in which more content can be presented, or in the content selection capabilities of the system. The highest correlation between summary length and a human rating is that for informativeness, which in hind sight is completely intuitive because the longer the summary,

the more information it includes. The exact same informativeness definition is used for the Newsroom leaderboard (Grusky et al., 2018)[6]. Clearly, a meaningful interpretation of the human scores will require normalization similar to the one we presented for ROUGE, with human ratings for random or lead summaries of different length, so the overall effectiveness of the system over these is measured in evaluation.

To mirror the analysis of ROUGE scores, we conduct another experiment where we present the workers with lead system of max length 50, 70, 90 and 110 as well as the reference. Complete sentences are extracted so that readability is maintained. Each HIT is assigned to 3 workers and only contains one summary-reference pair. The average length of these four systems are 38.0, 53.4, 75.1, 92.5 respectively. Workers are told that they may assume the reference summary captures all key points of the article, then we ask them to rate the informativeness and verbosity question again. Average ratings for each length can be seen in Table 5. Much like ROUGE, human evaluation of informativeness is also confounded by summary length and requires normalization for meaningful evaluation. We normalize the original human ratings for each system with the interpolated (*IN*) rating in table 5 and present it in table 6.

We also evaluated how the verbosity score behaves when applied to summaries of that length. We chose that because it has the lowest overall correlation with the informativeness and relevance evaluations introduced in prior work. Its (and its related evaluation of unnecessary content) correlation with length is not significant but still appears high. Better sense of the relationship can be obtained in future work when a larger number of system can be evaluated.

Unlike informativeness, verbosity human scores fluctuate with length, increasing and

---

[6] https://summari.es

decreasing without clear pattern. This suggests future human evaluations should involve more similar judgments likely to capture precision in content selection, which are currently missing in the field.

6 Conclusion

We have shown that plain ROUGE F1 scores are not ideal for comparing current neural systems which on average produce different lengths. This is due to a non-linear pattern between ROUGE F1 and summary length. To alleviate the effect of length during evaluation, we have proposed a new method which normalizes the ROUGE F1 scores of a system by that of a random system with same average output length. A pilot human evaluation has shown that humans prefer short summaries in terms of the verbosity of a summary but overall consider longer summaries to be of higher quality. While human evaluations are more expensive in time and resources, it is clear that normalization, such as the one we proposed for automatic evaluation, will make human evaluations more meaningful. Finally, human evaluations related to content precision are needed for fully evaluating abstractive summarization systems.

References

Federico Barrios, Federico López, Luis Argerich, and Rosa Wachenchauzer. 2016. Variations of the similarity function of textrank for automated summarization. *arXiv preprint arXiv:1602.03606*.

Steven Bird, Ewan Klein, and Edward Loper. 2009. *Natural language processing with Python: analyzing text with the natural language toolkit.* " O'Reilly Media, Inc.".

Daniel Cer, Yinfei Yang, Sheng-yi Kong, Nan Hua, Nicole Limtiaco, Rhomni St. John, Noah Constant, Mario Guajardo-Cespedes, Steve Yuan, Chris Tar, Brian Strope, and Ray Kurzweil. 2018. Universal sentence encoder for english. In *Proceedings of the 2018 Conference on Empirical Methods in Natural Language Processing: System Demonstrations*, pages 169–174. Association for Computational Linguistics.

James Clarke and Mirella Lapata. 2007. Modelling compression with discourse constraints. In *Proceedings of the 2007 Joint Conference on Empirical Methods in Natural Language Processing and Computational Natural Language Learning (EMNLP-CoNLL)*.

Alexis Conneau, Douwe Kiela, Holger Schwenk, Loïc Barrault, and Antoine Bordes. 2017. Supervised learning of universal sentence representations from natural language inference data. In *Proceedings of the 2017 Conference on Empirical Methods in Natural Language Processing*, pages 670–680, Copenhagen, Denmark. Association for Computational Linguistics.

John M Conroy and Dianne P O'leary. 2001. Text summarization via hidden markov models. In *Proceedings of the 24th annual international ACM SIGIR conference on Research and development in information retrieval*, pages 406–407. ACM.

Günes Erkan and Dragomir R Radev. 2004. Lexrank: Graph-based lexical centrality as salience in text summarization. *Journal of artificial intelligence research*, 22:457–479.

Sebastian Gehrmann, Yuntian Deng, and Alexander Rush. 2018. Bottom-up abstractive summarization. In *Proceedings of the 2018 Conference on Empirical Methods in Natural Language Processing*, pages 4098–4109. Association for Computational Linguistics.

Jade Goldstein, Mark Kantrowitz, Vibhu O. Mittal, and Jaime G. Carbonell. 1999. Summarizing text documents: Sentence selection and evaluation metrics. In *SIGIR '99: Proceedings of the 22nd Annual International ACM SIGIR Conference on Research and Development in Information Retrieval, August 15-19, 1999, Berkeley, CA, USA*, pages 121–128.

Jade Goldstein, Vibhu Mittal, Jaime Carbonell, and Mark Kantrowitz. 2000. Multi-document summarization by sentence extraction. In *Proceedings of the 2000 NAACL-ANLP Workshop on Automatic summarization*, pages 40–48. Association for Computational Linguistics.

Yihong Gong and Xin Liu. 2001. Generic text summarization using relevance measure and latent semantic analysis. In *Proceedings of the 24th annual international ACM SIGIR conference on Research and development in information retrieval*, pages 19–25. ACM.

Max Grusky, Mor Naaman, and Yoav Artzi. 2018. Newsroom: A dataset of 1.3 million summaries with diverse extractive strategies. In *Proceedings of the 2018 Conference of the North American Chapter of the Association for Computational Linguistics: Human Language Technologies, Volume 1 (Long Papers)*, pages 708–719. Association for Computational Linguistics.

Kai Hong, John M. Conroy, Benoît Favre, Alex Kulesza, Hui Lin, and Ani Nenkova. 2014. A repository of state of the art and competitive baseline summaries for generic news summarization. In *Proceedings of the Ninth International Conference on Language Resources and Evaluation, LREC 2014, Reykjavik, Iceland, May 26-31, 2014.*, pages 1608–1616.

Michael Kaisser, Marti A. Hearst, and John B. Lowe. 2008. Improving search results quality by customizing summary lengths. In *ACL 2008, Proceedings of the 46th Annual Meeting of the Association for Computational Linguistics, June 15-20, 2008, Columbus, Ohio, USA*, pages 701–709.

Yuta Kikuchi, Graham Neubig, Ryohei Sasano, Hiroya Takamura, and Manabu Okumura. 2016. Controlling output length in neural encoder-decoders. In *Proceedings of the 2016 Conference on Empirical Methods in Natural Language Processing*, pages 1328–1338. Association for Computational Linguistics.

Chin-Yew Lin and Eduard Hovy. 2000. The automated acquisition of topic signatures for text summarization. In *Proceedings of the 18th conference on Computational linguistics-Volume 1*, pages 495–501. Association for Computational Linguistics.

Yizhu Liu, Zhiyi Luo, and Kenny Zhu. 2018. Controlling length in abstractive summarization using a convolutional neural network. In *Proceedings of the 2018 Conference on Empirical Methods in Natural Language Processing*, pages 4110–4119.

Tengfei Ma and Hiroshi Nakagawa. 2013. Automatically determining a proper length for multi-document summarization: A bayesian nonparametric approach. In *Proceedings of the 2013 Conference on Empirical Methods in Natural Language Processing*, pages 736–746.

Inderjeet Mani, David House, Gary Klein, Lynette Hirschman, Therese Firmin, and Beth Sundheim. 1999. The tipster summac text summarization evaluation. In *Proceedings of the ninth conference on European chapter of the Association for Computational Linguistics*, pages 77–85. Association for Computational Linguistics.

Ryan McDonald. 2006. Discriminative sentence compression with soft syntactic evidence. In *11th Conference of the European Chapter of the Association for Computational Linguistics*.

Rada Mihalcea. 2004. Graph-based ranking algorithms for sentence extraction, applied to text summarization. In *Proceedings of the ACL 2004 on Interactive poster and demonstration sessions*, page 20. Association for Computational Linguistics.

Tomas Mikolov, Ilya Sutskever, Kai Chen, Greg S Corrado, and Jeff Dean. 2013. Distributed representations of words and phrases and their compositionality. In *Advances in neural information processing systems*, pages 3111–3119.

Ramesh Nallapati, Bowen Zhou, Cicero dos Santos, Caglar Gulcehre, and Bing Xiang. 2016. Abstractive text summarization using sequence-to-sequence rnns and beyond. In *Proceedings of The 20th SIGNLL Conference on Computational Natural Language Learning*, pages 280–290. Association for Computational Linguistics.

Courtney Napoles, Matthew R. Gormley, and Benjamin Van Durme. 2012. Annotated gigaword. In *AKBC-WEKEX@NAACL-HLT*.

Courtney Napoles, Benjamin Van Durme, and Chris Callison-Burch. 2011. Evaluating sentence compression: Pitfalls and suggested remedies. In *Proceedings of the Workshop on Monolingual Text-To-Text Generation*, pages 91–97, Portland, Oregon. Association for Computational Linguistics.

Paul Over, Hoa Dang, and Donna Harman. 2007. DUC in context. *Inf. Process. Manage.*, 43(6):1506–1520.

Kishore Papineni, Salim Roukos, Todd Ward, and Wei-Jing Zhu. 2002. Bleu: a method for automatic evaluation of machine translation. In *Proceedings of the 40th annual meeting on association for computational linguistics*, pages 311–318. Association for Computational Linguistics.

Dragomir R Radev, Hongyan Jing, Małgorzata Styś, and Daniel Tam. 2004. Centroid-based summarization of multiple documents. *Information Processing & Management*, 40(6):919–938.

Alexander M. Rush, Sumit Chopra, and Jason Weston. 2015. A neural attention model for abstractive sentence summarization. In *Proceedings of the 2015 Conference on Empirical Methods in Natural Language Processing*, pages 379–389. Association for Computational Linguistics.

Abigail See, Peter J. Liu, and Christopher D. Manning. 2017. Get to the point: Summarization with pointer-generator networks. In *Proceedings of the 55th Annual Meeting of the Association for Computational Linguistics (Volume 1: Long Papers)*, pages 1073–1083. Association for Computational Linguistics.

Ori Shapira, David Gabay, Hadar Ronen, Judit Bar-Ilan, Yael Amsterdamer, Ani Nenkova, and Ido Dagan. 2018. Evaluating multiple system summary lengths: A case study. In *Proceedings of the 2018 Conference on Empirical Methods in Natural Language Processing*, pages 774–778. Association for Computational Linguistics.

Ashish Vaswani, Noam Shazeer, Niki Parmar, Jakob Uszkoreit, Llion Jones, Aidan N. Gomez, Lukasz Kaiser, and Illia Polosukhin. 2017. Attention is all you need. In *NIPS*.

Xingxing Zhang, Mirella Lapata, Furu Wei, and Ming Zhou. 2018. Neural latent extractive document summarization. In *Proceedings of the 2018 Conference on Empirical Methods in Natural Language Processing*, pages 779–784. Association for Computational Linguistics.

A Normalizing ROUGE with truncated random selection

System	Len.	Sys. F1	Rand. F1	Norm.
latent_cmpr	43	$0.362_{[+2]}$	$0.256_{[+0]}$	$1.413_{[+13]}$
baseline	48	$0.311_{[-1]}$	$0.267_{[+0]}$	$1.165_{[-1]}$
textrank_50	50	$0.345_{[-1]}$	$0.270_{[+0]}$	$1.280_{[+0]}$
mask_lo	51	$0.371_{[+2]}$	$0.273_{[+0]}$	$1.359_{[+7]}$
BU_trans	53	$0.410_{[+10]}$	$0.275_{[-1]}$	$1.491_{[+10]}$
bottom_up	55	$\mathbf{0.412}_{[+10]}$	$0.274_{[+1]}$	$\mathbf{1.505}_{[+10]}$
pointer-gen	56	$0.362_{[-3]}$	$0.279_{[+0]}$	$1.295_{[-3]}$
lead-pointer	56	$0.377_{[+0]}$	$0.280_{[+0]}$	$1.347_{[+2]}$
mask_hi	58	$0.377_{[+0]}$	$0.281_{[+0]}$	$1.344_{[-1]}$
DiffMask	58	$0.380_{[+0]}$	$0.283_{[+0]}$	$1.344_{[-1]}$
lead-cov	61	$0.383_{[+0]}$	$0.286_{[-1]}$	$1.340_{[-5]}$
pointer-cov	62	$0.392_{[+0]}$	$0.285_{[+1]}$	$1.378_{[+1]}$
multitask	63	$0.376_{[-6]}$	$0.286_{[+0]}$	$1.317_{[-8]}$
textrank_70	71	$0.363_{[-9]}$	$0.291_{[+0]}$	$1.245_{[-12]}$
latent_ext	82	$0.409_{[-1]}$	$0.298_{[+0]}$	$1.374_{[-3]}$
lead3	**85**	$0.401_{[-3]}$	$\mathbf{0.299}_{[+0]}$	$1.342_{[-9]}$
Rank change	-	48	4	86
Spearman	-	0.500	0.944	-0.115
Pearson	-	0.491	0.994	-0.047

Table 7: System performance on the CNN/DailyMail test set, including average summary length, system ROUGE-1 F1 score, ROUGE-1 F1 for the random system with same average length. Systems are ordered by length. Values in the last three columns are subscripted by the difference in rank when sorted by corresponding item as compared to when sorted by length. In the bottom of the table, we show the sum of absolute rank change, Spearman and Pearson correlation between corresponding values and length.

BERT has a Mouth, and It Must Speak:
BERT as a Markov Random Field Language Model

Alex Wang
New York University
`alexwang@nyu.edu`

Kyunghyun Cho
New York University
Facebook AI Research
CIFAR Azrieli Global Scholar
`kyunghyun.cho@nyu.edu`

Abstract

We show that BERT (Devlin et al., 2018) is a Markov random field language model. This formulation gives way to a natural procedure to sample sentences from BERT. We generate from BERT and find that it can produce high-quality, fluent generations. Compared to the generations of a traditional left-to-right language model, BERT generates sentences that are more diverse but of slightly worse quality.

1 Introduction

BERT (Devlin et al., 2018) is a recently released sequence model used to achieve state-of-art results on a wide range of natural language understanding tasks, including constituency parsing (Kitaev and Klein, 2018) and machine translation (Lample and Conneau, 2019). Early work probing BERT's linguistic capabilities has found it surprisingly robust (Goldberg, 2019).

BERT is trained on a *masked language modeling* objective. Unlike a traditional language modeling objective of predicting the next word in a sequence given the history, masked language modeling predicts a word given its left and right context. Because the model expects context from both directions, it is not immediately obvious how BERT can be used as a traditional language model (i.e., to evaluate the probability of a text sequence) or how to sample from it.

We attempt to answer these questions by showing that BERT is a combination of a Markov random field language model (MRF-LM, Jernite et al., 2015; Mikolov et al., 2013) with pseudo log-likelihood (Besag, 1977) training. This formulation automatically leads to a sampling procedure based on Gibbs sampling.

2 BERT as a Markov Random Field

Let $X = (x_1, \ldots, x_T)$ be a sequence of random variables x_i, each of which is categorical in that it can take one of M items from a vocabulary $V = \{v_1, \ldots, v_M\}$. These random variables form a fully-connected graph with undirected edges, indicating that each variable x_i is dependent on all the other variables.

Joint Distribution To define a Markov random field (MRF), we start by defining a potential over cliques. Among all possible cliques, we only consider the clique corresponding to the full graph. All other cliques will be assigned a potential of 1 (i.e. $\exp(0)$). The potential for this full-graph clique decomposes into a sum of T log-potential terms:

$$\phi(X) = \prod_{t=1}^{T} \phi_t(X) = \exp\left(\sum_{t=1}^{T} \log \phi_t(X)\right),$$

where we use X to denote the fully-connected graph created from the original sequence. Each log-potential $\phi_t(X)$ is defined as

$$\log \phi_t(X) = \begin{cases} \mathrm{1h}(x_t)^\top f_\theta(X_{\backslash t}), & \text{if } [\text{MASK}] \notin \\ & \qquad X_{1:t-1} \cup X_{t+1:T} \\ 0, & \text{otherwise}, \end{cases} \tag{1}$$

where $f_\theta(X_{\backslash t}) \in \mathbb{R}^M$, $\mathrm{1h}(x_t)$ is a one-hot vector with index x_t set to 1, and

$$X_{\backslash t} = (x_1, \ldots, x_{t-1}, [\text{MASK}], x_{t+1}, \ldots, x_T)$$

From this log-potential, we can define a probability of a given sequence X as

$$p_\theta(X) = \frac{1}{Z(\theta)} \prod_{t=1}^{T} \phi_t(X), \tag{2}$$

Proceedings of the Workshop on Methods for Optimizing and Evaluating Neural Language Generation (NeuralGen), pages 30–36
Minneapolis, Minnesota, USA, June 6, 2019. ©2019 Association for Computational Linguistics

where

$$Z(\theta) = \sum_{X'} \prod_{t=1}^{T} \phi_t(X'),$$

for all X'. This normalization constant is unfortunately impractical to compute exactly, rendering exact maximum log-likelihood intractable.

Conditional Distribution Given a fixed $X_{\setminus t}$, the conditional probability of x_t is derived to be

$$p(x_t|X_{\setminus t}) = \frac{1}{Z(X_{\setminus t})} \exp(1\mathrm{h}(x_t)^\top f_\theta(X_{\setminus t})),$$

$$(3)$$

where

$$Z(X_{\setminus t}) = \sum_{m=1}^{M} \exp(1\mathrm{h}(m)^\top f_\theta(X_{\setminus t})).$$

This derivation follows from the peculiar formulation of the log-potential in Eq. (1). It is relatively straightforward to compute, as it is simply softmax normalization over M terms (Bridle, 1990).

(Stochastic) Pseudo Log-Likelihood Learning One way to avoid the issue of intractability in computing the normalization constant $Z(\theta)$ above[1] is to resort to an approximate learning strategy. BERT uses pseudo log-likelihood learning, where the pseudo log-likelihood is defined as:

$$\mathrm{PLL}(\theta; D) = \frac{1}{|D|} \sum_{X \in D} \sum_{t=1}^{|X|} \log p(x_t|X_{\setminus t}), . \quad (4)$$

where D is a set of training examples. We maximize the predictability of each token in a sequence given all the other tokens, instead of the joint probability of the entire sequence.

It is still expensive to compute the pseudo log-likelihood in Eq. (4) for even one example, especially when f_θ is not linear. This is because we must compute $|X|$ forward passes of f_θ for each sequence, when $|X|$ can be long and f_θ be computationally heavy. Instead we could stochastically

---

[1] In BERT it is not intractable in the strictest sense, since the amount of computation is bounded (by $T = 500$) each iteration. It however requires computation up to $\exp(500)$ which is in practice impossible to compute exactly.

estimate it by

$$\frac{1}{|X|} \sum_{t=1}^{|X|} \log p(x_t|X_{\setminus t})$$

$$= \mathbb{E}_{t \sim \mathcal{U}(\{1,\ldots,|X|\})} \left[\log p(x_t|X_{\setminus t}) \right]$$

$$\approx \frac{1}{K} \sum_{k=1}^{K} \log p(x_{\tilde{t}_k}|X_{\setminus \tilde{t}_k}),$$

where $\tilde{t}_k \sim \mathcal{U}(\{1,\ldots,|X|\})$. Let us refer to this as stochastic pseudo log-likelihood learning.

In Reality The stochastic pseudo log-likelihood learning above states that we "mask out" one token in a sequence at a time and let f_θ predict it based on all the other "observed" tokens in the sequence. Devlin et al. (2018) however proposed to "mask out" multiple tokens at a time and predict all of them given both all "observed" and "masked out" tokens in the sequence. This brings the original BERT closer to a denoising autoencoder (Vincent et al., 2010), which could still be considered as training a Markov random field with (approximate) score matching (Vincent, 2011).

3 Using BERT as an MRF-LM

The discussion so far implies that BERT is a Markov random field language model (MRF-LM) and that it learns a distribution over sentences (of some given length). This framing suggests that we can use BERT not only as parameter initialization for finetuning but as a generative model of sentences to either score a sentence or sample a sentence.

Ranking Let us fix the length T. Then, we can use BERT to rank a set of sentences. We cannot compute the exact probabilities of these sentences, but we can compute their unnormalized log-probabilities according to Eq. (2):

$$\sum_{t=1}^{T} \log \phi_t(X).$$

These unnormalized probabilities can be used to find the most likely sentence within the set or to sort the sentences according to their probabilities.

Sampling Sampling from a Markov random field is less trivial than is from a directed graphical model which naturally admits ancestral sampling. One of the most widely used approaches

the nearest regional centre is alemanno , with another connection to potenza and maradona , and the nearest railway station is in bergamo , where the line terminates on its northern end	for all of thirty seconds , she was n't going to speak . maybe this time , she 'd actually agree to go . thirty seconds later , she 'd been speaking to him in her head every
' let him get away , mrs . nightingale . you could do it again . ' ' he - ` ' no , please . i have to touch him . and when you do , you run .	" oh , i 'm sure they would be of a good service , " she assured me . " how are things going in the morning ? is your husband well ? " " yes , very well
he also " turned the tale [of] the marriage into a book " as he wanted it to " be elegiac " . both sagas contain stories of both couple and their wedding night ;	" i know . " she paused ." did he touch you ? " " no . " " ah . " " oh , no , " i said , confused , not sure why
" i had a bad dream . " " about an alien ship ? who was it ? " i check the text message that 's been only partially restored yet, the one that says love .	i watched him through the glass , wondering if he was going to attempt to break in on our meeting . but he did n't seem to even bother to knock when he entered the room . i was n't
replaced chris hall (st . louis area manager) . june 9 : mike howard (syndicated " good morning " , replaced steve koval , replaced dan nickolas , and replaced phil smith) ;	" how long has it been since you have made yourself an offer like that ? " asked planner . " oh " was the reply . planner had heard of some of his other business associates who had

Table 1: Random sample generations from BERT base (left) and GPT (right).

is Markov-chain Monte-Carlo (MCMC) sampling (Neal, 1993; Swendsen and Wang, 1986; Salakhutdinov, 2009; Desjardins et al., 2010; Cho et al., 2010). In this report, we only consider Gibbs sampling which fits naturally with (stochastic) pseudo log-likelihood learning.

In Gibbs sampling, we start with a random initial state X^0, which we initialize to be an all-mask sequence, i.e., ([MASK], ..., [MASK]), though we could with a sentence consisting of randomly sampled words or by retrieving a sentence from data. At each iteration i, we sample the position t^i uniformly at random from $\{1, ..., T\}$ and mask out the selected location, i.e., $x_{t^i}^i = $ [MASK], resulting in $X_{\setminus t^i}^i$. We now compute $p(x_{t^i} | X_{\setminus t^i}^i)$ according to Eq. (3), sample $\tilde{x}_{t^i}$ from it[2], and construct the next sequence by

$$X^{i+1} = (x_1^i, ..., x_{t^i-1}^i, \tilde{x}_{t^i}, x_{t^i+1}^i, ..., x_T^i).$$

We repeat this procedure many times, preferably with thinning.[3] Because Gibbs sampling, as well as any MCMC sampler with a local proposal distribution, tends to get stuck in a mode of the distribution, we advise running multiple chains of Gibbs sampling or using different sentence initializations.

Sequential Sampling The undirectedness of the MRF-LM and the bidirectional nature of BERT do not naturally admit sequential sampling, but given that the dominant approach to text generation is left-to-right, we experiment with generating from BERT in such a manner.

As with our non-sequential sampling scheme, we can begin with a seed sentence of either all masks or a random sentence. Whereas previously we sampled a position $t \in \{1, ..., T\}$ to mask out and generate for at each time step, in the sequential setting, at each time step t, we mask out x_t^t, generate a word for that position, and substitute it into the sequence. After T timesteps, we have a sampled a token at each position, at which we point we can terminate or repeat the process from the current sentence.

4 Experiments

Our experiments demonstrate the potential of using BERT as a *standalone* language model rather than as a parameter initializer for transfer learning (Devlin et al., 2018; Lample and Conneau, 2019; Nogueira and Cho, 2019). We show that sentences sampled from BERT are well-formed and are assigned high probabilities by an off-the-shelf language model. We take pretrained BERT models trained on a mix of Toronto Book Corpus (TBC, Zhu et al., 2015) and Wikipedia provided by Devlin et al. (2018) and its PyTorch implementation[4] provided by HuggingFace. We experiment with both the base and large BERT configuations.

4.1 Evaluation

We consider several evaluation metrics to estimate the quality and diversity of the generations.

---

[2] In practice, one can imagine sampling from the k-most probable words (Fan et al., 2018). We find $k = 100$ to be effective in early experiments.

[3] Thinning refers to the procedure of selecting a sample only once a while during MCMC sampling.

[4] https://github.com/huggingface/pytorch-pretrained-BERT

Model	Self-BLEU ($\downarrow$)	% Unique n-grams ($\uparrow$)								
		Self			WT103			TBC		
		n=2	n=3	n=4	n=2	n=3	n=4	n=2	n=3	n=4
BERT (large)	9.43	63.15	92.38	98.01	59.91	91.86	98.43	64.59	93.27	98.59
BERT (base)	10.06	60.76	91.76	98.14	57.90	91.72	98.55	60.94	92.04	98.56
GPT	40.02	31.13	67.01	87.28	33.71	72.86	91.12	25.74	65.04	88.42
WT103	9.80	70.29	94.36	99.05	56.19	88.05	97.44	68.35	94.20	99.23
TBC	12.51	62.19	92.70	98.73	55.30	91.08	98.81	44.75	82.06	96.31

Table 2: Self-BLEU and percent of generated n-grams that are unique relative to own generations (left) WikiText-103 test set (middle) a sample of 5000 sentences from Toronto Book Corpus (right). For the WT103 and TBC rows, we sample 1000 sentences from the respective datasets.

Quality To automatically measure the quality of the generations, we follow Yu et al. (2017) by computing BLEU (Papineni et al., 2002) between the generations and the original data distributions to measure how similar the generations are. We use a random sample of 5000 sentences from the test set of WikiText-103 (WT103, Merity et al., 2016) and a random sample of 5000 sentences from TBC as references.

We also use the perplexity of a trained language model evaluated on the generations as a rough proxy for fluency. Specifically, we use the Gated Convolutional Language Model (Dauphin et al., 2016) pretrained on WikiText-103[5].

Diversity To measure the diversity of each model's generations, we compute self-BLEU (Zhu et al., 2018): for each generated sentence, we compute BLEU treating the rest of the sentences as references, and average across sentences. Self-BLEU measures how similar each generated sentence is to the other generations; high self-BLEU indicates that the model has low sample diversity.

We also evaluate the percentage of n-grams that are unique, when compared to the original data distribution and within the corpus of generations. We note that this metric is somewhat in opposition to BLEU between generations and data, as fewer unique n-grams implies higher BLEU.

Methodology We use the non-sequential sampling scheme with sampling from the top $k = 100$ most frequent words at each time step, as empirically this led to the most coherent generations. We show generations from the sequential sampler in Table 4 in the appendix. We compare against generations from a high-quality neural language model, the OpenAI Generative Pre-Training

[5]https://github.com/pytorch/fairseq/tree/master/examples/conv_lm

Model	Corpus-BLEU ($\uparrow$)		PPL ($\downarrow$)
	WT103	TBC	
BERT (large)	5.05	7.60	331.47
BERT (base)	7.80	7.06	279.10
GPT	10.81	30.75	154.29
WT103	17.48	6.57	54.00
TBC	10.05	23.05	314.28

Table 3: Quality metrics of model generations. Perplexity (PPL) is measured using an additional language model (Dauphin et al., 2016). For the WT103 and TBC rows, we sample 1000 sentences from the respective datasets.

Transformer (Radford et al., 2018, GPT), which was trained on TBC and has approximately the same number of parameters as the base configuration of BERT. For BERT, we pad each input with special symbols [CLS] and [SEP]. For GPT, we start with a start of sentence token and generate left to right. For all models, we generate 1000 uncased sequences of length 40. Finally, as a trivial baseline, we sample 1000 sentences from TBC and the training split of WT103 and compute all automatic metrics against these samples.

5 Results

We present sample generations, quality results, and diversity results respectively in Tables 1, 2, 3.

We find that, compared to GPT, the BERT generations are of worse quality, but are more diverse. Surprisingly, the outside language model, which was trained on Wikipedia, is less perplexed by the GPT generations than the BERT generations, even though GPT was only trained on romance novels and BERT was trained on romance novels and Wikipedia. On actual data from TBC, the outside language model is about as perplexed as on the BERT generations, which suggests that domain shift is an issue in using a trained language

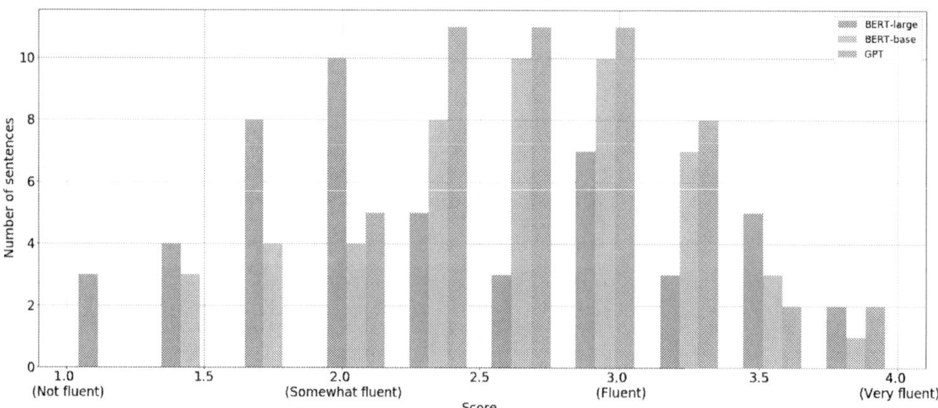

Figure 1: Fluency scores for 100 sentences samples from each of BERT large, BERT base, and GPT, as judged by human annotators according to a four-point Likert scale.

model for evaluating generations and that the GPT generations might have collapsed to fairly generic and simple sentences. This observation is further bolstered by the fact that the GPT generations have a higher corpus-BLEU with TBC than TBC has with itself. The perplexity on BERT samples is not absurdly high, and in reading the samples, we find that many are fairly coherent. The corpus-BLEU between BERT models and the datasets is low, particularly with WT103.

We find that BERT generations are more diverse than GPT generations. GPT has high n-gram overlap (smaller percent of unique n-grams) with TBC, but surprisingly also with WikiText-103, despite being trained on different data. Furthermore, GPT generations have greater n-gram overlap with these datasets than these datasets have with themselves, further suggesting that GPT is relying significantly on generic sentences. BERT has lower n-gram overlap with both corpora, with similar degrees of n-gram overlap as the samples of the data.

For a more rigorous evaluation of generation quality, we collect human judgments on sentence fluency for 100 samples from BERT large, BERT base, and GPT using a four point Likert scale. For each sample we ask three annotators to rate the sentence on its fluency and take the average of the three judgments as the sentence's fluency score. We present a histogram of the results in Figure 1. For BERT large, BERT base, and GPT we respectively get mean scores over the samples of 2.37 ($\sigma = 0.83$), 2.65 ($\sigma = 0.65$), and 2.80 ($\sigma = 0.51$). All means are within a standard deviation of each other. BERT base and GPT have similar unimodal distributions with BERT base having a slightly more non-fluent samples. BERT large has a bimodal distribution.

6   Conclusion

We show that BERT is a Markov random field language model. Formulating BERT in this way gives rise to a practical algorithm for generating from BERT based on Gibbs sampling that does not require any additional parameters or training. We verify in experiments that the algorithm produces diverse and fairly fluent generations. The power of this framework is in allowing the principled application of Gibbs sampling, and potentially other MCMC algorithms, for generating from BERT.

Future work might explore these improved sampling methods, especially those that do not need to run the model over the entire sequence each iteration and that more robustly handle variable-length sequences. To facilitate such investigation, we release our code on GitHub at `https://github.com/nyu-dl/bert-gen` and a demo as a Colab notebook at `https://colab.research.google.com/drive/1MxKZGtQ9SSBjTK5ArsZ5LKhkztzg52RV`.

Acknowledgements

We thank Ilya Kulikov and Nikita Nangia for their help, as well as reviewers for insightful comments. AW is supported by an NSF Fellowship. KC is partly supported by Samsung Advanced Institute of Technology (Next Generation Deep Learning: from Pattern Recognition to AI) and Samsung Electronics (Improving Deep Learning using Latent Structure).

References

Julian Besag. 1977. Efficiency of pseudolikelihood estimation for simple gaussian fields. *Biometrika*, pages 616–618.

John S Bridle. 1990. Probabilistic interpretation of feedforward classification network outputs, with relationships to statistical pattern recognition. In *Neurocomputing*, pages 227–236. Springer.

KyungHyun Cho, Tapani Raiko, and Alexander Ilin. 2010. Parallel tempering is efficient for learning restricted boltzmann machines. In *Neural Networks (IJCNN), The 2010 International Joint Conference on*, pages 1–8. IEEE.

Yann N Dauphin, Angela Fan, Michael Auli, and David Grangier. 2016. Language modeling with gated convolutional networks. *arXiv preprint:1612.08083*.

Guillaume Desjardins, Aaron Courville, Yoshua Bengio, Pascal Vincent, and Olivier Delalleau. 2010. Tempered markov chain monte carlo for training of restricted boltzmann machines. In *Proceedings of the thirteenth international conference on artificial intelligence and statistics*, pages 145–152.

Jacob Devlin, Ming-Wei Chang, Kenton Lee, and Kristina Toutanova. 2018. Bert: Pre-training of deep bidirectional transformers for language understanding. *arXiv preprint:1810.04805*.

Angela Fan, Mike Lewis, and Yann Dauphin. 2018. Hierarchical neural story generation. *arXiv preprint:1805.04833*.

Yoav Goldberg. 2019. Assessing bert's syntactic abilities.

Yacine Jernite, Alexander Rush, and David Sontag. 2015. A fast variational approach for learning markov random field language models. In *International Conference on Machine Learning*, pages 2209–2217.

Nikita Kitaev and Dan Klein. 2018. Multilingual constituency parsing with self-attention and pre-training.

Guillaume Lample and Alexis Conneau. 2019. Cross-lingual Language Model Pretraining. *arXiv e-prints*, page arXiv:1901.07291.

Stephen Merity, Caiming Xiong, James Bradbury, and Richard Socher. 2016. Pointer sentinel mixture models.

Tomas Mikolov, Kai Chen, Greg Corrado, and Jeffrey Dean. 2013. Efficient estimation of word representations in vector space. *arXiv preprint:1301.3781*.

Radford M Neal. 1993. Probabilistic inference using markov chain monte carlo methods.

Rodrigo Nogueira and Kyunghyun Cho. 2019. Passage re-ranking with bert. *arXiv preprint:1901.04085*.

Kishore Papineni, Salim Roukos, Todd Ward, and Wei-Jing Zhu. 2002. Bleu: a method for automatic evaluation of machine translation. In *Proceedings of the 40th annual meeting on association for computational linguistics*, pages 311–318. Association for Computational Linguistics.

Alec Radford, Karthik Narasimhan, Tim Salimans, and Ilya Sutskever. 2018. Improving language understanding by generative pre-training. *URL https://s3-us-west-2. amazonaws. com/openai-assets/research-covers/languageunsupervised/language understanding paper. pdf*.

Ruslan R Salakhutdinov. 2009. Learning in markov random fields using tempered transitions. In *Advances in neural information processing systems*, pages 1598–1606.

Robert H Swendsen and Jian-Sheng Wang. 1986. Replica monte carlo simulation of spin-glasses. *Physical review letters*, 57(21):2607.

Pascal Vincent. 2011. A connection between score matching and denoising autoencoders. *Neural computation*, 23(7):1661–1674.

Pascal Vincent, Hugo Larochelle, Isabelle Lajoie, Yoshua Bengio, and Pierre-Antoine Manzagol. 2010. Stacked denoising autoencoders: Learning useful representations in a deep network with a local denoising criterion. *Journal of machine learning research*, 11(Dec):3371–3408.

Lantao Yu, Weinan Zhang, Jun Wang, and Yong Yu. 2017. Seqgan: Sequence generative adversarial nets with policy gradient. In *AAAI*, pages 2852–2858.

Yaoming Zhu, Sidi Lu, Lei Zheng, Jiaxian Guo, Weinan Zhang, Jun Wang, and Yong Yu. 2018. Texygen: A benchmarking platform for text generation models. *arXiv preprint:1802.01886*.

Yukun Zhu, Ryan Kiros, Richard Zemel, Ruslan Salakhutdinov, Raquel Urtasun, Antonio Torralba, and Sanja Fidler. 2015. Aligning books and movies: Towards story-like visual explanations by watching movies and reading books. In *arXiv preprint:1506.06724*.

A Other Sampling Strategies

We explored two other sampling strategies: left-to-right and generating for all positions at each time step. See Section 3 for an explanation of the former. For the latter, we start with an initial sequence of all masks, and at each time step, we would not mask any positions but would generate for all positions. This strategy is designed to save on computation. However, we found that this tended to get stuck in non-fluent sentences that could not be recovered from. We present sample generations for the left-to-right strategy in Table 4.

all the good people , no more , no less . no more . for ... the kind of better people ... for ... for ... for ... for ... for ... for ... as they must become again .

sometimes in these rooms , here , back in the castle . but then : and then , again , as if they were turning , and then slowly , and and then and then , and then suddenly .

other available songs for example are the second and final two complete music albums among the highest played artists , including : the one the greatest ... and the last recorded album , " this sad heart " respectively .

6 that is i ? ? and the house is not of the lord . i am well ... the lord is ... ? , which perhaps i should be addressing : ya is then , of ye ? ?

four - cornered rap . big screen with huge screen two of his friend of old age . from happy , happy , happy . left ? left ? left ? right . left ? right . right ? ?

Table 4: Random sample generations from BERT base using a sequential, left-to-right sampling strategy.

Neural Text Simplification in Low-Resource Conditions
Using Weak Supervision

Alessio Palmero Aprosio
Fondazione Bruno Kessler
Trento, Italy
aprosio@fbk.eu

Sara Tonelli
Fondazione Bruno Kessler
Trento, Italy
satonelli@fbk.eu

Marco Turchi
Fondazione Bruno Kessler
Trento, Italy
turchi@fbk.eu

Matteo Negri
Fondazione Bruno Kessler
Trento, Italy
negri@fbk.eu

Mattia Di Gangi
Fondazione Bruno Kessler
Trento, Italy
digangi@fbk.eu

Abstract

Neural text simplification has gained increasing attention in the NLP community thanks to recent advancements in deep sequence-to-sequence learning. Most recent efforts with such a data-demanding paradigm have dealt with the English language, for which sizeable training datasets are currently available to deploy competitive models. Similar improvements on less resource-rich languages are conditioned either to intensive manual work to create training data, or to the design of effective automatic generation techniques to bypass the data acquisition bottleneck. Inspired by the machine translation field, in which synthetic parallel pairs generated from monolingual data yield significant improvements to neural models, in this paper we exploit large amounts of heterogeneous data to automatically select simple sentences, which are then used to create synthetic simplification pairs. We also evaluate other solutions, such as oversampling and the use of external word embeddings to be fed to the neural simplification system. Our approach is evaluated on Italian and Spanish, for which few thousand gold sentence pairs are available. The results show that these techniques yield performance improvements over a baseline sequence-to-sequence configuration.

1 Introduction

Text simplification aims at making a text more readable by reducing its lexical and structural complexity while preserving the meaning. (Chandrasekar and Bangalore, 1997; Carroll et al., 1998; Vickrey and Koller, 2008; Crossley et al., 2012; Shardlow, 2014). Neural approaches to the task have gained increasing attention in the NLP community thanks to recent advancements of deep,

sequence-to-sequence approaches. However, all recent improvements have dealt with English. The main reason is that such data-hungry approaches require large training sets (in the order of hundred thousand instances) and sizable datasets have been developed and made available only for this language. Indeed, the only available datasets composed of a complex and a simple version of the same document, which are large enough to experiment with deep neural systems, are Newsela (Xu et al., 2015) and the aligned version of simple and standard English Wikipedia (Zhu et al., 2010). These data have become the common benchmark for evaluating new approaches to neural text simplification. These methods rely on the use of deep reinforcement learning (Zhang and Lapata, 2017), memory-augmented neural networks (Vu et al., 2018), the combination of semantic parsing and neural approaches (Sulem et al., 2018) and the personalisation to specific grade levels (Scarton and Specia, 2018). Due to data paucity, none of them can be tested on other languages, for which less data-intensive, rule-based solutions have been proposed (Brouwers et al., 2012; Bott et al., 2012; Barlacchi and Tonelli, 2013). The main disadvantage of such solutions, however, is a reduced portability and scalability to new scenarios, which require the creation of new sets of rules each time a new language (or a new domain with specific idiosyncrasies) has to be covered.

To alleviate the data bottleneck issue, enabling the development of neural solutions also for languages other than English, we explore data augmentation techniques for creating task-specific training data. Our experiments range from simple oversampling techniques to weakly supervised data augmentation methods inspired by recent

Proceedings of the Workshop on Methods for Optimizing and Evaluating Neural Language Generation (NeuralGen), pages 37–44
Minneapolis, Minnesota, USA, June 6, 2019. ©2019 Association for Computational Linguistics

works in other NLP tasks (Bérard et al., 2016; Ding and Balog, 2018), in particular Machine Translation (MT) (Sennrich et al., 2016b). In a nutshell, taking an opposite direction to simplification, we proceed by *i)* automatically selecting simple sentences from a large pool of monolingual data, and *ii)* synthetically creating complex sentences. These artificially created sentences will be then used as the "source" side of new *difficult–simple* training pairs fed into an MT-like encoder-decoder architecture.

Our hypothesis is that, though sub-optimal due to possible errors introduced in the automatic generation of complex sentences, these training pairs represent useful material for building our sequence-to-sequence text simplification models. Under this hypothesis, any noise in the source side of the pairs can still be treated as an approximation of text difficulty that, paired with its correct simplified counterpart, can contribute to model training.

We run our experiments on Italian and Spanish, two languages for which only small datasets of manually curated simplifications are available. The main contributions of this work are:

- We explore different approaches for augmenting training data for neural text simplification using weak supervision;

- We test them in under-resourced conditions on Italian and Spanish.

2   Related work

The lack of data for training sequence-to-sequence models is a problem that has been addressed in several NLP tasks. In MT, for instance, synthetic parallel data for low-resource settings have been generated by automatically translating sentences from the target language into the source language (Sennrich et al., 2016b,a). In speech translation, recent works (Bérard et al., 2016; Jia et al., 2018) have shown that end-to-end models can be successfully trained on artificial *source_audio–target_text* pairs built from synthesized speech data and/or machine-translated text.

For keyword-to-question generation, small training data have been first inverted to create a question-to-keyword dataset and then used to artificially generate keywords given a large quantity of questions (Ding and Balog, 2018).

In all these tasks, when added to the original data, the synthetic sets always result in significant improvements in performance. Even if suboptimal due to variable noise introduced on the source side by automatic processing, large "silver" data provide a valuable additional complement to small "gold" training corpora.

Regarding neural text simplification, we are not aware of previous work on extending small training corpora with synthetic data. Indeed, the lack of training instances has been a major issue in the development of such applications for languages other than English.

3   Neural sentence simplification system

Our sentence simplification approach is based on the attentional encoder-decoder model (Bahdanau et al., 2014) initially proposed for MT. It takes as input a complex sentence and outputs its simplified version (Nisioi et al., 2017). Cast as a (monolingual) translation task, it provides a comprehensive solution to address both lexical and structural simplification, since the model does not only learn single term replacements, but also more complex structural changes. Initially, a sequence of words is fed to the encoder, which maps it into a sequence of continuous representations (the hidden states of the encoder) providing increasing levels of abstraction. At each time step, based on these continuous representations and the generated word in the previous time step, the decoder generates the next word. This process continues until the decoder generates the end-of-sentence symbol. This sequence-to-sequence model is extended by adding a pointer-generator network that allows both copying words via pointing to the source sentence, and generating words from a fixed vocabulary (See et al., 2017). At each time step, the network estimates the probability of generating a word and uses this probability as a gate to decide whether to generate or copy the word. To apply this pointer-generator network, a shared vocabulary containing all the words in the complex and simple training sentences is used. This architecture is implemented in the OpenNMT platform (Klein et al., 2017).

4   Data augmentation

Our experimentation starts from the availability of a limited quantity (few tens of thousand complex-to-simple sentence pairs) of high-quality gold standard data that is used to train and evaluate our pointer-generator network baseline.

To satisfy the need of much larger training sets required to exploit the generalization capabilities of neural approaches,[1] we explore three different data augmentation strategies:

Oversampling: In line with the work in MT-related tasks like automatic post-editing (Chatterjee et al., 2017), we increase the size of the training set by multiplying the whole original training corpus (5 and 10 times) to maximize the use of the few "gold" sentence pairs available.

Simple-to-simple synthetic pairs creation: Starting from large monolingual corpora, we automatically extract the simplest sentences using different heuristics, and then duplicate them to create simple-to-simple pairs. These are then used as synthetic data to train the simplification system. The intuition behind this strategy is to add information that can be beneficial to the creation of better word embedding representations and to introduce a bias in the decoder towards producing simple outputs.

Simple-to-complex synthetic pairs creation: We convert the gold data into a set of simple-to-complex pairs inspired by the work in MT (Sennrich et al., 2016b) and in keyword-to-question (Ding and Balog, 2018), and then use the Open-NMT toolkit to train a "complexifier" system. Then, we run it on the set of simple sentences selected to create the simple-to-simple pairs (see above) to obtain additional simple-to-complex pairs. Finally, we revert the pairs again and use them as synthetic data to train the simplification system. The intuition behind this strategy is to maintain the human-generated simplified sentences in the target side of the parallel data to improve the generation of simplified sentences. This comes at the cost of accepting the low quality of automatically "complicated" source sentences. Due to the limited amount of training data available, we do not expect that complicating a sentence is an easier task than making it simpler, so the quality of the automatic complex sentences can be limited. With this method, however, we are interested in checking if the neural network approach is able to infer useful information from low-quality data when dealing with few gold-standard sentence pairs. We expect that, similar to MT, a neural simplification model can be trained even if the source data is not of high quality, given that the sentences on the target side are correct.

Additionally, we explore also whether large scale **pre-trained embeddings** can improve text simplification models. A similar setting was evaluated on English (Nisioi et al., 2017) and did not yield remarkable improvements. However, our intuition is that pre-trained embeddings may be more beneficial in low-resource conditions, providing additional information that cannot be extracted from small training corpora.

5 Experimental Setup

We run our experiments on two languages, Italian and Spanish. Below, we describe for each language the gold standard and the simple monolingual data extraction process to augment our training data.

5.1 Italian

To obtain the Italian gold standard, we merge three available data sets, namely:

- The SIMPITIKI corpus (Tonelli et al., 2016), a manually curated corpus with $1,166$ complex–simple pairs extracted from Italian Wikipedia and from documents in the administrative domain;

- The corpus presented in (Brunato et al., 2015), another manually curated corpus comprising $1,690$ sentence pairs from the educational domain;

- A subset of the PaCCSS-it corpus (Brunato et al., 2016), which contains $63,000$ complex-to-simple sentence pairs automatically extracted from the Web. In order to extract only the pairs of higher quality, we pre-processed the corpus by discarding sentence pairs with special characters, misspellings, non-matching numerals or dates, and a cosine similarity below 0.5.

The final gold standard contains $32,210$ complex-to-simple pairs.

The set of simple sentences used to create the synthetic pairs is obtained from a large monolingual corpus covering both formal and infor-

---

[1] In speech recognition and MT, for instance, the impressive performance obtained by end-to-end systems is the result of resource-intensive training, respectively on thousands of hours of transcribed speech (Chiu et al., 2018) and tens of millions of parallel sentences (Hassan et al., 2018).

Pretr. Emb.	Copied	Complic.	ITA x1	ITA x5	ITA x10	SPA x1	SPA x5	SPA x10
-	-	-	44.6	48.5	48.1	28.4	27.4	27.6
✓	-	-	47.3	48.8	49.5	**29.1**	28.2	28.1
-	✓	-	44.4	49.4	49.1	23.1	24.3	28.6
✓	✓	-	44.2	49.2	49.2	24.6	25.0	27.2
-	-	✓	**48.0**	49.9	49.8	28.6	28.6	30.6
✓	-	✓	47.9	**49.9**	**50.0**	28.6	28.7	**30.8**
-	✓	✓	45.6	49.3	49.5	29.0	**29.1**	26.2
✓	✓	✓	45.2	**49.9**	49.7	24.9	25.0	26.2

Table 1: Results of neural simplification experiments on Italian and Spanish data (SARI)

mal language, including Italian Opensubtitles,[2] the Paisà corpus (Lyding et al., 2014), Wikipedia and the collection of Italian laws.[3] This merging process results in around 1.3B words and 125M sentences. We rank all sentences by readability level according to the best features described in (Dell'Orletta et al., 2014) and keep the $500,000$ most readable (i.e. simplest) sentences to create the synthetic pairs. This process is needed due to the lack of an Italian equivalent of the Simple English Wikipedia,[4] which is widely used as a source of simple monolingual data when dealing with English text simplification (Zhu et al., 2010; Woodsend and Lapata, 2011). From the large corpus described above, before filtering only simple sentences, we also create word embeddings with 300 dimensions using word2vec (Mikolov et al., 2013).

5.2 Spanish

The Spanish gold standard is obtained from the Spanish Newsela corpus,[5] containing $1,221$ documents manually annotated by professionals for different proficiency levels. We align complex–simple pairs using the CATS-Align[6] tool (Štajner et al., 2018) and discard the pairs coupled with an alignment accuracy below 0.5. The gold standard contains $55,890$ complex-to-simple pairs.

The set of simple sentences used to create the synthetic pairs is extracted from a large monolin-gual corpus covering different domains, obtained from websites written in simple Spanish for language learners.[7] The documents are then ranked based on the Flesch-Szigriszt readability score for Spanish (Szigriszt, 1993)[8] and all sentences belonging to the most readable ones are included in the set of simple monolingual data ($484,325$ simple sentences in total, from a set of about 1.2M sentences). For Spanish, we do not rank directly the sentences because there is no specific study to identify metrics at sentence level similar to the one for Italian presented in (Dell'Orletta et al., 2014).

The Spanish embeddings used in the simplification process are those obtained from the Spanish Billion Word Corpus, that is widely used in NLP experiments on Spanish (Zea et al., 2016; Quirós et al., 2016).[9] To favour the extraction of word embeddings from simple texts, we increase the Spanish Billion Word Corpus by adding our extracted simple Spanish texts. In total, Spanish word embeddings are extracted from a corpus of nearly 1.5B words.

5.3 System configuration

OpenNMT is run on a Nvidia Tesla K80 GPU using stochastic gradient descent (Robbins and Monro, 1951) optimization with learning rate 1. Each run is repeated three times with different seeds, then the average value is considered. Since the source and target languages are the same, in

---

[2] www.opensubtitles.org

[3] www.gazzettaufficiale.it

[4] simple.wikipedia.org/wiki/Simple_English_Wikipedia.

[5] newsela.com/data

[6] The tool (github.com/neosyon/SimpTextAlign) includes several lexical and semantic text similarity methods and alignment strategies for simplified text alignment at different text representation levels (paragraph, sentence, and sentence with paragraph pre-alignment).

[7] For example www.cuentosinfantiles.net or www.mundoprimaria.com

[8] This score is an adaptation of the Flesch Index (Flesch, 1946), which provides a readability measure combining word and sentence length in a 1-100 scale (the closer the score is to 100, the easier the text is to read). The Flesch-Szigriszt adaptation refines the original Flesch equation by also considering the number of syllables and phrases in the text.

[9] github.com/uchile-nlp/spanish-word-embeddings

the preprocessing phase their vocabulary is shared. We split data into train/dev/test with ratio 90/5/5 respectively. For Italian, this results in a split of $29,260/1,475/1,475$ sentence pairs, while for Spanish it is $50,301/2,794/2,795$.

6 Evaluation

We report in Table 1 the results of Italian and Spanish text simplification using different settings and data augmentation techniques. For each language, we evaluate the results using the gold training set as is, and expanding it through oversampling (i.e. repetition of the same sentence pairs 5 and 10 times). In addition, we evaluate the impact of: *i)* adding pre-trained word embeddings built on large monolingual corpora (*Pretr.Emb*), *ii)* using the simple-to-simple pairs for data augmentation (*Copied*), and *iii)* using, for the same purpose, the simple-to-complex synthetic pairs (*Complic.*). We also explore the addition of different combinations of the aforementioned resources. The evaluation is performed by computing the SARI score (Xu et al., 2016) on the test set.

Our results show that adding only pre-trained word embeddings trained on large monolingual corpora achieves, in general, better performance than the baseline (max: +2.73 SARI points for Italian, +0.8 for Spanish). Our experiments show also that the usefulness of simple-to-simple pairs cannot be generalised: they are beneficial for all results on Italian and *SPAx10*, while they are harmful for *SPAx1* and *SPAx5*. Our intuition is that the copied data pushed the system in the direction of learning to copy the source sentence in the output instead of simplifying it, which can create some instability in the model during training. The addition of simple-to-simple pairs and of pre-trained word embeddings does not yield large improvements, confirming the idea that the copied pairs mainly affect the quality of the word embedding representations instead of the relation between complex and simple sentences (i.e. attention network).

The largest gains in performance are obtained when using the simple-to-complex synthetic pairs. Both in isolation and when paired with pre-trained embeddings, they make the neural model able to outperform the baseline up to +3.4 SARI points. The best results for both languages are obtained by multiplying the training data by 10 and adding the simple-to-complex synthetic data. These configurations outperform the standard settings (*ITAx1* and *SPAx1*) by +5.4 SARI points for Italian and and +2.4 for Spanish.

When concatenating all the synthetic and real data, and the pre-trained embeddings are used, the performance is comparable with the one obtained using the simple-to-complex synthetic pairs, but at the cost of using a larger quantity of training data.

Although we cannot make a direct comparison of the SARI scores across different languages, Italian and Spanish are typologically very similar, and therefore we can argue that our models for neural simplification in Italian works better than the Spanish ones. This may depend on several reasons. For Italian, the selection of $500,000$ simple sentences is based on sentence-specific features correlated with high readability, emerged from the analysis in (Dell'Orletta et al., 2014). On the contrary, extracting simple monolingual sentences based on the readability score at document level, as we did for Spanish, is more prone to inconsistencies. Other differences may be due to the quality of gold standard data: although the Spanish gold standard is bigger than the Italian one ($55,890$ complex-simple sentence pairs vs. $32,210$ pairs respectively), its language is generally more complex, since it contains news articles, while the Italian gold standard includes to a large extent stories for children and textbooks. Besides, while some of the Italian sentences were manually aligned, the Spanish gold data were obtained by automatically extracting complex-to-simple pairs from the Newsela corpus, in which the alignment had been done at document level.

As a comparison, we evaluate on the same test set also the MUSST syntactic simplifier (Scarton et al., 2017), a freely available system implementing a set of simplification rules for Italian and Spanish. We obtain 20.16 SARI for Italian and 21.24 for Spanish. Our results show that, despite some issues described before, low-resource neural simplification is still a promising research direction to pursue, especially with data augmentation. This is particularly true for Spanish MUSST, which includes a richer set of rules than the Italian version, but that achieves nevertheless -9.56 SARI points than the best neural model for Spanish.

7 Conclusions

We presented several techniques to augment the amount of training data for neural text simplification through weak supervision. Our solutions were evaluated on Italian and Spanish using a sequence-to-sequence approach. Our results show that using external embeddings is generally beneficial in a low-resource setting, since they provide additional information that cannot be extracted from a limited amount of training pairs. Another gain in performance is achieved using complex-to-simple synthetic pairs created with a 'complexifier' system.

In the future, we plan to extend both the languages of the experiments and the data augmentation techniques, for example by applying machine translation to increase the amount of gold sentence pairs across languages, or by using bootstrapping techniques.

Acknowledgments

This work has been partially supported by the European Commission project SIMPATICO (H2020-EURO-6-2015, grant number 692819).

References

Dzmitry Bahdanau, Kyunghyun Cho, and Yoshua Bengio. 2014. Neural machine translation by jointly learning to align and translate. *arXiv preprint arXiv:1409.0473*.

Gianni Barlacchi and Sara Tonelli. 2013. ERNESTA: A Sentence Simplification Tool for Children's Stories in Italian. In *Computational Linguistics and Intelligent Text Processing: 14th International Conference, CICLing 2013, Samos, Greece, March 24-30, 2013, Proceedings, Part II*, pages 476–487, Berlin, Heidelberg. Springer Berlin Heidelberg.

Alexandre Bérard, Olivier Pietquin, Laurent Besacier, and Christophe Servan. 2016. Listen and Translate: A Proof of Concept for End-to-End Speech-to-Text Translation. In *NIPS Workshop on end-to-end learning for speech and audio processing*, Barcelona, Spain.

Stefan Bott, Horacio Saggion, and David Figueroa. 2012. A Hybrid System for Spanish Text Simplification. In *Proceedings of the Third Workshop on Speech and Language Processing for Assistive Technologies*, pages 75–84.

Laetitia Brouwers, Delphine Bernhard, Anne-Laure Ligozat, and Thomas François. 2012. Simplification syntaxique de phrases pour le français (Syntactic Simplification for French Sentences) [in French]. In *Proceedings of the Joint Conference JEP-TALN-RECITAL 2012, volume 2: TALN*, pages 211–224. ATALA/AFCP.

Dominique Brunato, Andrea Cimino, Felice Dell'Orletta, and Giulia Venturi. 2016. PaCCSS-IT: A Parallel Corpus of Complex-Simple Sentences for Automatic Text Simplification . In *Proceedings of the 2016 Conference on Empirical Methods in Natural Language Processing*, pages 351–361. Association for Computational Linguistics.

Dominique Brunato, Felice Dell'Orletta, Giulia Venturi, and Simonetta Montemagni. 2015. Design and Annotation of the First Italian Corpus for Text Simplification. In *Proceedings of The 9th Linguistic Annotation Workshop*, pages 31–41, Denver, Colorado, USA. Association for Computational Linguistics.

John Carroll, Guido Minnen, Yvonne Canning, Siobhan Devlin, and John Tait. 1998. Practical Simplification of English Newspaper Text to Assist Aphasic Readers. In *In Proc. of AAAI-98 Workshop on Integrating Artificial Intelligence and Assistive Technology*, pages 7–10.

Raman Chandrasekar and Srinivas Bangalore. 1997. Automatic induction of rules for text simplification. *Knowledge-Based Systems*, 10(3):183–190.

Rajen Chatterjee, M. Amin Farajian, Matteo Negri, Marco Turchi, Ankit Srivastava, and Santanu Pal. 2017. Multi-source Neural Automatic Post-Editing: FBK's Participation in the WMT 2017 APE Shared Task . In *Proceedings of the Second Conference on Machine Translation*, pages 630–638. Association for Computational Linguistics.

Chung-Cheng Chiu, Tara Sainath, Yonghui Wu, Rohit Prabhavalkar, Patrick Nguyen, Zhifeng Chen, Anjuli Kannan, Ron J. Weiss, Kanishka Rao, Katya Gonina, Navdeep Jaitly, Bo Li, Jan Chorowski, and Michiel Bacchiani. 2018. State-of-the-art Speech Recognition With Sequence-to-Sequence Models. In *Proceedings of the IEEE International Conference on Acoustics, Speech and Signal Processing, (ICASSP) 2018*, pages 4774–4778, Calgary, Alberta, Canada.

Scott A. Crossley, David Allen, and Danielle S. McNamara. 2012. Text simplification and comprehensible input: A case for an intuitive approach. *Language Teaching Research*, 16(1):89–108.

Felice Dell'Orletta, Martijn Wieling, Giulia Venturi, Andrea Cimino, and Simonetta Montemagni. 2014. Assessing the Readability of Sentences: Which Corpora and Features? In *Proceedings of the Ninth Workshop on Innovative Use of NLP for Building Educational Applications*.

Heng Ding and Krisztian Balog. 2018. Generating Synthetic Data for Neural Keyword-to-Question Models. In *Proceedings of the 2018 ACM SIGIR International Conference on Theory of Information Retrieval, ICTIR*, pages 51–58.

Rudolf Flesch. 1946. *The Art of plain talk*. Harper.

Hany Hassan, Anthony Aue, Chang Chen, Vishal Chowdhary, Jonathan Clark, Christian Federmann, Xuedong Huang, Marcin Junczys-Dowmunt, William Lewis, Mu Li, Shujie Liu, Tie-Yan Liu, Renqian Luo, Arul Menezes, Tao Qin, Frank Seide, Xu Tan, Fei Tian, Lijun Wu, Shuangzhi Wu, Yingce Xia, Dongdong Zhang, Zhirui Zhang, and Ming Zhou. 2018. Achieving Human Parity on Automatic Chinese to English News Translation. *ArXiv e-prints arXiv:1803.05567v2*.

Ye Jia, Melvin Johnson, Wolfgang Macherey, Ron-J. Weiss, Yuan Cao, Chung-Cheng Chiu, Stella-Laurenzo Ari, and Yonghui Wu. 2018. Leveraging Weakly Supervised Data to Improve End-to-End Speech-to-Text Translation. *ArXiv e-prints arXiv:1811.02050*.

Guillaume Klein, Yoon Kim, Yuntian Deng, Jean Senellart, and Alexander M. Rush. 2017. Open-NMT: Open-Source Toolkit for Neural Machine Translation. In *Proceedings of ACL*.

Verena Lyding, Egon Stemle, Claudia Borghetti, Marco Brunello, Sara Castagnoli, Felice Dell'Orletta, Henrik Dittmann, Alessandro Lenci, and Vito Pirrelli. 2014. The PAISÀ Corpus of Italian Web Texts. In *Proceedings of the 9th Web as Corpus Workshop, WaC@EACL 2014, Gothenburg, Sweden, April 26, 2014*, pages 36–43. Association for Computational Linguistics.

Tomas Mikolov, Ilya Sutskever, Kai Chen, Greg Corrado, and Jeffrey Dean. 2013. Distributed Representations of Words and Phrases and Their Compositionality. In *Proceedings of the 26th International Conference on Neural Information Processing Systems - Volume 2*, NIPS'13, pages 3111–3119, USA. Curran Associates Inc.

Sergiu Nisioi, Sanja Stajner, Simone Paolo Ponzetto, and Liviu P. Dinu. 2017. Exploring Neural Text Simplification Models. In *Proceedings of the 55th Annual Meeting of the Association for Computational Linguistics, ACL 2017, Vancouver, Canada, July 30 - August 4, Volume 2: Short Papers*, pages 85–91. Association for Computational Linguistics.

Antonio Quirós, Isabel Segura-Bedmar, and Paloma Martínez. 2016. LABDA at the 2016 TASS Challenge Task: Using Word Embeddings for the Sentiment Analysis Task. In *TASS@ SEPLN*, pages 29–33.

Herbert Robbins and Sutton Monro. 1951. A stochastic approximation method. *The annals of mathematical statistics*, pages 400–407.

Carolina Scarton, Alessio Palmero Aprosio, Sara Tonelli, Tamara Martín Wanton, and Lucia Specia. 2017. MUSST: A Multilingual Syntactic Simplification Tool. In *Proceedings of the IJCNLP 2017, System Demonstrations*, pages 25–28. Association for Computational Linguistics.

Carolina Scarton and Lucia Specia. 2018. Learning Simplifications for Specific Target Audiences. In *Proceedings of the 56th Annual Meeting of the Association for Computational Linguistics (Volume 2: Short Papers)*, pages 712–718. Association for Computational Linguistics.

Abigail See, Peter J. Liu, and Christopher D. Manning. 2017. Get To The Point: Summarization with Pointer-Generator Networks. In *Proceedings of the 55th Annual Meeting of the Association for Computational Linguistics (Volume 1: Long Papers)*, pages 1073–1083. Association for Computational Linguistics.

Rico Sennrich, Barry Haddow, and Alexandra Birch. 2016a. Edinburgh Neural Machine Translation Systems for WMT 16. In *Proceedings of the First Conference on Machine Translation*, pages 371–376, Berlin, Germany. Association for Computational Linguistics.

Rico Sennrich, Barry Haddow, and Alexandra Birch. 2016b. Improving Neural Machine Translation Models with Monolingual Data. In *Proceedings of the 54th Annual Meeting of the Association for Computational Linguistics (Volume 1: Long Papers)*, pages 86–96. Association for Computational Linguistics.

Matthew Shardlow. 2014. A survey of automated text simplification. *International Journal of Advanced Computer Science and Applications(IJACSA), Special Issue on Natural Language Processing 2014*, 4(1).

Elior Sulem, Omri Abend, and Ari Rappoport. 2018. Simple and Effective Text Simplification Using Semantic and Neural Methods. In *Proceedings of the 56th Annual Meeting of the Association for Computational Linguistics (Volume 1: Long Papers)*, pages 162–173. Association for Computational Linguistics.

Francisco Szigriszt. 1993. *Sistemas predictivos de legibilidad del lenguaje escrito*. Ph.D. thesis, Tesis doctoral. Madrid: Universidad Complutense de Madrid.

Sara Tonelli, Alessio Palmero Aprosio, and Francesca Saltori. 2016. SIMPITIKI: a Simplification Corpus for Italian. In *Proceedings of the 3rd Italian Conference on Computational Linguistics (CLiC-it)*, volume 1749 of *CEUR Workshop Proceedings*.

David Vickrey and Daphne Koller. 2008. Applying Sentence Simplification to the CoNLL-2008 Shared Task. In *Proceedings of the Twelfth Conference on Computational Natural Language Learning, CoNLL*, pages 268–272, Manchester, UK.

Sanja Štajner, Marc Franco-Salvador, Paolo Rosso, and Simone Paolo Ponzetto. 2018. CATS: A Tool for Customized Alignment of Text Simplification Corpora. In *Proceedings of the Eleventh International Conference on Language Resources and Evaluation*

(LREC 2018), Miyazaki, Japan. European Language Resources Association (ELRA).

Tu Vu, Baotian Hu, Tsendsuren Munkhdalai, and Hong Yu. 2018. Sentence Simplification with Memory-Augmented Neural Networks. In *Proceedings of the 2018 Conference of the North American Chapter of the Association for Computational Linguistics: Human Language Technologies, Volume 2 (Short Papers)*, pages 79–85. Association for Computational Linguistics.

Kristian Woodsend and Mirella Lapata. 2011. Learning to Simplify Sentences with Quasi-Synchronous Grammar and Integer Programming. In *Proceedings of the 2011 Conference on Empirical Methods in Natural Language Processing*, pages 409–420, Edinburgh, Scotland, UK. Association for Computational Linguistics.

Wei Xu, Chris Callison-Burch, and Courtney Napoles. 2015. Problems in Current Text Simplification Research: New Data Can Help. *Transactions of the Association for Computational Linguistics*, 3:283–297.

Wei Xu, Courtney Napoles, Ellie Pavlick, Quanze Chen, and Chris Callison-Burch. 2016. Optimizing Statistical Machine Translation for Text Simplification. *Transactions of the Association for Computational Linguistics*, 4:401–415.

Jenny Linet Copara Zea, Jose Eduardo Ochoa Luna, Camilo Thorne, and Goran Glavaš. 2016. Spanish NER with Word Representations and Conditional Random Fields. In *Proceedings of the Sixth Named Entity Workshop*, pages 34–40.

Xingxing Zhang and Mirella Lapata. 2017. Sentence Simplification with Deep Reinforcement Learning. In *Proceedings of the 2017 Conference on Empirical Methods in Natural Language Processing, EMNLP 2017, Copenhagen, Denmark, September 9-11, 2017*, pages 584–594. Association for Computational Linguistics.

Zhemin Zhu, Delphine Bernhard, and Iryna Gurevych. 2010. A Monolingual Tree-based Translation Model for Sentence Simplification. In *Proceedings of the 23rd International Conference on Computational Linguistics (Coling 2010)*, pages 1353–1361.

Paraphrase Generation for Semi-Supervised Learning in NLU

Eunah Cho
Amazon, Alexa AI
eunahch@amazon.com

He Xie
Amazon, Alexa AI
hexie@amazon.com

William M. Campbell
Amazon, Alexa AI
cmpw@amazon.com

Abstract

Semi-supervised learning is an efficient way to improve performance for natural language processing systems. In this work, we propose Para-SSL, a scheme to generate candidate utterances using paraphrasing and methods from semi-supervised learning. In order to perform paraphrase generation in the context of a dialog system, we automatically extract paraphrase pairs to create a paraphrase corpus. Using this data, we build a paraphrase generation system and perform one-to-many generation, followed by a validation step to select only the utterances with good quality. The paraphrase-based semi-supervised learning is applied to five functionalities in a natural language understanding system.

Our proposed method for semi-supervised learning using paraphrase generation does not require user utterances and can be applied prior to releasing a new functionality to a system. Experiments show that we can achieve up to 19% of relative semantic error reduction without an access to user utterances, and up to 35% when leveraging live traffic utterances.

1 Introduction

Task-oriented dialog systems are used frequently, either providing mobile support (e.g. Siri, Bixby) or at-home service (e.g. Alexa, Google Home). Natural language understanding (NLU) technology is one of the components for dialog systems, producing interpretation for an input utterance. Namely, an NLU system takes recognized speech input and produces intents, domains, and slots for the utterance to support the user request (Tur and De Mori, 2011). For example, for a user request "turn off the lights in living room," the NLU system would generate domain *Device*, intent *Light-Control*, and slot values of "off" for *OffTrigger* and "living room" for *Location*. In this work, we define *functionality* as a dialog system's capability

given NLU output (e.g., turning off a light, playing a user's playlist).

It is crucial for applications to add support for new functionalities and improve them continuously. An efficient method for this is semi-supervised learning (SSL), where the model learns from both unlabeled as well as labeled data. One SSL method for NLU is to find functionality-relevant user utterances in live traffic and use them to augment the training data. In this work, we explore an alternative SSL approach "Para-SSL," where we generate functionality-relevant utterances and augment them by applying a conservative validation. To generate functionality-relevant utterances, we use paraphrasing, a task to generate an alternative surface form to express the same semantic content (Madnani and Dorr, 2010). Paraphrasing has been used for many natural language processing (NLP) tasks to additionally generate training data (Callison-Burch et al., 2006).

We view the generation work as a translation task (Quirk et al., 2004; Bannard and Callison-Burch, 2005), where we *translate* an utterance into its paraphrase that supports the same functionality. In our task, it is crucial to perform one-to-many generation so that we can obtain a bigger candidate pool for utterance augmentation. In this work, we use beam search to generate n-best list from paraphrase generation model. We then apply a validation step for utterances in the generated n-best list and augment the ones that could be successfully validated.

In order to model paraphrases that fit to the style of dialog system, we build a paraphrase corpus for NLU modeling by automatically extracting paraphrases in terms of NLU functionality. Experiments on five functionalities of our dialog system show that we can achieve up to 35% of relative error reduction by using generated paraphrases for semi-supervised learning.

45

Proceedings of the Workshop on Methods for Optimizing and Evaluating Neural Language Generation (NeuralGen), pages 45–54
Minneapolis, Minnesota, USA, June 6, 2019. ©2019 Association for Computational Linguistics

2   Related Work

SSL has been used in various tasks in NLP with self-training (Ma et al., 2006; Tur et al., 2005; McClosky et al., 2006; Reichart and Rappoport, 2007). Previous work also investigated learning representations from implicit information (Collobert and Weston, 2008; Peters et al., 2018). Oliver et al. (2018) showed that using SSL in a production setting poses a distinctive challenge for evaluation.

Paraphrase modeling has been viewed as a machine translation (MT) task in previous work. Approaches include ones based on statistical machine translation (SMT) (Quirk et al., 2004; Bannard and Callison-Burch, 2005) as well as syntax-based SMT (Callison-Burch, 2008). Mallinson et al. (2017) showed that neural machine translation (NMT) systems perform better than phrase-based MT systems in paraphrase generation tasks.

In Wang et al. (2018), authors show that paraphrase generation using the transformer leads to better performance compared to two other state-of-the-art techniques, a stacked residual LSTM (Prakash et al., 2016) and a nested variational LSTM (Gupta et al., 2018). Yu et al. (2016) showed that text generation task can be achieved using a generative network, where the generator is modeled as a stochastic policy. Later the model was explored and compared to maximum likelihood estimation, as well as scheduled sampling in Kawthekar et al. (2017). Authors noted that training generative adversarial networks (GANs) is a hard problem for textual input due to its discrete nature, which makes mini updates for models to learn difficult. Iyyer et al. (2018) proposed encoder-decoder model-based, syntactically controlled paraphrase networks to generate syntactically adversarial examples.

Paraphrase extraction using bilingual pivoting was proposed in Bannard and Callison-Burch (2005), where they assume that two English strings e_1 and e_2, whose translation in a foreign language f is the same, have the same meaning. Inspired by this, we apply monolingual pivoting based on NLU interpretations. If two strings e_1 and e_2 share the same set of NLU interpretations (represented by domain, intent and slot sets), they are considered to be paraphrases. Details will be given in Section 4.

The encoder-decoder based MT approach has been applied to generate paraphrases for addi-tional training data for NLU (Sokolov and Filimonov, 2019). They trained the encoder on a traditional, bilingual MT task, fixed it and trained decoder for paraphrase task. Authors showed that using generated paraphrases can help to improve NLU performance for a given feature. Our work distinguishes itself from this work from two perspectives. First, we show that paraphrase generation for NLU can be modeled in a shared monolingual space by leveraging pivoting based on NLU interpretations. Second, we show that generating many variants of paraphrase and applying a validation step is an effective way to apply semi-supervised learning and improves model performance greatly.

3   Para-SSL

In this section, we describe two approaches for semi-supervised learning in NLU. The first one utilizes user utterances, while the second approach uses generated paraphrases.

3.1   Semi-supervised Learning for NLU

Our conventional semi-supervised learning approach has largely two steps: filtering and validation. We first find functionality-relevant utterances from live traffic (filtering) and augment them using the current NLU model (validation). In order to find the functionality-relevant utterances, we rely on a high-throughput, low complexity linear logistic regression classifier. To train the 1-vs-all classifier, we use available target functionality utterances as in-class examples, and the rest for out-of-class examples. As feature of the classifier, we use n-grams from the examples.

The filtered utterances are augmented and validated through NLU model. Utterances with confidence score above a threshold are added into training. Throughout the paper, we will call this approach *SSL*.

3.2   Paraphrase Generation for SSL

Another approach for SSL is to generate functionality-relevant utterances, instead of filtering them from live traffic. The SSL technique described in Section 3.1 has an advantage that the filtered utterances are indeed actual utterances from dialog system users. Thus, it ensures the quality of filtered utterances in terms of fluency and context fit for our dialog system. On the other hand, it requires live traffic utterances for the target functionality. Therefore, the above-mentioned SSL technique is not applicable when the functionality is not yet released.

In this work, we explore generation of functionality-relevant utterance for SSL. Generated utterances are validated in the same method as in conventional SSL, by running them through an NLU model and selecting utterances whose hypothesis confidence is higher than a threshold.

Inspired by its good performance in paraphrase generation task, we use the model constructed with self-attention encoders and decoders, known as the Transformer (Vaswani et al., 2017). Unlike other paraphrase tasks (Wang et al., 2018; Yu et al., 2016), our application requires one-to-many generation. Namely, when we input one in-class functionality utterance, we expect to have many paraphrases who are likely to invoke the same functionality. In order to generate multiple paraphrases for an input utterance, we use beam search and generate n-best lists (Tillmann and Ney, 2003), where we fix $n = 50$ in this work. Throughout this paper, we will call this approach *Para-SSL*.

3.3 Benchmarks

In order to evaluate the impact of generated paraphrases in NLU modeling we set up benchmarks on five functionalities. The details of the functionalities will be discussed in Section 6. In each benchmark, we simulate the NLU functionality development cycle by adding an increasing amount of training data on the target functionality.

The first version for each benchmark represents the *bootstrap phase*. On top of the training data for other functionalities that the dialog system supports, we have synthetically created training data for the target functionality. As the functionality is not yet launched, there is no training data coming from actual user utterances.

In the following *live phase*, we add 10%, 20%, 50%, 80%, or 100% of the annotated training data of the target functionality on top of the bootstrap phase version. We will refer to them as *annotation increments* in this paper. Using the annotation increments, we aim to simulate how support for the target functionality improves as we have more user utterances available for training.

The SSL algorithm on the benchmark is shown in Algorithm 1. The starting dialog system D is trained with the bootstrap data B for the func-

---

Algorithm 1 Algorithm for SSL

Require: Bootstrap data B
Require: Annotated $A_i, i = \{10, 20, 50, 80, 100\}$
Require: Training data for other functionalities T
Require: Dialog system D, trained on $d = T \cup B$
1: **for** each increment A_i **do**
2:     train D with $d = T \cup B \cup A_i$
3:     find candidate utterances C_{Ai} from user traffic
4:     hypotheses from dialog system $H \leftarrow D(C_{Ai})$ with model confidence score for each hypothesis c_{hi}
5:     $S \leftarrow \emptyset$
6:     **for** $h_i \in H$ **do**
7:         **if** $c_{hi} > \theta_{cSSL}$ **then**
8:             $S \leftarrow S \cup h_i$
9:     train D with $d = T \cup B \cup A_i \cup S$, evaluate

Algorithm 2 Algorithm for Para-SSL

Require: Bootstrap data B
Require: Annotated $A_t, t = \{10, 20, 50, 80, 100\}$
Require: Training data for other functionalities T
Require: Dialog system D, trained on $d = T \cup B$
1: $S_B \leftarrow \emptyset$
2: **for** each input in $U = \{B, A\}$ **do**
3:     **if** $U_i = B$ **then**
4:         train D with $d = T \cup B$
5:     **else**
6:         train D with $d = T \cup B \cup U_i$
7:     generate paraphrases $P \leftarrow para(U_i)$
8:     hypotheses from dialog system $H \leftarrow D(P)$ with model confidence score for each hypothesis c_{hi}
9:     $S \leftarrow S_B$
10:    **for** $h_i \in H$ **do**
11:        **if** $c_{hi} > \theta_{cPara-SSL}$ **then**
12:           $S \leftarrow S \cup h_i$
13:           **if** $U_i = B$ **then**
14:              $S_B \leftarrow S_B \cup h_i$
15:    **if** $U_i = B$ **then**
16:        train D with $d = T \cup B \cup S$, evaluate
17:    **else**
18:        train D with $d = T \cup B \cup U_i \cup S$, evaluate

---

tionality and other data T for other functionalities that it supports. As we have more annotation data available, we find and validate candidate utterances C_A. We then update D using the additional training data for the functionality. Note that the bootstrap data B is continuously used throughout the live phase in order to secure a broad support for the functionality.

We perform Para-SSL as shown in Algorithm 2. As Para-SSL does not require live traffic utterances, we can start augmenting more utterances using bootstrap data only. Note that during the live phase ($U_i \in A$), we continue to use the bootstrap data B (line 6). Instead of the step to find candidate utterances C_A in SSL (line 3 in Algorithm 1), Para-SSL enables generation of utterances given input group (line 7 in Algorithm 2). Both algorithms have a validation step to threshold NLU interpretations based on model score. For each annotation increment in Para-SSL, we can also leverage the validated data from bootstrap phase $\mathcal{S}_B$ by setting $\mathcal{S}$ to always include $\mathcal{S}_B$ (see line 9).

Based upon preliminary experiments to set $\theta_{cPara-SSL}$, we fixed $\theta_{cPara-SSL}$ at 0.9 in this work. For θ_{cSSL}, we took the model's reject threshold of each functionality. When an NLU interpretation has a confidence score lower than the reject threshold, it will not be accepted by the downstream process in the dialog system. The reject threshold is set differently for each functionality to minimize false rejects as described in Su et al. (2018) and varies from 0.13 to 0.35.

4   Dialog Paraphrase Corpus

How users interact with a spoken dialog system is very distinguishable in terms of style of the speech. Thus, it is crucial to use a corpus that contains such style of utterances. Since we do not have a hand-annotated paraphrase corpus for our dialog system, we automatically created a paraphrase corpus from user interaction with the dialog system.

4.1   Definition

In order to pair up existing utterances with NLU interpretation with their paraphrases, we first have to define what makes **paraphrase** in this work. We define utterances that invoke the same functionality from our spoken dialog system with same entities are paraphrase of each other. For example, an utterance *Play Adele in my living room* is a paraphrase of *I would like to listen to Adele in my living room*. However, such paraphrases that share the same entities in granularity would be sparse throughout the corpus. Thus, we propose a concept of **para-carrier phrase**, which groups utterances that invoke the same functionality of the dialog system but not necessarily share the entities. For example, *Play Adele in my living room* can be a para-carrier phrase of an utterance *I would like to listen to Lady Gaga in my kitchen*.

4.2   Paraphrase Pairs

For paraphrase pair extraction, we used NLU training data that was available before any of the five functionalities we consider in this work were designed or launched. Thereby, we aim to simulate scenarios where a new functionality does not have similar or related utterances in the training data of the paraphrase model. In order to avoid potential annotation errors, we first applied frequency-based de-noising to the data, removing annotated utterances whose frequency is lower than m times throughout the corpus. For annotated utterances from live traffic, we apply $m = 3$ and for synthetic utterances we apply $m = 6$. Given de-noised utterances, we pair up utterances that are para-carrier phrase of each other. Once they are paired, we masked their entities with their slot type. Our previous example will become a para-carrier phrase pair *Play Artist in HomeLocation - I would like to listen to Artist in HomeLocation* in this step. We then randomly sample entities from an internal catalog for each slot type in order to make them into a paraphrase pair that shares the same entities. In this way, we obtained around 1M paraphrase pairs. This data is used as an in-domain data for paraphrase generation system.

5   System Description

5.1   Neural Machine Translation

For training data of the paraphrase generation system, we use both general and in-domain paraphrase corpora. The in-domain paraphrase corpus, as described in Section 4, contains 1M paraphrase pairs that fit the style and genre of the dialog system. For the general domain data, we use a back-translated English paraphrase corpus (Wieting and Gimpel, 2017). Out of a 50M pair parallel corpus, we first selected 30M pairs whose score are the highest. We then randomly selected 10M parallel sentences. The general and in-domain corpora are shuffled so that each batch can be exposed to both of them. For development data, we randomly chose 3K sentences from the in-domain data. Prior to training, we apply BPE (Sennrich et al., 2015) at operation size 40K for both source and target side concatenated.

We use a transformer (Vaswani et al., 2017) for the task, using the implementation in Klein et al. (2017). Our hyper-parameters follow the *Base* configuration of the original work, with several alterations. We use 512 as the hidden layer size, and 2048 for the inner size of the feed-forward network. We added sinusoidal position encoding to each embedding. The model is trained for $200,000$ steps, with the Adam optimizer (Kingma and Ba, 2014). We set 0.998 for β_2 in Adam optimizer and $8,000$ for warm-up steps. As our source and target languages are the same, we shared the embeddings between encoder and decoder.

Funct.	Domain	#Intent	#Slot (new)	Test
Announce	Comms.	1	17 (1)	1.3K
Quotes	Info	1	12 (5)	1.4K
Playlist	Music	2	32 (0)	1.9K
Donate	General	1	7 (3)	1.3K
Chat	General	1	1 (1)	2.7K

Table 1: Five functionalities considered in this work

5.2 Natural Language Understanding

Our NLU model consists of a domain classifier (DC), an intent classifier (IC), and a named entity classifier (NER). For this experiment, we used statistical models for the three components. A DC model outputs whether a given input utterance is intended for the target domain (e.g. Book). We trained our DC with a maximum entropy (ME) classifier, using n-grams extracted from the training data as input features. An intent of the input utterance is classified in IC. Trained with a multi-class ME classifier, the IC outputs the intent for each utterance (e.g. ReadBook). The model uses n-grams as features. The NER is used to identify named entities in the utterance (e.g. "Harry Potter" for BookTitle). We used conditional random fields for NER tagging, using n-grams extracted from training data.

Each component outputs labels and corresponding confidence scores. The overall model confidence is obtained by multiplying the three confidence scores. We also applied a reranker scheme to integrate outputs from the components and provide a list of hypotheses. A detailed description of the reranker scheme as well as the NLU system can be found in Su et al. (2018).

6 Experimental Setup

We apply paraphrase generation to five functionalities of our spoken dialog system, where each functionality consists of one to two intents (e.g. PlayMusic, PlayVideo, etc.). Five functionalities come from four different domains, as shown in Table 1. By applying paraphrase generation to various functionalities across multiple domains, we show the applicability of the technique.

Table 1 shows the number of intents and slots covered by each functionality. Additionally, the number of new slots introduced by modeling this functionality is shown in parentheses. Each functionality has a designated test set, which contains 1k to 3k functionality-specific utterances of live traffic data annotated. Table 1 shows test set size for each functionality.

In this work, we evaluate the impact of generated paraphrases in terms of the NLU model performance, measured in Semantic Error Rate (SemER) (Makhoul et al., 1999). There are three types of slot errors in a hypothesis with respect to reference interpretation: substitution error (S), insertion error (I), and deletion error (D). We treat intent of NLU interpretation as one of slots using the metric, where an intent error is considered as a substitution. SemER is calculated as follows:

$$SemER = \frac{S + I + D}{S + D + C} \quad (1)$$

where C denotes the number of correct slots/intents. Numbers we report in this work are the relative performance in terms of SemER.

6.1 Bootstrap Phase

We apply the paraphrase generation technique to two phases of spoken dialog system. The first phase is bootstrap phase where the functionality is in development. Thus, we do not have any actual user utterances in the training data but only synthetically-created training data. In our experiment, we rely on FST-generated synthetic data for a new functionality. We will call this data *bootstrap data*. We use the bootstrap data as an input to the paraphrase generation system.

Note that we can only apply Para-SSL for the bootstrap phase, as SSL requires live traffic utterances.

6.2 Live Phase

The second phase we consider in this work is the live phase, where we have user utterances annotated for training. We apply our SSL approaches on the benchmarks, as described in Section 3.3.

For live phase experiments, we compare three methods against the baseline where no additional data was used. In Para-SSL, we use live annotation data as an input for paraphrase generation and validate the output using the NLU model. In SSL, we show the results of conventional SSL where we use an n-gram based filter to find functionality-related utterances and validate them using NLU model. In Combined, we use the validated utterances from SSL as an additional input for paraphrase generation model. The validated paraphrases from both SSL and Para-SSL are added for the system with SSL for each annotation increment.

Funct.	Bootstrap	Para	Valid.	Ratio
Announce	90.0K	2.0M	460.6K	22.5%
Quotes	50.0K	1.6M	538.6K	32.8%
Playlist	21.6K	928.8K	79.2K	8.5%
Donate	5.0K	202.0K	74.8K	37.0%
Chat	150.0K	2.0M	811.8K	41.4%

Table 2: Data statistics for paraphrase generation in the bootstrap phase, including the number of utterances and validation ratio.

Funct.	Para-SSL	ω Boot.
Announce	-18.99%	-7.85%
Quotes	-3.49%	+0.56%
Playlist	-5.33%	-8.72%
Donate	-5.09%	-6.16%
Chat	-17.39%	-9.49%

Table 3: Relative SemER reduction for target functionality when adding generated paraphrases in bootstrap phase, compared to the model with bootstrap data only.

7 Results

7.1 Bootstrap Phase

Table 2 shows data statistics of the generated paraphrases for the bootstrap phase. In the second column, we show how many utterances we used for the bootstrap data. Note that this data contains duplicate utterances. Para column in the table shows how many unique paraphrases are generated when inputting the bootstrap data into paraphrase model. The next two columns show the number of validated utterances and the corresponding ratio.

We then added the validated paraphrases into the NLU training. In second column of Table 3, we show how much relative improvement in SemER we can achieve by adding the validated paraphrases. Relative performance is evaluated against the baseline where no validated paraphrases were used. We can see that all functionalities' performances is improved greatly, with relative SemER reduction ranges from -3.5% up to -18.99% .

Additionally, we investigated whether we can achieve comparable performance by up-weighting the existing bootstrap training data. For this experiment, we randomly sample existing bootstrap data to the same amount as the validated paraphrases. Instead of the validated utterances, we then used the up-weighted bootstrap data (the ωBoot. column in Table 3). Especially for the functionalities where we obtained a big improvement using paraphrases (Announce, Chat), up-weighting bootstrap data did not lead to comparable result. This result shows the potential of Para-SSL in bootstrap phase to improve functionality performance without using user interactions.

7.2 Live Phase

Table 4 shows the number of validated paraphrases, for each functionality and annotation increment. As expected, we obtain more validated utterances as annotation increment increases. We can see that for most of the functionalities SSL obtains a bigger pool of validated utterances, compared to Para-SSL. It is noticeable that Combined sometimes obtains a smaller number of utterances validated, compared to SSL (e.g. Live10 for Quotes). Note that SSL and Combined rely on two different NLU models to augment and validate the utterances. For validation, Combined uses the model trained with validated paraphrases of bootstrap data. Adding generated paraphrases from bootstrap data changes decision boundary for the model, shifting confidence score ranges as well.

Table 5 shows the impact when we generate paraphrases given live annotation data and add the validated ones into training data. For each functionality, we present three systems' performance against the baseline where only annotated training data is available. We can see that using Para-SSL can effectively improve NLU performance for most of the functionalities. Note that Para-SSL benefits from its capability of utilizing bootstrap data, in live phase as well. Even when the amount of validated utterances from Para-SSL is much smaller than the ones from SSL, we often observe comparative results.

On the other hand, Para-SSL did not bring a great improvement for Playlist, possibly due to the low validation rate throughout bootstrap and live phase, compared to other functionalities. We believe that the model is less prone to provide a high confidence score for a complex functionality such as Playlist. As shown in Table 1, Playlist involves the highest number of slots and intents. Also, there is no new slot involved for the modeling of this functionality. Thus, the model has to learn existing slots in a different context, which may lead to a generally lower confidence score range for the functionality.

In Combined, we observe that Para-SSL and SSL bring complementary improvements. It is also noticeable that even when we have less amount of utterances validated, Combined outperforms SSL. Figure 1 depicts utterances from vari-

Functionality	System	Live10	Live20	Live50	Live80	Live100
	Para-SSL	1.0K	1.8K	1.9K	6.0K	27.8K
Announce	SSL	6.1K	6.5K	9.9K	9.5K	29.6K
	Combined	10.9K	21.1K	34.8K	44.6K	111.5K
	Para-SSL	0.2K	0.6K	2.0K	5.5K	9.5K
Quotes	SSL	45.4K	55.6K	68.9K	120.6K	176.7K
	Combined	15.2K	98.9K	198.7K	378.7K	298.7K
	Para-SSL	40	0.2K	0.5K	1.6K	3.2K
Playlist	SSL	32.7K	96.3K	260.3K	398.9K	725.1K
	Combined	10.0K	69.3K	173.3K	664.4K	1.4M
	Para-SSL	0.2K	0.3K	0.7K	1.8K	3.0K
Donate	SSL	0.2K	0.2K	0.4K	0.5K	1.2K
	Combined	1.1K	1.6K	2.6K	4.8K	10.0K
	Para-SSL	0.5K	0.8K	1.5K	2.5K	3.8K
Chat	SSL	30.7K	22.4K	36.1K	52.8K	103.6K
	Combined	137.1K	147.7K	243.1K	330.4K	579.2K

Table 4: Data statistics on the number of validated utterances in live phase, per annotation increment

Functionality	System	Live10	Live20	Live50	Live80	Live100
	Para-SSL	-19.11%	-16.49%	-14.40%	-15.96%	-22.71%
Announce	SSL	-20.27%	-19.12%	-16.78%	-10.74%	-17.73%
	Combined	-27.44%	-31.13%	-29.40%	-29.55%	-35.73%
	Para-SSL	-11.08%	-9.65%	-2.42%	-4.92%	-5.01%
Quotes	SSL	-16.71%	-15.51%	-12.46%	-13.50%	-18.45%
	Combined	-21.38%	-28.26%	-21.90%	-18.62%	-22.19%
	Para-SSL	-1.55%	-2.98%	-1.63%	-0.89%	-0.61%
Playlist	SSL	-18.43%	-13.50%	-18.19%	-13.20%	-15.45%
	Combined	-19.40%	-16.24%	-19.85%	-14.02%	-15.68%
	Para-SSL	-4.92%	-2.24%	-5.22%	-6.85%	-13.52%
Donate	SSL	-4.92%	-4.36%	-6.04%	-6.69%	-12.78%
	Combined	-8.03%	-11.9%	-15.82%	-19.17%	-29.92%
	Para-SSL	-9.55%	-15.03%	-12.59%	-13.75%	-16.76%
Chat	SSL	-25.14%	-16.50%	-17.90%	-20.50%	-24.39%
	Combined	-30.95%	-30.90%	-26.72%	-32.27%	-35.27%

Table 5: Relative SemER reduction for target functionality when adding generated paraphrases in live phase.

ous sources in an embedding space[1]. We can see that generated paraphrases from Combined fill the gap between data points for bootstrap, live annotation, and SSL.

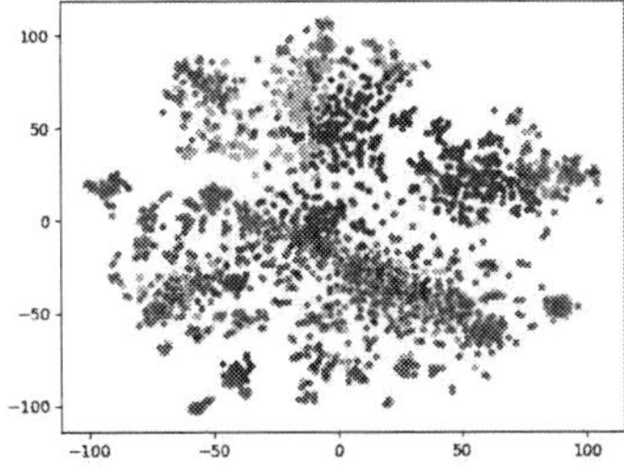

Figure 1: Embedding depiction of utterances for Announce functionality. Blue = bootstrap data, red = live annotation data, green = SSL, cyan = Combined

<hr>

[1]1K utterances are randomly sampled from each source. We train embeddings using 89 million utterances in production (Pagliardini et al., 2017). For visualization we used t-SNE (Maaten and Hinton, 2008).

8   Analysis

First, we quantified the quality of generated utterances in n-best list in terms of their validation yield. Figure 2 shows the validation rate for each functionality. Validation rate is calculated for each n in the n-best list, by dividing the number of validated paraphrases by the number of generated ones, given all input utterances. Solid line represents semantic fidelity trend as n increases, showing how many of the generated utterances for each n are validated through. The dashed line shows the diversity trend in the n-best list. It represents how many of the generated utterances are unique utterances within the generated data assuming that we are adding new utterances starting from top to bottom in n-best lists for all utterances.

As expected, the general trend of the yield decreases (thus semantic fidelity likely decreases as well) as n grows. However, note that it does not drastically drop, but instead it reaches a plateau. The varying level of yield rate for different func-

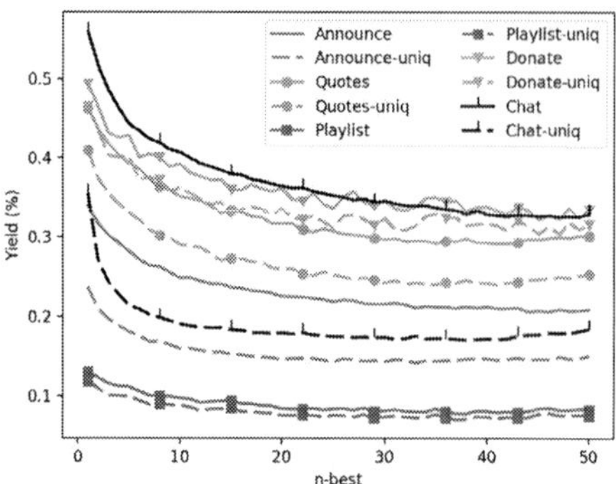

Figure 2: Validation rate for n in n-best list. Dashed line represents how many of the validated utterances are unique utterances. Paraphrases are generated by inputting bootstrap training data for each functionality.

Validated	Filtered-out
Announce that supper is ready	Declare that supper is ready
Get me a famous quote from Obama	I'd like to order a famous quote from Obama
Put on a dance pop song from the nineties to the playlist	Put on a dance pop song from the nineties

Table 6: Examples of validated and filtered-out paraphrases.

tionalities also indicates that validation is a necessary step in order to use generated paraphrases into training data. We believe a further analysis will be beneficial to understand the trade-off between computational complexity and diversity of validated utterances when increasing size of n.

Additionally, we share examples of validated and filtered-out utterances in Table 6. We can see that validation step can successfully filter out paraphrases that do not conform well to the context of dialog system. A vague paraphrase in terms of NLU functionality (e.g. add a song to playlist vs. play a song) could also be filtered out.

For the second analysis, we looked into the necessity of keeping paraphrases of bootstrap data, especially when the model is trained with more live annotation data. As shown in Algorithm 2, we kept using the validated paraphrases of bootstrap data in live phase, in order to benefit from Para-SSL's applicability in bootstrap phase. As bootstrap data is often relatively larger than the annotated live data, we would keep the big corpus throughout the cycle of functionality development, potentially increasing the computational cost. For

Funct.	Live80	Live100
Announce	-29.05%	-35.31%
Quotes	-15.35%	-18.96%
Playlist	-13.17%	-15.18%
Donate	-17.92%	-26.27%
Chat	-32.34%	-37.96%

Table 7: Retiring paraphrases from bootstrap data, from Combined experiments. Numbers are reported in relative SemER reduction.

this analysis, we remove the validated paraphrases of bootstrap data and retrained the model.

The analysis is applied for Combined experiments. Table 7 shows the result for annotation increments 80 and 100. Comparison to the numbers in the same increments shown in Table 5 shows that there is no substantial degradation caused by retiring the generated paraphrases from bootstrap data, when model is trained with sufficient live annotation data.

Experiment showed that we still benefit from augmenting and validating paraphrases using the Combined system, without retiring the validated paraphrases of bootstrap data. When we use the system with data retirement, we reached a worse performance in live phase. This indicates that we can use a better-performing but potentially computationally expensive model for utterance augmentation and validation, and for production we can use a lighter system with a comparable performance.

9   Conclusion

In this work, we investigated the impact of paraphrase generation for semi-supervised learning in NLU. The proposed method has an advantage over the conventional SSL that it does not require actual user utterances. Using Para-SSL, thus, we can improve the support for a new functionality effectively prior to launching it.

We applied Para-SSL on five functionalities in an NLU system. In addition to compare the results with the conventional SSL, we also combined the two SSL methods to achieve even better performance. Experiments show that Para-SSL leads up to 19% of relative error reduction without an access to user utterances, and up to 35% when combined with SSL method, leveraging live traffic utterances.

References

Colin Bannard and Chris Callison-Burch. 2005. Paraphrasing with bilingual parallel corpora. In *Proceedings of the 43rd Annual Meeting on Association for Computational Linguistics*, pages 597–604. Association for Computational Linguistics.

Chris Callison-Burch. 2008. Syntactic constraints on paraphrases extracted from parallel corpora. In *Proceedings of the Conference on Empirical Methods in Natural Language Processing*, pages 196–205. Association for Computational Linguistics.

Chris Callison-Burch, Philipp Koehn, and Miles Osborne. 2006. Improved statistical machine translation using paraphrases. In *Proceedings of the main conference on Human Language Technology Conference of the North American Chapter of the Association of Computational Linguistics*, pages 17–24. Association for Computational Linguistics.

Ronan Collobert and Jason Weston. 2008. A unified architecture for natural language processing: Deep neural networks with multitask learning. In *Proceedings of the 25th international conference on Machine learning*, pages 160–167. ACM.

Ankush Gupta, Arvind Agarwal, Prawaan Singh, and Piyush Rai. 2018. A deep generative framework for paraphrase generation. In *Thirty-Second AAAI Conference on Artificial Intelligence*.

Mohit Iyyer, John Wieting, Kevin Gimpel, and Luke Zettlemoyer. 2018. Adversarial example generation with syntactically controlled paraphrase networks. In *North American Association for Computational Linguistics*.

Prasad Kawthekar, Raunaq Rewari, and Suvrat Bhooshan. 2017. Evaluating generative models for text generation.

Diederik P Kingma and Jimmy Ba. 2014. Adam: A method for stochastic optimization. *arXiv preprint arXiv:1412.6980*.

Guillaume Klein, Yoon Kim, Yuntian Deng, Jean Senellart, and Alexander M. Rush. 2017. OpenNMT: Open-source toolkit for neural machine translation. In *Proc. ACL*.

Jeff Ma, Spyros Matsoukas, Owen Kimball, and Richard Schwartz. 2006. Unsupervised training on large amounts of broadcast news data. In *Acoustics, Speech and Signal Processing, 2006. ICASSP 2006 Proceedings. 2006 IEEE International Conference on*, volume 3, pages III–III. IEEE.

Laurens van der Maaten and Geoffrey Hinton. 2008. Visualizing data using t-sne. *Journal of machine learning research*, 9(Nov):2579–2605.

Nitin Madnani and Bonnie J Dorr. 2010. Generating phrasal and sentential paraphrases: A survey of data-driven methods. *Computational Linguistics*, 36(3):341–387.

John Makhoul, Francis Kubala, Richard Schwartz, Ralph Weischedel, et al. 1999. Performance measures for information extraction.

Jonathan Mallinson, Rico Sennrich, and Mirella Lapata. 2017. Paraphrasing revisited with neural machine translation. In *Proceedings of the 15th Conference of the European Chapter of the Association for Computational Linguistics: Volume 1, Long Papers*, volume 1, pages 881–893.

David McClosky, Eugene Charniak, and Mark Johnson. 2006. Effective self-training for parsing. In *Proceedings of the main conference on human language technology conference of the North American Chapter of the Association of Computational Linguistics*, pages 152–159. Association for Computational Linguistics.

Avital Oliver, Augustus Odena, Colin Raffel, Ekin D Cubuk, and Ian J Goodfellow. 2018. Realistic evaluation of deep semi-supervised learning algorithms. *arXiv preprint arXiv:1804.09170*.

Matteo Pagliardini, Prakhar Gupta, and Martin Jaggi. 2017. Unsupervised learning of sentence embeddings using compositional n-gram features. *arXiv preprint arXiv:1703.02507*.

Matthew E Peters, Mark Neumann, Mohit Iyyer, Matt Gardner, Christopher Clark, Kenton Lee, and Luke Zettlemoyer. 2018. Deep contextualized word representations. *arXiv preprint arXiv:1802.05365*.

Aaditya Prakash, Sadid A Hasan, Kathy Lee, Vivek Datla, Ashequl Qadir, Joey Liu, and Oladimeji Farri. 2016. Neural paraphrase generation with stacked residual lstm networks. *arXiv preprint arXiv:1610.03098*.

Chris Quirk, Chris Brockett, and Bill Dolan. 2004. Monolingual machine translation for paraphrase generation.

Roi Reichart and Ari Rappoport. 2007. Self-training for enhancement and domain adaptation of statistical parsers trained on small datasets. In *Proceedings of the 45th Annual Meeting of the Association of Computational Linguistics*, pages 616–623.

Rico Sennrich, Barry Haddow, and Alexandra Birch. 2015. Neural machine translation of rare words with subword units. *arXiv preprint arXiv:1508.07909*.

Alex Sokolov and Denis Filimonov. 2019. Neural machine translation for paraphrase generation. *2nd Conversational AI*.

Chengwei Su, Rahul Gupta, Shankar Ananthakrishnan, and Spyros Matsoukas. 2018. A re-ranker scheme for integrating large scale nlu models. *arXiv preprint arXiv:1809.09605*.

Christoph Tillmann and Hermann Ney. 2003. Word reordering and a dynamic programming beam search algorithm for statistical machine translation. *Computational linguistics*, 29(1):97–133.

Gokhan Tur and Renato De Mori. 2011. *Spoken language understanding: Systems for extracting semantic information from speech*. John Wiley & Sons.

Gokhan Tur, Dilek Hakkani-Tür, and Robert E Schapire. 2005. Combining active and semi-supervised learning for spoken language understanding. *Speech Communication*, 45(2):171–186.

Ashish Vaswani, Noam Shazeer, Niki Parmar, Jakob Uszkoreit, Llion Jones, Aidan N Gomez, Łukasz Kaiser, and Illia Polosukhin. 2017. Attention is all you need. In *Advances in Neural Information Processing Systems*, pages 5998–6008.

Su Wang, Rahul Gupta, Nancy Chang, and Jason Baldridge. 2018. A task in a suit and a tie: paraphrase generation with semantic augmentation. *arXiv preprint arXiv:1811.00119*.

John Wieting and Kevin Gimpel. 2017. Paranmt-50m: Pushing the limits of paraphrastic sentence embeddings with millions of machine translations. *arXiv preprint arXiv:1711.05732*.

Lantao Yu, Weinan Zhang, Jun Wang, and Yong Yu Seqgan. 2016. sequence generative adversarial nets with policy gradient. arxiv preprint. *arXiv preprint arXiv:1609.05473*, 2(3):5.

Bilingual-GAN: A Step Towards Parallel Text Generation

Ahmad Rashid, Alan Do-Omri, Md. Akmal Haidar, Qun Liu and Mehdi Rezagholizadeh
Huawei Noah's Ark Lab
ahmad.rashid@huawei.com , alan.do.omri@huawei.com,
md.akmal.haidar@huawei.com, qun.liu@huawei.com,
mehdi.rezagholizadeh@huawei.com

Abstract

Latent space based GAN methods and attention based sequence to sequence models have achieved impressive results in text generation and unsupervised machine translation respectively. Leveraging the two domains, we propose an adversarial latent space based model capable of generating parallel sentences in two languages concurrently and translating bidirectionally. The bilingual generation goal is achieved by sampling from the latent space that is shared between both languages. First two denoising autoencoders are trained, with shared encoders and back-translation to enforce a shared latent state between the two languages. The decoder is shared for the two translation directions. Next, a GAN is trained to generate synthetic 'code' mimicking the languages' shared latent space. This code is then fed into the decoder to generate text in either language. We perform our experiments on Europarl and Multi30k datasets, on the English-French language pair, and document our performance using both supervised and unsupervised machine translation.

1 Introduction

Many people in the world are fluent in at least two languages, yet most computer applications and services are designed for a monolingual audience. Fully bilingual people do not think about a concept in one language and translate it to the other language but are adept at generating words in either language.

Inspired by this bilingual paradigm, the success of attention based neural machine translation (NMT) and the potential of Generative Adversarial Networks (GANs) for text generation we propose Bilingual-GAN, an agent capable of deriving a shared latent space between two languages, and then generating from that space in either language.

Attention based NMT (Bahdanau et al., 2014; Gehring et al., 2017; Vaswani et al., 2017) has achieved state of the art results on many different language pairs and is used in production translation systems (Wu et al., 2016). These systems generally consist of an encoder-decoder based sequence to sequence model where at least the decoder is auto-regressive. Generally, they require massive amount of parallel data but recent methods that use shared autoencoders (Lample et al., 2017, 2018) and cross-lingual word embeddings (Conneau et al., 2017a) have shown promise even without using parallel data.

Deep learning based text generation systems can be divided into three categories: Maximum Likelihood Estimation (MLE)-based, GAN-based and reinforcement learning (RL)-based. MLE-based methods (Sutskever et al., 2014) model the text as an auto-regressive generative process using Recurrent Neural Networks (RNNs) but generally suffer from exposure bias (Bengio et al., 2015). A number of solutions have been proposed including scheduled sampling (Bengio et al., 2015), Gibbs sampling (Su et al., 2018) and Professor forcing (Lamb et al., 2016).

Recently, researchers have used GANs (Goodfellow et al., 2014) as a potentially powerful generative model for text (Yu et al., 2017; Gulrajani et al., 2017; Haidar and Rezagholizadeh, 2019), inspired by their great success in the field of image generation. Text generation using GANs is challenging due to the discrete nature of text. The discretized text output is not differentiable and if the softmax output is used instead it is trivial for the discriminator to distinguish between that and real text. One of the proposed solutions (Zhao et al., 2017) is to generate the latent space of the autoencoder instead of generating the sentence and has shown impressive results.

We use the concept of shared encoders and

Proceedings of the Workshop on Methods for Optimizing and Evaluating Neural Language Generation (NeuralGen), pages 55–64
Minneapolis, Minnesota, USA, June 6, 2019. ©2019 Association for Computational Linguistics

multi-lingual embeddings to learn the aligned latent representation of two languages and a GAN that can generate this latent space. Particularly, our contributions are as follows:

- We introduce a GAN model, Bilingual-GAN, which can generate parallel sentences in two languages concurrently.

- Bilingual-GAN can match the latent distribution of the encoder of an attention based NMT model.

- We explore the ability to generate parallel sentences when using only monolingual corpora.

2 Related Work

2.1 Latent space based Unsupervised NMT

A few works (Lample et al., 2017; Artetxe et al., 2017; Lample et al., 2018) have emerged recently to deal with neural machine translation without using parallel corpora, i.e sentences in one language have no matching translation in the other language. The common principles of such systems include learning a language model, encoding sentences from different languages into a shared latent representation and using back-translation (Sennrich et al., 2015a) to provide a pseudo supervision. Lample et al. (2017) use a word by word translation dictionary learned in an unsupervised way (Conneau et al., 2017b) as part of their back-translation along with an adversarial loss to enforce language independence in latent representations. Lample et al. (2018) improves this by removing these two elements and instead use Byte Pair Encoding (BPE) sub-word tokenization (Sennrich et al., 2015b) with joint embeddings learned using FastText (Bojanowski et al., 2017), so that the sentences are embedded in a common space. Artetxe et al. (2017) uses online back translation and cross-lingual embeddings to embed sentences in a shared space. They also decouple the decoder so that one is used per language.

2.2 Latent space based Adversarial Text Generation

Researchers have conventionally utilized the GAN framework in image applications (Salimans et al., 2016) with great success. Inspired by their success, a number of works have used GANs in various NLP applications such as machine transla-tion (Wu et al., 2017; Yang et al., 2017a), dialogue models (Li et al., 2017), question answering (Yang et al., 2017b), and natural language generation (Gulrajani et al., 2017; Kim et al., 2017). However, applying GAN in NLP is challenging due to the discrete nature of text. Consequently, back-propagation would not be feasible for discrete outputs and it is not straightforward to pass the gradients through the discrete output words of the generator. A latent code based solution for this problem, ARAE, was proposed in Kim et al. (2017), where a latent representation of the text is derived using an autoencoder and the manifold of this representation is learned via adversarial training of a generator. Another version of the ARAE method which proposes updating the encoder based on discriminator loss function was introduced in (Spinks and Moens, 2018). Gagnon-Marchand et al. (2019) introduced a self-attention based GAN architecture to the ARAE and Haidar et al. (2019) explore a hybrid approach generating both a latent representation and the text itself.

3 Methodology

The Bilingual-GAN comprises of a translation module and a text generation module. The complete architecture is illustrated in Figure 1.

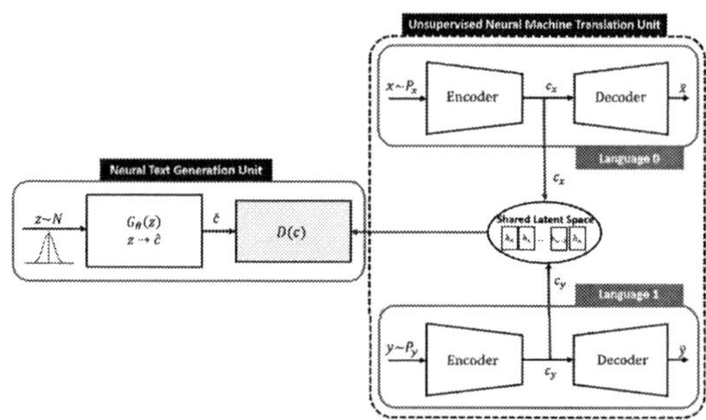

Figure 1: The complete architecture for our unsupervised bilingual text generator (Bilingual-GAN)

3.1 Translation Unit

The translation system is a sequence-to-sequence model with an encoder and a decoder extended to support two languages. This first translation component is inspired by the unsupervised neural machine translation system by Lample et al. (2017). We have one corpus in language 1 and another in language 2 (they need not be translations of each other), an encoder and a decoder shared between the two languages. The weights of the encoder are shared across the two languages, only their embedding tables are different. For the decoder, the weights are also shared except for the last language specific projection layer.

The loss function which is used to compare two sentences is the same as the standard sequence-to-sequence loss: the token wise cross-entropy loss between the sentences, that we denote by $\Delta(\text{sentence a}, \text{sentence b})$. For our purpose, let s_{l_i} be a sentence in language i with $i \in \{1, 2\}$. The encoding of sentence s_{l_i} is denoted by $\text{enc}\left(s_{l_i}\right)$ in language i using the word embeddings of language i to convert the input sentence s_{l_i}. Similarly, denote by $\text{dec}\left(x, l_i\right)$ the decoding of the code x (typically the output of the encoder) into language l_i using the word embeddings of target language i.

Then, the system is trained with three losses aimed to allow the encoder-decoder pair to reconstruct inputs (reconstruction loss), to translate correctly (cross-domain loss) and for the encoder to encode language independent codes (adversarial loss).

Reconstruction Loss This is the standard autoencoder loss which aims to reconstruct the input:

$$\mathcal{L}_{\text{recon}} = \Delta\left(s_{l_i}, \overbrace{\text{dec}\left(\text{enc}\left(s_{l_i}\right), l_i\right)}^{\hat{s}_{l_i} :=}\right)$$

This loss can be seen in Figure 2.

Cross-Domain Loss This loss aims to allow translation of inputs. It is similar to back-translation (Sennrich et al., 2015a). For this loss, denote by $\text{transl}\left(s_{l_i}\right)$ the translation of sentence s_{l_i} from language i to language $1 - i$. The implementation of the translation is explained in subsection 3.1.1 when we address supervision.

$$\mathcal{L}_{\text{cd}} = \Delta\left(s_{l_i}, \underbrace{\text{dec}\left(\text{enc}\left(\text{transl}\left(s_{l_i}\right)\right), l_i\right)}_{\tilde{s}_{l_i} :=}\right) \tag{1}$$

In this loss, we first translate the original sentence s_{l_i} into the other language and then check if we can recreate the original sentence in its original language. This loss can be seen in Figure 2.

Adversarial Loss This loss is to enforce the encoder to produce language independent code which is believed to help in decoding into either language. This loss was only present in Lample et al. (2017) and removed in Lample et al. (2018) as it was considered not necessary by the authors and even harmful. Our results show a similar behaviour.

Input Noise In order to prevent the encoder-decoder pair to learn the identity function and to make the pair more robust, noise is added to the input of the encoder. On the input sentences, the noise comes in the form of random word drops (we use a probability of 0.1) and of random shuffling but only moving each word by at most 3 positions. We also add a Gaussian noise of mean 0 and standard deviation of 0.3 to the input of the decoder.

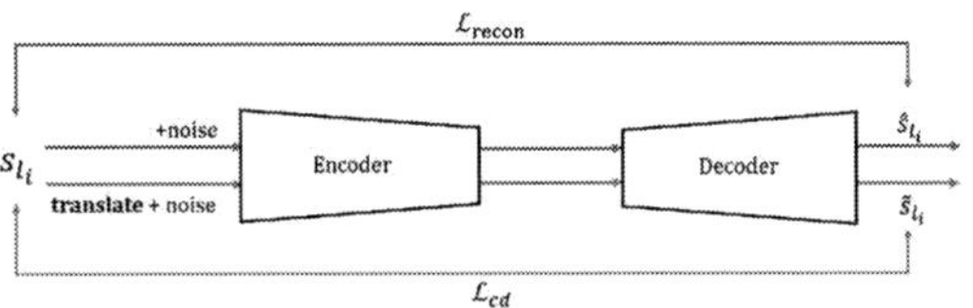

Figure 2: The translation unit of the Bilingual-GAN.

3.1.1 Supervision

The choice of the translation function $\text{transl}\left(s_{l_i}\right)$ directly affects the amount of supervision in the trained model. If the translation function $\text{transl}()$ is a lookup of a word-by-word translation dictionary learned in an unsupervised fashion as in Conneau et al. (2017b), then the whole system is trained in an unsupervised manner since we have no groundtruth information about s_{l_i}. After a couple of epochs, the encoder-decoder model should be good enough to move beyond simple word-by-word translation. At that point the translation function can be changed to using the model itself to translate input sentences. This is what's done in Lample et al. (2017) where they change the translation function from word-by-word to model prediction after 1 epoch. In our case, we get the word-by-word translation lookup table by taking each word in the vocabulary and looking up the closest word in the other language in the multilingual embedding space created by Conneau et al. (2017a).

If the translation function $\text{transl}()$ is able to get the ground truth translation of the sentence, for example if we have an aligned dataset, then $\text{transl}\left(s_{l_i}\right) = s_{l_j}$ which is encoded and decoded into the original language i and compared with s_{l_i} getting the usual supervised neural machine translation loss.

3.1.2 Embeddings

There are a few choices for embedding the sentence words before feeding into the encoder. In particular, we use randomly initialized embeddings, embeddings trained with FastText (Bojanowski et al., 2017) and both pretrained and self-trained cross-lingual embeddings (Conneau et al., 2017a).

3.2 Bilingual Text Generation Unit

The proposed bilingual generator is a GAN trained to learn the latent state manifold of the encoder of the translation unit. We use the Improved Wasserstein GAN gradient penalty (IWGAN) (Gulrajani et al., 2017) loss function in our experiments:

$$L = \mathbb{E}_{\hat{c} \sim \mathbb{P}_g}[D(\hat{c})] - \mathbb{E}_{c \sim \mathbb{P}_r}[D(c)] \\ + \lambda \mathbb{E}_{\bar{c} \sim \mathbb{P}_{\bar{g}}}[(\|\nabla_{\bar{c}} D(\bar{c})\|_2 - 1)^2]) \tag{2}$$

where $\mathbb{P}_r$ is the is the real distribution, c represents the 'code' or the latent space representation of the input text, $\mathbb{P}_g$ is the fake or mimicked distribution, $\hat{c}$ represents the generated code representation. The last term is the gradient penalty where $[\bar{c} \sim \mathbb{P}_{\bar{g}}(\bar{c})] \leftarrow \alpha \, [c \sim \mathbb{P}_r(c)] + (1-\alpha) \, [\hat{c} \sim \mathbb{P}_g(\hat{c})]$ and it is a random latent code obtained by sampling uniformly along a line connecting pairs of the generated code and the encoder output. λ is a constant. We used $\lambda = 10$ in our experiments.

3.2.1 Matrix-based code representation

In latent-space based text generation, where the LSTM based encoder-decoder architectures do not use attention, a single code vector is generally employed which summarizes the entire hidden sequence (Zhao et al., 2017). A variant of the approach is to employ global mean pooling to produce a representative encoding (Semeniuta et al., 2018). We take advantage of our attention based architecture and our bidirectional encoder to concatenate the forward and backward latent states depth-wise and produce a code matrix which can be attended to by our decoder. The code matrix is obtained by concatenating the latent code of each time steps. Consequently, the generator tries to mimic the entire concatenated latent space. We found that this richer representation improves the quality of our sentence generation.

3.2.2 Training

First we pre-train our NMT system (see section 3.1). In order to train the GAN, we used the encoder output of our NMT system as 'real' code. The encoder output is a latent state space matrix which captures all the hidden states of the LSTM encoder. Next we generate noise which is upsampled and reshaped to match the dimensions of the encoder output. This is then fed into a generator neural network comprising 1 linear layer and 5 1-d convolutional with residual connections. Finally we pass it through a non-linearity and output the fake code. The 'real' code and the fake code are then fed into the discriminator neural network, which also consists of 5 convolutional and 1 linear layer. The last layer of the discriminator is a linear layer which ouputs a score value. The discriminator output is used to calculate the generator and discriminator losses. The losses are optimized using Adam (Kingma and Ba, 2014). Unlike the GAN update in (Gulrajani et al., 2017), we use 1 discriminator update per generator update. We think that because we train our GAN on the latent distribution of machine translation we get a better signal to train our GAN on and don't require multiple discriminator updates to one generator update like in Zhao et al. (2017)

In one training iteration, we feed both an English and a French sentence to the encoder and produce two real codes. We generate one fake code by using the generator and calculate losses against both the real codes. We average out the two losses. Although, the NMT is trained to align the latent spaces and we can use just one language to train the GAN, we use both real codes to reduce any biases in our NMT system. We train our GAN on both the supervised and unsupervised NMT scenarios. In the supervised scenario, we feed English and French parallel sentences in each training iteration. In the unsupervised scenario, our corpus does not contain parallel sentences.

Once the GAN is trained, the generator code can be decoded in either language using the pretrained decoder of the NMT system.

4 Experiments

This section presents the different experiments we did, on both translation and bilingual text generation, and the datasets we worked on.

4.1 Datasets

The Europarl and the Multi30k datasets have been used for our experimentation. The Europarl dataset is part of the WMT 2014 parallel corpora (Koehn, 2005) and contains a little more than 2 millions French-English aligned sentences. The Multi30k dataset is used for image captioning (Elliott et al., 2017) and consists of 29k images and their captions. We only use the French and English paired captions.

As preprocessing steps on the Europarl dataset, we removed sentences longer than 20 words and those with a ratio of number of words between translations is bigger than 1.5. Then, we tokenize the sentence using the Moses tokenizer (Koehn et al., 2007). For the Multi30k dataset, we use the supplied tokenized version of the dataset with no further processing. For the BPE experiments, we use the sentencepiece subword tokenizer by Google [1]. Consequentially, the decoder also predicts subword tokens. This results in a common embeddings table for both languages since English and French share the same subwords. The BPE was trained on the training corpora that we created.

For the training, validation and test splits, we used 200k, after filtering, randomly chosen sentences from the Europarl dataset for training and 40k sentences for testing. When creating the splits for unsupervised training, we make sure that the sentences taken in one language have no translations in the other language's training set by randomly choosing different sentences for each of them with no overlap. For the validation set in that case, we chose 80k sentences. In the supervised case, we randomly choose the same sentences in both languages with a validation set of 40k. For the Multi30k dataset, we use 12 850 and 449 sentences for training and validation respectively for each language for the unsupervised case and the whole provided split of 29k and 1014 sentences for training and validation respectively in the supervised case. In both cases, the test set is the provided 1k sentences Flickr 2017 one. For the hyperparameter search phase, we chose a vocabulary size of 8k for the Europarl, the most common words appearing in the training corpora and for the final experiments with the best hyperparameters, we worked with a vocabulary size of 15k. For Multi30k, we used the 6800 most common words

as vocabulary.

4.2 System Specifications

NMT Unit The embeddings have size 300, the encoder consists of either 1 or 2 layers of 256 bidirectional LSTM cells, the decoder is equipped with attention (Bahdanau et al., 2014) and consists of a single layer of 256 LSTM cells. The discriminator, when the adversarial loss is present, is a standard feed-forward neural network with 3 layers of 1024 cells with ReLU activation and one output layer of one cell with Sigmoid activation.

We used Adam with a β_1 of 0.5, a β_2 of 0.999, and a learning rate of 0.0003 to train the encoder and the decoder whereas we used RMSProp with a learning rate of 0.0005 to train the discriminator. Most of the specifications here were taken from Lample et al. (2017).

NTG Unit The Generator and Discriminator are trained using Adam with a a β_1 of 0.5, a β_2 of 0.999, and a learning rate of 0.0001.

4.3 Quantitative Evaluation Metrics

Corpus-level BLEU We use the BLEU-N scores to evaluate the fluency of the generated sentences according to Papineni et al. (2002),

$$\text{BLEU-N} = \text{BP} \cdot \exp(\sum_{n=1}^{N} w_n \log(p_n)) \quad (3)$$

where p_n is the probability of n-gram and $w_n = \frac{1}{n}$. The results is described in Table 3. Here, we set BP to 1 as there is no reference length like in machine translation. For the evaluations, we generated 40 000 sentences for the model trained on Europarl and 1 000 on the model trained on Multi30k.

Perplexity is also used to evaluate the fluency of the generated sentences. For the perplexity evaluations, we generated 100 000 and 10 000 sentences for the Europarl and the Multi30k datasets respectively. The forward and reverse perplexities of the LMs trained with maximum sentence length of 20 and 15 using the Europarl and he Multi30k datasets respectively are described in Table 4. The forward perplexities (F-PPL) are calculated by training an RNN language model (RNNLM) (Zaremba et al., 2015) on real training data and evaluated on the generated samples. This measure describe the fluency of the synthetic samples. We also calculated the reverse perplexities (R-PPL) by training an RNNLM on the synthetic

---

[1] https://github.com/google/sentencepiece

samples and evaluated on the real test data. The results are illustrated in Table 4.

4.4 Translation

MTF	the epoch at which we stop using the `transl()` function and instead start using the model
NC	a new concatenation method used to combine the bidirectional encoder output: concatenate either the forward and backward states lengthwise or depthwise
FastText	the use of FastText (Bojanowski et al., 2017) to train our embeddings
Xlingual	refers to the use of cross-lingual embeddings using (Conneau et al., 2017a) either trained on our own (**Self-Trained**) or pretrained (**Pretrain.**) ones.
BPE	the use of subword tokenization learned as in (Sennrich et al., 2015b)
NoAdv	not using the adversarial loss to train the translation part described in section 3.1
2Enc	using a 2 layers of 256 cells each bidirectional LSTM encoder

Table 1: Notations that are used for this experiment

This section of the results focuses on the scores we have obtained while training the neural machine translation system. The results in Table 2 will show the BLEU scores for translation on a held out test set for the WMT'14 Europarl corpus and for the official Flickr test set 2017 for the Multi30k dataset. The notations that are used in Table 2 are described in Table 1. The baseline is our implementation of the architecture from Lample et al. (2017). From Table 2, we notice first that removing the adversarial loss helps the model. It's possible that the shared encoder and decoder weights are enough to enforce a language independent code space. We note that using 2 layers for the encoder is beneficial but that was to be expected. We also note that the new concatenation method improved upon the model. A small change for a small improvement that may be explained by the fact that both the forward and the backward states are combined and explicitly represent each word of the input sentence rather than having first only the forward states and then only the backward states.

Surprisingly, BPE gave a bad score on English to French. We think that this is due to French being a harder language than English but the score difference is too big to explain that. Further investigation is needed. We see also good results with train-

able FastText embeddings trained on our training corpora. Perhaps using pre-trained ones might be better in a similar fashion as pre-trained cross-lingual embeddings helped over the self-trained ones. The results also show the importance of letting the embeddings change during training instead of fixing them.

4.5 Text Generation

We evaluated text generation on both the fluency of the sentences in English and French and also on the degree to which concurrently generated sentences are valid translations of each other. We fixed our generated sentence length to a maximum of length 20 while training on Europarl and to a maximum of length 15 while training on Multi30k. We measured our performance both on the supervised and unsupervised scenario. The supervised scenario uses a pre-trained NMT trained on parallel sentences and unsupervised uses a pre-trained NMT trained on monolingual corpora. The baseline is our implementation of Zhao et al. (2017) with two additions. We change the Linear layers to 1-d convolutions with residual connections and our generator produces a distributed latent representation which can be paired with an attention based decoder.

Corpus-level BLEU scores are measured using the two test sets. The results are described in Table 3. The higher BLEU scores demonstrate that the GAN can generate fluent sentences both in English and French. We can note that the English sentences have a higher BLEU score which could be a bias from our translation system. On Europarl our BLEU score is much higher than the baseline indicating that we can improve text generation if we learn from the latent space of translation rather than just an autoencoder. This however, requires further investigation. The BLEU scores for the Multi30k are lower because of the smaller test size.

Perplexity result is presented in Table 4. We can easily compare different models by using the forward perplexities whereas it is not possible by using the reverse perplexities as the models are trained using the synthetic sentences with different vocabulary sizes. We put the baseline results only for the English generated sentences to show the superiority of our proposed Bilingual generated sentences. The forward perplexities (F-PPL) of the LMs using real data are 140.22 (En), 136.09 (Fr)

Europarl			
	FR to EN	**EN to FR**	**Mean**
Supervised + Train. Pretrain. Xlingual + NC + 2Enc + NoAdv*	**26.78**	**26.07**	**26.43**
Supervised + NC	24.43	24.89	24.66
Unsupervised + Train. Pretrain. Xlingual + NC + MTF 5 + 2Enc + NoAdv*	**20.82**	**21.20**	**21.01**
Unsupervised + Train. Self-Trained FastText Embeddings + NC + MTF 5	18.12	17.74	17.93
Unsupervised + Train. Pretrain. Xlingual + NC + MTF 5	17.42	17.34	17.38
Unsupervised + NC + MTF 4	16.45	16.56	16.51
Unsupervised + Train. Self-Trained Xlingual + NC + MTF 5	15.91	16.00	15.96
Baseline (Unsupervised + Fixed Pretrain. Xlingual + NC + MTF 5)	15.22	14.34	14.78
Multi30k			
Supervised + Train. Pretrain. Xlingual + NC + 2Enc + NoAdv	**36.67**	**42.52**	**39.59**
Unsupervised + Train. Pretrain. Xlingual + NC + MTF 5 + 2Enc + NoAdv	**10.26**	**10.98**	**10.62**

Table 2: The BLEU-4 scores for French to English and English to French translation. The *'ed experiments use a vocabulary size of 15k words. The Multi30k experiments use the best hyperparameters found when training on the Europarl dataset and a vocabulary size of 6800 words.

Europarl					
	English			French	
	Bilingual-GAN (Supervised)	Bilingual-GAN (Unsupervised)	Baseline (ARAE)	Bilingual-GAN (Supervised)	Bilingual-GAN (Unsupervised)
B-2	89.34	86.06	88.55	82.86	77.40
B-3	73.37	70.52	70.79	65.03	58.32
B-4	52.94	50.22	48.41	44.87	38.70
B-5	34.26	31.63	29.07	28.10	23.63
Multi30k					
B-2	68.41	68.36	72.17	60.23	61.94
B-3	47.60	47.69	51.56	41.31	41.76
B-4	29.89	30.38	33.04	25.24	25.60
B-5	17.38	18.18	19.31	14.21	14.52

Table 3: Corpus-level BLEU scores for Text Generation on Europarl and Multi30k Datasets

and 59.29 (En), 37.56 (Fr) for the Europarl and the Multi30k datasets respectively reported in F-PPL column. From the tables, we can note the models with lower forward perplexities (higher fluency) for the synthetic samples tend to have higher reverse perplexities. For the Europarl dataset, the lower forward perplexities for the Bilingual-GAN and the baseline models than the real data indicate the generated sentences by using these models has less diversity than the training set . For the Multi30k dataset, we cannot see this trend as the size of the test set is smaller than the number of synthetic sentences.

4.6 Human Evaluation

The subjective judgments of the generated sentences of the models trained using the Europarl and the Multi30k datasets with maximum sentence length of size 20 and 15 is reported in Table 6. As we do not have ground truth for our translation we measure parallelism between our generated sentences only based on human evaluation. We used 25 random generated sentences from each model and give them to a group of 4 bilingual people. We asked them to first rate the sentences based on a 5-point scale according to their fluency. The judges are asked to score 1 which corresponds to gibberish, 3 corresponds to understandable but ungrammatical, and 5 correspond to naturally constructed and understandable sentences (Semeniuta et al., 2018). Then, we ask ask them to measure parallelism of the generated samples assuming that the sentences are translations of each other. The scale is between 1 and 5 again with 1 corresponding to no parallelism, 3 to some parallelism and 5 to fully parallel sentences. From Table 6, we can note that on text quality human evaluation results corresponds to our other quantitative metrics. Our generated sentences show some parallelism even in the unsupervised scenario. Some example generated sentences are shown in Table 5. As expected, sentences generated by the supervised models exhibit more parallelism compared to ones generated by unsupervised models.

5   Conclusion

This work proposes a novel way of modelling NMT and NTG whereby we consider them as a

Europarl

	English		French	
	F-PPL	*R-PPL*	*F-PPL*	*R-PPL*
Real	140.22	-	136.09	-
Bilingual-GAN (Supervised)	64.91	319.32	66.40	428.52
Bilingual-GAN (Unsupervised)	65.36	305.96	82.75	372.27
Baseline (ARAE)	73.57	260.18	-	-

Multi30k

Real	59.29	-	37.56	-
Bilingual-GAN (Supervised)	65.97	169.19	108.91	179.12
Bilingual-GAN (Unsupervised)	83.49	226.16	105.94	186.97
Baseline (ARAE)	64.4	222.89	-	-

Table 4: Forward (F) and Reverse (R) perplexity (PPL) results for the Europarl and Multi30k datasets using synthetic sentences of maximum length 20 and 15 respectively. F-PPL: Perplexity of a language model trained on real data and evaluated on synthetic samples. R-PPL: Perplexity of a language model trained on the synthetic samples from Bilingual-GAN and evaluated on the real test data.

English	French
Europarl Supervised	
the vote will take place tomorrow at 12 noon tomorrow.	le vote aura lieu demain à 12 heures.
mr president, i should like to thank mr. unk for the report.	monsieur le président, je tiens à remercier tout particulièrement le rapporteur.
i think it is now as a matter of trying to make it with a great political action.	je pense dès lors qu'une deuxième fois, je pense que nous pouvons agir à une bonne manière que nous sommes une bonne politique.
the debate is closed.	le débat est clos.
Europarl Unsupervised	
the report maintains its opinion, the objective of the european union.	la commission maintient son rapport de l ' appui, tout son objectif essentiel.
the question is not on the basis of which the environmental application which we will do with.	le principe n'est pas sur la loi sur laquelle nous avons besoin de l'application de la législation.
i have no need to know that it has been adopted in a democratic dialogue.	je n'ai pas besoin de ce qu'il a été fait en justice.
Multi30k Supervised	
a child in a floral pattern, mirrored necklaces, walking with trees in the background.	un enfant avec un mannequin, des lunettes de soleil, des cartons, avec des feuilles.
two people are sitting on a bench with the other people.	deux personnes sont assises sur un banc et de la mer.
a man is leaning on a rock wall.	un homme utilise un mur de pierre.
a woman dressed in the rain uniforms are running through a wooden area	une femme habille'e en uniformes de soleil marchant dans une jungle
Multi30k Unsupervised	
three people walking in a crowded city.	trois personnes marchant dans une rue animée.
a girl with a purple shirt and sunglasses are eating.	un homme et une femme mange un plat dans un magasin local.
a woman sleeping in a chair with a graffiti lit street.	une femme âgée assise dans une chaise avec une canne en nuit.

Table 5: Examples of aligned generated sentences

Europarl

	Fluency		Parallelism
	(EN)	**(FR)**	
Real	4.89	4.81	4.63
Bilingual-GAN (Sup.)	4.14	3.8	3.05
Bilingual-GAN (Unsup.)	3.88	3.52	2.52
Multi30k			
Real	4.89	4.82	4.95
Bilingual-GAN (Sup.)	3.41	3.2	2.39
Bilingual-GAN (Unsup.)	4.07	3.24	1.97

Table 6: Human evaluation on the generated sentences by Bilingual-GAN using the Europarl and the Multi30k dataset.

joint problem from the vantage of a bilingual person. It is a step towards modeling concepts and ideas which are language agnostic using the latent representation of machine translation as the basis.

We explore the versatility and the representation power of latent space based deep neural architectures which can align different languages and give us a principled way of generating from this shared space. Using quantitative and qualitative evaluation metrics we demonstrate that we can generate fluent sentences which exhibit parallelism in our two target languages. Future work will consist of improving the quality of the generated sentences, increasing parallelism specially without using parallel data to train the NMT and adding more languages. Other interesting extensions include using our model for conditional text generation and multi-modal tasks such as image captioning.

References

Mikel Artetxe, Gorka Labaka, Eneko Agirre, and Kyunghyun Cho. 2017. Unsupervised neural machine translation. *CoRR*, abs/1710.11041.

Dzmitry Bahdanau, Kyunghyun Cho, and Yoshua Bengio. 2014. Neural machine translation by jointly learning to align and translate. *CoRR*, abs/1409.0473.

Samy Bengio, Oriol Vinyals, Navdeep Jaitly, and Noam Shazeer. 2015. Scheduled sampling for sequence prediction with recurrent neural networks. *CoRR*, abs/1506.03099.

Piotr Bojanowski, Edouard Grave, Armand Joulin, and Tomas Mikolov. 2017. Enriching word vectors with subword information. *Transactions of the Association for Computational Linguistics*, 5:135–146.

Alexis Conneau, Guillaume Lample, Marc'Aurelio Ranzato, Ludovic Denoyer, and Hervé Jégou. 2017a. Word translation without parallel data. *arXiv preprint arXiv:1710.04087*.

Alexis Conneau, Guillaume Lample, Marc'Aurelio Ranzato, Ludovic Denoyer, and Hervé Jégou. 2017b. Word translation without parallel data. *CoRR*, abs/1710.04087.

Desmond Elliott, Stella Frank, Loïc Barrault, Fethi Bougares, and Lucia Specia. 2017. Findings of the second shared task on multimodal machine translation and multilingual image description. In *Proceedings of the Second Conference on Machine Translation, Volume 2: Shared Task Papers*, pages 215–233, Copenhagen, Denmark. Association for Computational Linguistics.

Jules Gagnon-Marchand, Hamed Sadeghi, Md. Akmal Haidar, and Mehdi Rezagholizadeh. 2019. Salsatext: self attentive latent space based adversarial text generation. In *Canadian AI 2019*.

Jonas Gehring, Michael Auli, David Grangier, Denis Yarats, and Yann N. Dauphin. 2017. Convolutional sequence to sequence learning. *CoRR*, abs/1705.03122.

Ian Goodfellow, Jean Pouget-Abadie, Mehdi Mirza, Bing Xu, David Warde-Farley, Sherjil Ozair, Aaron Courville, and Yoshua Bengio. 2014. Generative adversarial nets. In *Advances in neural information processing systems*, pages 2672–2680.

Ishaan Gulrajani, Faruk Ahmed, Martin Arjovsky, Vincent Dumoulin, and Aaron Courville. 2017. Improved training of wasserstein gans. *arXiv preprint arXiv:1704.00028*.

Md. Akmal Haidar and Mehdi Rezagholizadeh. 2019. Textkd-gan: Text generation using knowledge distillation and generative adversarial networks. In *Canadian AI 2019*.

Md. Akmal Haidar, Mehdi Rezagholizadeh, Alan Do-Omri, and Ahmad Rashid. 2019. Latent code and text-based generative adversarial networks for soft-text generation. In *NAACL-HLT 2019*.

Yoon Kim, Kelly Zhang, Alexander M Rush, Yann LeCun, et al. 2017. Adversarially regularized autoencoders for generating discrete structures. *arXiv preprint arXiv:1706.04223*.

Diederik P. Kingma and Jimmy Ba. 2014. Adam: A method for stochastic optimization. *CoRR*, abs/1412.6980.

Philipp Koehn. 2005. Europarl: A parallel corpus for statistical machine translation. In *MT summit*, volume 5, pages 79–86.

Philipp Koehn, Hieu Hoang, Alexandra Birch, Chris Callison-Burch, Marcello Federico, Nicola Bertoldi, Brooke Cowan, Wade Shen, Christine Moran, Richard Zens, Chris Dyer, Ondřej Bojar, Alexandra Constantin, and Evan Herbst. 2007. Moses: Open source toolkit for statistical machine translation. In *Proceedings of the 45th Annual Meeting of the ACL on Interactive Poster and Demonstration Sessions*, ACL '07, pages 177–180, Stroudsburg, PA, USA. Association for Computational Linguistics.

Alex M Lamb, Anirudh Goyal ALIAS PARTH GOYAL, Ying Zhang, Saizheng Zhang, Aaron C Courville, and Yoshua Bengio. 2016. Professor forcing: A new algorithm for training recurrent networks. In *Advances In Neural Information Processing Systems*, pages 4601–4609.

Guillaume Lample, Ludovic Denoyer, and Marc'Aurelio Ranzato. 2017. Unsupervised machine translation using monolingual corpora only. *CoRR*, abs/1711.00043.

Guillaume Lample, Myle Ott, Alexis Conneau, Ludovic Denoyer, and Marc'Aurelio Ranzato. 2018. Phrase-based & neural unsupervised machine translation. *arXiv preprint arXiv:1804.07755*.

Jiwei Li, Will Monroe, Tianlin Shi, Alan Ritter, and Dan Jurafsky. 2017. Adversarial learning for neural dialogue generation. *arXiv preprint arXiv:1701.06547*.

Kishore Papineni, Salim Roukos, Todd Ward, and Wei-Jing Zhu. 2002. Bleu: a method for automatic evaluation of machine translation. In *ACL*, pages 311–318.

Tim Salimans, Ian Goodfellow, Wojciech Zaremba, Vicki Cheung, Alec Radford, and Xi Chen. 2016. Improved techniques for training gans. In *Advances in Neural Information Processing Systems*, pages 2234–2242.

Stanislau Semeniuta, Aliaksei Severyn, and Sylvain Gelly. 2018. On accurate evaluation of gans for language generation. *arXiv preprint arXiv:1806.04936*.

Rico Sennrich, Barry Haddow, and Alexandra Birch. 2015a. Improving neural machine translation models with monolingual data. *CoRR*, abs/1511.06709.

Rico Sennrich, Barry Haddow, and Alexandra Birch. 2015b. Neural machine translation of rare words with subword units. *CoRR*, abs/1508.07909.

Graham Spinks and Marie-Francine Moens. 2018. Generating continuous representations of medical texts. In *NAACL-HLT*, pages 66–70.

Jinyue Su, Jiacheng Xu, Xipeng Qiu, and Xuanjing Huang. 2018. Incorporating discriminator in sentence generation: a gibbs sampling method. *CoRR*, abs/1802.08970.

Ilya Sutskever, Oriol Vinyals, and Quoc V Le. 2014. Sequence to sequence learning with neural networks. In *Advances in neural information processing systems*, pages 3104–3112.

Ashish Vaswani, Noam Shazeer, Niki Parmar, Jakob Uszkoreit, Llion Jones, Aidan N. Gomez, Lukasz Kaiser, and Illia Polosukhin. 2017. Attention is all you need. *CoRR*, abs/1706.03762.

Lijun Wu, Yingce Xia, Li Zhao, Fei Tian, Tao Qin, Jianhuang Lai, and Tie-Yan Liu. 2017. Adversarial neural machine translation. *arXiv preprint arXiv:1704.06933*.

Yonghui Wu, Mike Schuster, Zhifeng Chen, Quoc V Le, Mohammad Norouzi, Wolfgang Macherey, Maxim Krikun, Yuan Cao, Qin Gao, Klaus Macherey, et al. 2016. Google's neural machine translation system: Bridging the gap between human and machine translation. *arXiv preprint arXiv:1609.08144*.

Zhen Yang, Wei Chen, Feng Wang, and Bo Xu. 2017a. Improving neural machine translation with conditional sequence generative adversarial nets. *arXiv preprint arXiv:1703.04887*.

Zhilin Yang, Junjie Hu, Ruslan Salakhutdinov, and William W Cohen. 2017b. Semi-supervised qa with generative domain-adaptive nets. *arXiv preprint arXiv:1702.02206*.

Lantao Yu, Weinan Zhang, Jun Wang, and Yong Yu. 2017. Seqgan: Sequence generative adversarial nets with policy gradient. In *AAAI*, pages 2852–2858.

Wojciech Zaremba, Ilya Sutskever, and Oriol Vinyals. 2015. Recurrent neural network regularization. *arXiv preprint arXiv:1409.2329*.

Junbo Jake Zhao, Yoon Kim, Kelly Zhang, Alexander M. Rush, and Yann LeCun. 2017. Adversarially regularized autoencoders for generating discrete structures. *CoRR*, abs/1706.04223.

Designing a Symbolic Intermediate Representation for Neural Surface Realization

Henry Elder
ADAPT Centre
Dublin City University
`henry.elder@adaptcentre.ie`

Jennifer Foster
ADAPT Centre
Dublin City University
`jennifer.foster@dcu.ie`

James Barry
ADAPT Centre
Dublin City University
`james.barry@adaptcentre.ie`

Alexander O'Connor
Autodesk, inc.
`alex.oconnor@autodesk.com`

Abstract

Generated output from neural NLG systems often contain errors such as hallucination, repetition or contradiction. This work focuses on designing a symbolic intermediate representation to be used in multi-stage neural generation with the intention of reducing the frequency of failed outputs. We show that surface realization from this intermediate representation is of high quality and when the full system is applied to the E2E dataset it outperforms the winner of the E2E challenge. Furthermore, by breaking out the surface realization step from typically end-to-end neural systems, we also provide a framework for non-neural content selection and planning systems to potentially take advantage of semi-supervised pretraining of neural surface realization models.

1 Introduction

For Natural Language Generation (NLG) systems to be useful in practice, they must generate utterances that are adequate, that is, the utterances need to include all relevant information. Furthermore the information should be expressed correctly and fluently, as if written by a human. The rule and template based systems which dominate commercial NLG systems are limited in their generation capabilities and require much human effort to create but are reliably adequate and known for widespread usage in areas such as financial journalism and business intelligence. By contrast, neural NLG systems need only a well collected dataset to train their models and generate fluent sounding utterances but have notable problems, such as hallucination and a general lack of adequacy (Wiseman et al., 2017). There was a marked absence of neural NLG in any of the finalist systems in either the 2017 or 2018 Alexa Prize (Fang et al., 2017; Chen et al., 2018).

Following prior work in the area of multi-stage neural NLG (Dušek and Jurcicek, 2016; Daniele et al., 2017; Puduppully et al., 2018; Hajdik et al., 2019; Moryossef et al., 2019), and inspired by more traditional pipeline data-to-text generation (Reiter and Dale, 2000; Gatt and Krahmer, 2018), we present a system which splits apart the typically end-to-end data-driven neural model into separate utterance planning and surface realization models using a symbolic intermediate representation. We focus in particular on surface realization and introduce a new symbolic intermediate representation which is based on an underspecified universal dependency tree (Mille et al., 2018b). In designing our intermediate representation, we are driven by the following constraints:

1. The intermediate representation must be suitable for processing with a neural system.

2. It must not make the surface realization task too difficult because we are interested in understanding the limitations of neural generation even under favorable conditions.

3. It must be possible to parse a sentence into this representation so that a surface realization training set can be easily augmented with additional in-domain data.

Focusing on English and using the E2E dataset, we parse the reference sentences into our intermediate representation. We then train a surface realization model to generate from this representation, comparing the resulting strings with the reference using both automatic and manual evaluation. We find that the quality of the generated text is high, achieving a BLEU score of 82.47. This increases to 83.38 when we augment the training data with sentences from the TripAdvisor corpus. A manual error analysis shows that in only a very small proportion ($\sim$5%) of the output sentences, the meaning of the reference is not fully recovered. This

Proceedings of the Workshop on Methods for Optimizing and Evaluating Neural Language Generation (NeuralGen), pages 65–73
Minneapolis, Minnesota, USA, June 6, 2019. ©2019 Association for Computational Linguistics

high level of adequacy is expected since the intermediate representations are generated directly from the reference sentences. An analysis of a sample of the adequate sentences shows that readability is on a par with the reference sentences.

Having established that surface realization from our intermediate representation achieves sufficiently high performance, we then test its efficacy as part of a pipeline system. On the E2E task, our system scores higher on automated results than the winner of the E2E challenge (Juraska et al., 2018). The use of additional training data in the surface realization stage results in further gains. These encouraging results suggest that pipelines can work well in the context of neural NLG.

2 Methods

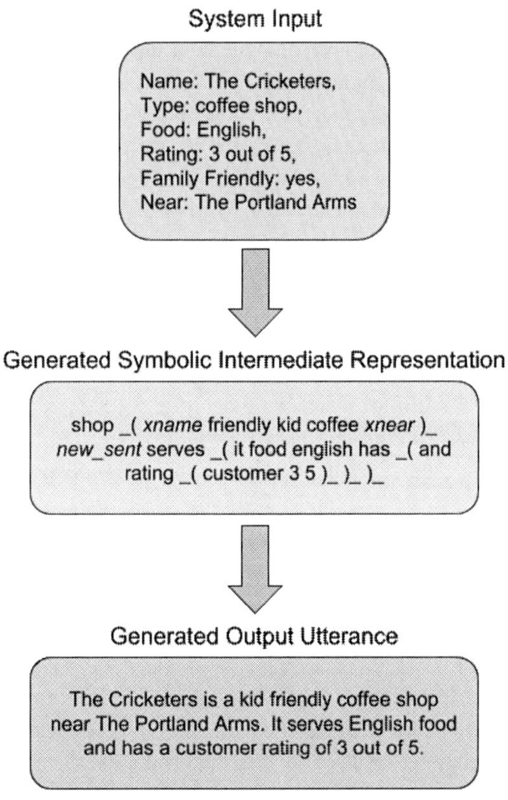

System Input

Generated Symbolic Intermediate Representation

Generated Output Utterance

Figure 1: Example of two stage generation using the pipeline system. Both are real examples generated by their respective models.

Our system consists of two distinct models. The first is an utterance planning model which takes as input some structured data and generates an intermediate representation of an utterance containing one or more sentences. The intermedi-

ate representation of each sentence in the utterance is then passed to a second surface realization model which generates the final natural language text. See Figure 1 for an example from the E2E dataset. Both models are neural based. We use a symbolic intermediate representation to pass information between the two models.

2.1 Symbolic Intermediate Representation

The symbolic intermediate representation used is the *deep*[1] Underspecified Universal Dependency (UUD) structure (Mille et al., 2018b). The UUD structure is a tree "containing only content words linked by predicate-argument edges in the PropBank/NomBank (Palmer et al., 2005; Meyers et al., 2004) fashion" (Mille et al., 2018b). Each UUD structure represents a single sentence. The UUD structure was designed to "approximate the kind of abstract meaning representations used in native NLG tasks" (Mille et al., 2018b). That is, the kind of output that a rule based system could be reasonably expected to generate as part of a pipeline NLG process. However, to the best of our knowledge, no such system has yet been developed or adapted to generate the deep UUD structure as output. Hence it was required to make a number of changes to the deep UUD structure during preprocessing to better suit a neural system designed to use the structure as a symbolic intermediate representation; namely we linearize the UUD tree, remove accompanying token features and use the surface form of each token, see Figure 2.

Linearization In order to use tree structures in a sequence-to-sequence model a linearization order for nodes in the tree must be determined. Following Konstas et al. (2017) tree nodes are ordered using depth first search. Scope markers are added before each child node. When a node has only one child node we omit scope markers. Though this can lead to moderate ambiguity it greatly reduces the length of the sequence (Konstas et al., 2017).

When two nodes appear at the same level in the tree their linearization order is typically chosen at random, or using some rule based heuristic or even a secondary model (Ferreira et al., 2018). In this system linearization of equivalent level tokens is

---

[1]*deep* here is not referring to deep learning but rather as a contrast with another UUD variant known as the *shallow* UUD. Shallow and deep surface realization tracks were used in both Surface Realization Shared Tasks (Mille et al., 2018a; Belz et al., 2011)

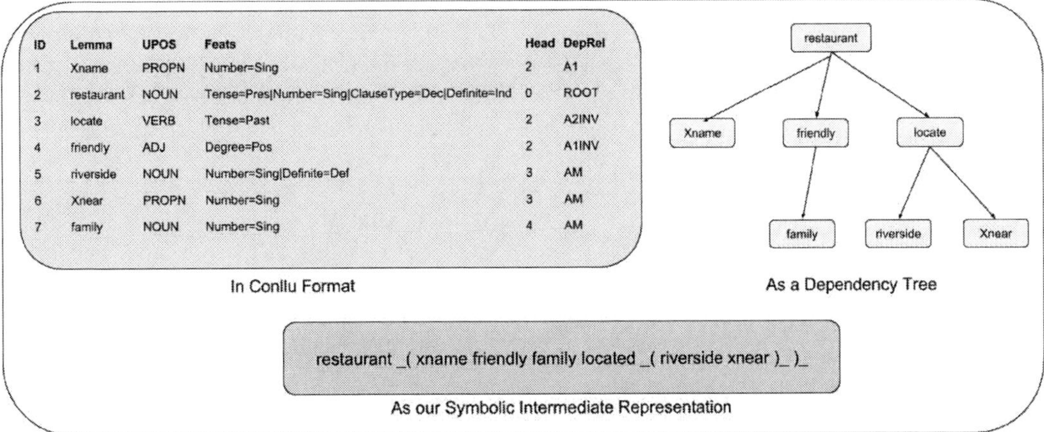

Figure 2: Different representations of the *Deep* Underspecified Universal Dependency structure

determined by the original order in which they appeared in the sentence. We chose to use a consistent, as opposed to random, ordering of equivalent level nodes for the symbolic intermediate representation as it has been shown in a number of papers (Konstas et al., 2017; Juraska et al., 2018) that neural models perform worse at given tasks when trained on symbolic intermediate representations sorted in random orders, even when that randomness is used to augment and increase the size of the data. We chose to use original sentence order of tokens as the basis for ordering sibling nodes. Though this is clearly a simplification, and gives the model additional information, it is an intuitive choice.

Features As well as the head id, tokens in the deep UUD structure are each associated with a number of additional features: dependency relations (DepRel), universal part-of-speech tag (UPOS) and lexical features (feats), see Figure 2. Other neural based work on surface realization from the deep UUD structure included this information using factor methods (Elder and Hokamp, 2018). However our symbolic intermediate representation does not include these additional features. By not including the additional features with each token we simplify the task of generating the symbolic intermediate representation using a neural model. Token features could be generated using multitask learning as in Dalvi et al. (2017)

but we leave this for future work.

Lemmas vs. Forms In the deep UUD structure the token provided is a lemma, the root of the original form of a token. Part-of-speech and lexical features are provided to enable a surface realization system to determine the form. As we do not include these features in our symbolic intermediary representation we use the original form of token instead. This is another simplification of the surface realization task. While we found that *lemma + part of speech tag + lexical features* typically provide enough information to reconstruct the original form, it is not a 100% accurate mapping.

3 Experiments

Datasets Experiments were performed with the E2E dataset (Novikova et al., 2017). Figure 1 contains an example of the E2E input. The E2E dataset contains a training set of 42,061 pairs of meaning representations and utterances. Training data for the surface realization model was augmented, for some experiments, with the TripAdvisor corpus (Wang et al., 2010), which was filtered for sentences with a 100% vocabulary overlap with the E2E corpus and a sentence length between 5 and 30 tokens, resulting in an additional 209,823 sentences, with an average sentence length of 10 tokens. By comparison the E2E corpus had sentence lengths ranging between 1 and

59 tokens with an average sentence length of 13 tokens.

Both corpora were sentence tokenized and parsed by the Stanford NLP universal dependency parser (Qi et al., 2018). The parsed sentences in CoNLL-U format were then further processed by a special deep UUD parser (Mille et al., 2018b). Utterances from the E2E corpus were delexicalised to anonymize restaurant names in both the *name* and *near* slots of the meaning representation. All tokens were lower cased before training.

Models For the neural NLG pipeline system we train two separate encoder-decoder models using the neural machine translation framework Open-NMT (Klein et al., 2017). We trained two separate encoder-decoder models for surface realization and content selection. However both used the same hyperparameters. A single layer LSTM (Hochreiter and Schmidhuber, 1997) with RNN size 450 and word vector size 300 was used. The models were trained using ADAM (Kingma and Ba, 2015) with a learning rate of 0.001. The only difference between the two models was that the surface realization model was trained with a copy attention mechanism (Vinyals et al., 2015).

For the full E2E task a single planning model was trained on the E2E corpus. However two different surface realization models were compared; one trained solely on sentences from the E2E corpus and another trained on a combined corpus of E2E and TripAdvisor sentences. For baselines on the full E2E task we compare with two encoder-decoder models which both use semantic rerankers on their generated utterances; TGen (Dušek and Jurcicek, 2016) the baseline system for the E2E challenge and Slug2Slug (Juraska et al., 2018) the winning system of the E2E challenge.

Automated Evaluation The E2E task is evaluated using an array of automated metrics[2]; BLEU (Papineni et al., 2002), NIST (Doddington, 2002), METEOR (Lavie and Agarwal, 2007), ROUGE (Lin, 2004), and CIDEr (Vedantam et al., 2015). The two surface realization models were evaluated on how well they were able to realize sentences from the E2E validation set using silver parsed intermediate representations. We report BLEU-4

scores[3] for the silver parse generated texts from the surface realization models. In both the E2E (Dušek et al., 2019) and WebNLG challenge (Shimorina, 2018) it was found that automated results did not correlate with the human evaluation *on the sentence level*. However in the Surface Realization shared task correlation between BLEU score and human evaluation was noted to be highly significant (Mille et al., 2018a).

Manual Analysis The importance of using human evaluation to get a more accurate understanding of the quality of text generated by an NLG system cannot be overstated. We perform human evaluation on the outputs of the surface realization model with a silver parse of the original utterances as input. We evaluate the outputs first in terms of meaning similarity and then readability and fluency.

To evaluate the surface realization model we compare generated utterances with the human references. For the meaning similarity human evaluation we remove sentences with no differences, only differences involving the presence or absence of hyphens or only capitalization differences. We evaluate meaning similarity between two utterances as whether they contain the same meaning. We treat this a binary Yes / No decision as the generated utterances are using a silver parse and ought to be able to reconstruct a sentence that, while possibly differently structured, does express the same meaning.

We manually analyze failure cases where semantic similarity is not achieved to discover where the issues arise. There may be failures in the method of obtaining the intermediate representation, in the surface realization model or some other issue with the intermediate representation.

We then pass on only those generated utterances deemed to have the same meaning with the reference utterance into the next stage of readability evaluation. To evaluate readability we perform pairwise comparisons between generated utterances and reference utterances. We randomize the order during evaluation so it is not clear what the origin of a particular utterance is. We define readability, sometimes called fluency, as how well a given utterances reads, "is it fluent English

---

[3]We input tokenized, lowercased and relexicalised sentences to the Moses multi-bleu perl script: `https://github.com/OpenNMT/OpenNMT-py/blob/master/tools/multi-bleu.perl`

or does it have grammatical errors, awkward constructions, etc." (Mille et al., 2018a). By investigating readability of utterances with meaning similarity, we hope to see how the surface realization model performs compared with a human written utterance. The surface realization model is required to at least match human level performance in order to be usable, if it does not then we need to investigate where it fails and why. We used Prodigy (Montani and Honnibal, 2018) as our data annotation tool.

4 Results

4.1 Surface Realization Analysis

	BLEU
E2E	0.8247
+ TripAdvisor	**0.8338**

Table 1: Automated evaluation of surface realization models on validation set sentences

Automated evaluation To initially establish if training on additional data from a different corpus was beneficial we performed automated evaluation. Each surface realization model is provided a parse of the target sentence. The BLEU score is slightly higher, see Table 1, when the model is trained with the additional corpus data.

	E2E	+ TripAdvisor
Exact matches	3807	3935
Punctuation and/or determiner differences	1242	1268

Table 2: Surface Realization of 8024 sentences in the E2E validation set

	E2E	+ TripAdvisor
Remaining sentences	2975	2821
Sentences analysed	325	325
Failed meaning similarities	76	45
Same readability as reference	198	208
Worse readability than reference	30	43
Better readability than reference	21	29

Table 3: Manual analysis of a subset of remaining sentences from the 8024 sentences in the E2E validation set

Manual analysis Starting with generated sentences from the E2E validation set, we first filter out exact or very close matches to the reference sentences, see Table 2. Then taking a subset of remaining generated sentences, we establish that they contain the same meaning as the reference sentence. Finally we compare the readability / naturalness of the generated text with the human reference sentences, see Table 3.

While the surface realization model trained on both E2E and Trip Advisor corpora generally outperforms the model trained on only E2E data, it has more sentences rated as *Worse readability than reference*. More detailed manual analysis is required to tell whether this is a statistical anomaly or a true insight into how the additional data is affecting model performance.

Analysis of failed meaning similarities Looking at examples where a generated sentence failed to correctly capture the meaning of the reference sentence we find the causes for this fall into a number of categories:

- Poor sentence tokenization

- Problems with the reference sentence

- Unusually phrased reference sentence

- Unknown words

- Generation model failures (repetition or missing words)

The model trained on the additional TripAdvisor corpus has a larger vocabulary and has seen a wider range of sentences, and thus fails less often. Most failures appear to be due to reference sentences containing unknown tokens or being phrased in a new or unusual way the model has not seen before. A smaller number of cases are attributable to issues directly with the generation model, namely repetition or absence of tokens from the intermediate representation. Figure 3 contains three examples of failed generation.

	BLEU	NIST	METEOR	ROUGE_L	CIDEr
Validation					
TGen	0.6925	8.4781	0.4703	0.7257	2.3987
Slug2Slug	0.6576	8.0761	0.4675	0.7029	-
Pipeline	0.7271	8.5680	0.4874	0.7546	2.5481
+ TripAdvisor	**0.7298**	**8.5891**	**0.4875**	**0.7557**	**2.5507**
Test					
TGen	0.6593	8.6094	0.4483	0.6850	2.2338
Slug2Slug	0.6619	8.6130	0.4454	0.6772	2.2615
Pipeline	0.6705	8.6737	**0.4573**	0.7114	2.2940
+ TripAdvisor	**0.6738**	**8.7277**	0.4572	**0.7152**	**2.2995**

Table 4: Automated results on end-to-end task

Ref: Do not go to The Punter near riverside.

IR: go _(not xname riverside)_

Gen: Not go to The Punter in riverside.

(a) Model generation failure

Ref: With only an average customer rating, and it being a no for families, it doesn't have much going for it.

IR: have _(rating _(only average customer no _(and it families)_)_it n't much _(going it)_)_

Gen: With a only average customer rating and its no families, it won't have much that going to it.

(b) Unusual phrasing in reference sentence

Ref: Have you heard of The Sorrento and The Wrestlers, they are the average friendly families.

IR: heard _(you xnear _(xname and)_families _(they average friendly)_)_

Gen: You can be heard near The Sorrento and The Wrestlers, they are average friendly families.

(c) Nonsensical reference sentence

Figure 3: Examples of reference sentences *(Ref)*, intermediate representations *(IR)* and generated texts *(Gen)* from three different scenarios.

4.2 End-to-End Analysis

We report results on the full E2E task in Table 4. Both our systems outperform the E2E challenge winning system Slug2Slug (Juraska et al., 2018), with the system using the surface realization model trained with additional data performing slightly better. Both surface realization models received the same set of intermediate representations from the single utterance planning model.

Further human evaluation may be required to establish the meaningfulness of these higher automated results.

5 Related Work

The work most similar to ours is (Dušek and Jurcicek, 2016). It is also in the domain of task oriented dialogue and they apply two-stage generation; first generating deep syntax dependency trees using a neural model and then generating the final utterance using a non-neural surface realizer. They found that while generation quality is initially higher from the two-stage model, when using a semantic reranker it is outperformed by an end-to-end seq2seq system.

Concurrent to this work is Moryossef et al. (2019). In this work they split apart the task of planning and surface realization. Conversely to Dušek and Jurcicek (2016) they employ a rule based utterance planner and a neural based surface realizer. They applied this system to the WebNLG corpus (Gardent et al., 2017) and found that, compared with a strong neural system, it performed roughly equally at surface realization but exceeded the neural system at adequately including information in the generated utterance.

Other work has looked for innovative ways to separate planning and surface realization from the end-to-end neural systems, most notably Wiseman et al. (2018) which learns template generation also on the E2E task, but does not yet match baseline performance, and He et al. (2018) which has a dialogue manager control decision making and passes this information onto a secondary language generator. Other work has attempted either multi-stage semi-unconstrained language generation, such as in the domain of story telling (Fan et al., 2019), or filling-in-the-blanks style sentence reconstruction (Fedus et al., 2018).

6 Discussion

Our system's automated results on the E2E task exceed that of the winning system. This shows that splitting apart utterance planning and surface realization in a fully neural system may have potential benefit. Our intuition is that by loosely separating the semantic and syntactic tasks of sentence planning and surface realization, our models are more easily able to learn alignments between source and target sequences in each distinct task than in a single model. More clear alignments may help as the E2E corpus is a relatively small dataset, at least compared with dataset sizes used for neural machine translation (Bojar et al., 2018) for which end-to-end neural models are the dominant paradigm. Further human analysis of the generated utterances' fluency and adequacy[4] could help determine what is driving the improved performance on automated metrics.

The design of our symbolic intermediate representation is such that additional training data can be easily collected for the surface realization model. Indeed we see marginally better results on the E2E task with a surface realization model trained on both the E2E and TripAdvisor corpuses. This approach could be further scaled beyond the relatively small number of additional sentences we automatically parsed from the TripAdvisor corpus. In the E2E challenge it was noted that a semantic reranker was requisite for high performing neural systems (Dušek et al., 2019). Adding a semantic reranker to our system could likely help improve performance of the utterance planning step.

While we made simplifications to the intermediate representation, namely including forms over lemmas and using the original sentence order to sort adjacent nodes, their generation was still required to be performed by a higher level model. It's possible that different higher level systems, for example a rule based utterance planning system, might prefer a more abstract intermediate representation. Indeed this trade off between what information ought to go into the intermediate representation is a highly practical one. A surface realization model trained using our automated representation could be made to work with a rule based system providing input.

7   Conclusion

We have designed a symbolic intermediate representation for use in a pipeline neural NLG system. We found the surface realization from this representation to be of high quality, and that results improved further when trained on additional data. When testing the full pipeline system automated results exceeded that of prior top perform-

---

[4]The generated utterance's coverage of the input meaning representation

ing neural systems, demonstrating the potential of breaking apart typically end-to-end neural systems into separate task-focused models.

Acknowledgements

This research is supported by Science Foundation Ireland in the ADAPT Centre for Digital Content Technology. The ADAPT Centre for Digital Content Technology is funded under the SFI Research Centres Programme (Grant 13/RC/2106) and is co-funded under the European Regional Development Fund.

References

Anja Belz, Michael White, Dominic Espinosa, Eric Kow, Deirdre Hogan, and Amanda Stent. 2011. The First Surface Realisation Shared Task: Overview and Evaluation Results. In *Proceedings of the European Workshop on Natural Language Generation*, December, pages 217–226.

Ondej Bojar, Christian Federmann, Mark Fishel, Yvette Graham, Barry Haddow, Matthias Huck, Philipp Koehn, and Christof Monz. 2018. Findings of the 2018 Conference on Machine Translation (WMT18). In *Proceedings of the Third Conference on Machine Translation, Volume 2: Shared Task Papers*, pages 272–307, Belgium, Brussels. Association for Computational Linguistics.

Chun-Yen Chen, Dian Yu, Weiming Wen, Yi Mang Yang, Jiaping Zhang, Mingyang Zhou, Kevin Jesse, Austin Chau, Antara Bhowmick, Shreenath Iyer, Giritheja Sreenivasulu, Runxiang Cheng, Ashwin Bhandare, and Zhou Yu. 2018. Gunrock: Building A Human-Like Social Bot By Leveraging Large Scale Real User Data.

Fahim Dalvi, Nadir Durrani, Hassan Sajjad, Yonatan Belinkov, and Stephan Vogel. 2017. Understanding and Improving Morphological Learning in the Neural Machine Translation Decoder. *IJCNLP*, pages 142–151.

Andrea F Daniele, Matthew R Walter, Mohit Bansal, and Matthew R Walter. 2017. Navigational Instruction Generation as Inverse Reinforcement Learning with Neural Machine Translation. In *Proceedings of HRI*.

George Doddington. 2002. Automatic Evaluation of Machine Translation Quality Using N-gram Co-occurrence Statistics. In *Proceedings of the Second International Conference on Human Language Technology Research*, pages 138–145, San Diego, CA, USA. ®.

Ondrej Dušek and Filip Jurcicek. 2016. Sequence-to-Sequence Generation for Spoken Dialogue via Deep Syntax Trees and Strings. In *Proceedings of the*

54th Annual Meeting of the Association for Computational Linguistics (Volume 2: Short Papers), pages 45–51. Association for Computational Linguistics.

Ondej Dušek, Jekaterina Novikova, and Verena Rieser. 2019. Evaluating the State-of-the-Art of End-to-End Natural Language Generation: The E2E NLG Challenge. *Under Review.*

Henry Elder and Chris Hokamp. 2018. Generating High-Quality Surface Realizations Using Data Augmentation and Factored Sequence Models. In *Proceedings of the 1st Workshop on Multilingual Surface Realisation (MSR), 56th Annual Meeting of the Association for Computational Linguistics (ACL).*

Angela Fan, Mike Lewis, and Yann Dauphin. 2019. Strategies for Structuring Story Generation. In *Forthcoming NAACL.*

Hao Fang, Hao Cheng, Elizabeth Clark, Ariel Holtzman, Maarten Sap, Mari Ostendorf, Yejin Choi, and Noah A Smith. 2017. Sounding Board University of Washingtons Alexa Prize Submission. In *1st Proceedings of Alexa Prize*, page 12.

William Fedus, Ian Goodfellow, and Andrew M Dai. 2018. MaskGAN: Better Text Generation via Filling in the______. In *International Conference on Learning Representations.*

Thiago Castro Ferreira, Sander Wubben, Emiel Krahmer, Thiago Castro Ferreira, Sander Wubben, and Emiel Krahmer. 2018. Surface Realization Shared Task 2018 (SR18): The Tilburg University Approach. In *Proceedings of the First Workshop on Multilingual Surface Realisation*, volume 2018, pages 35–38. Association for Computational Linguistics.

Claire Gardent, Anastasia Shimorina, Shashi Narayan, and Laura Perez-Beltrachini. 2017. The WebNLG Challenge: Generating Text from RDF Data. In *Proceedings of The 10th International Natural Language Generation conference*, pages 124–133.

Albert Gatt and Emiel Krahmer. 2018. Survey of the State of the Art in Natural Language Generation: Core tasks, applications and evaluation. *Journal of Artificial Intelligence Research*, 61(c):65–170.

Valerie Hajdik, Jan Buys, Michael W Goodman, and Emily M Bender. 2019. Neural Text Generation from Rich Semantic Representations. In *Forthcoming NAACL.*

He He, Derek Chen, Anusha Balakrishnan, and Percy Liang. 2018. Decoupling Strategy and Generation in Negotiation Dialogues. *Proceedings of the 2018 Conference on Empirical Methods in Natural Language Processing*, pages 2333–2343.

Sepp Hochreiter and Jurgen Schmidhuber. 1997. Long Short-Term Memory. *Neural Computation*, 9(8):1735–1780.

Juraj Juraska, Panagiotis Karagiannis, Kevin Bowden, and Marilyn Walker. 2018. A Deep Ensemble Model with Slot Alignment for Sequence-to-Sequence Natural Language Generation. In *Proceedings of the 2018 Conference of the North American Chapter of the Association for Computational Linguistics: Human Language Technologies, Volume 1 (Long Papers)*, pages 152–162, Stroudsburg, PA, USA. Association for Computational Linguistics.

Diederik P. Kingma and Jimmy Ba. 2015. Adam: A Method for Stochastic Optimization. In *International Conference on Learning Representations.*

Guillaume Klein, Yoon Kim, Yuntian Deng, Jean Senellart, and Alexander Rush. 2017. OpenNMT: Open-Source Toolkit for Neural Machine Translation. In *Proceedings of ACL 2017, System Demonstrations*, pages 67–72, Stroudsburg, PA, USA. Association for Computational Linguistics.

Ioannis Konstas, Srinivasan Iyer, Mark Yatskar, Yejin Choi, and Luke Zettlemoyer. 2017. Neural AMR: Sequence-to-Sequence Models for Parsing and Generation. In *Proceedings of the 55th Annual Meeting of the Association for Computational Linguistics (Volume 1: Long Papers)*, pages 146–157, Stroudsburg, PA, USA. Association for Computational Linguistics.

Alon Lavie and Abhaya Agarwal. 2007. Meteor: An Automatic Metric for MT Evaluation with High Levels of Correlation with Human Judgments. In *Proceedings of the Second Workshop on Statistical Machine Translation*, StatMT '07, pages 228–231, Stroudsburg, PA, USA.

C Y Lin. 2004. Rouge: A package for automatic evaluation of summaries. In *Proceedings of the workshop on text summarization branches out (WAS 2004)*, 1, pages 25–26.

Adam Meyers, Ruth Reeves, Catherine Macleod, Rachel Szekely, Veronika Zielinska, Brian Young, and Ralph Grishman. 2004. The NomBank project: An interim report. In *HLT-NAACL 2004 Workshop: Frontiers in Corpus Annotation, Boston, MA, May 2004*, pages 24–31.

Simon Mille, Anja Belz, Bernd Bohnet, Yvette Graham, Emily Pitler, and Leo Wanner. 2018a. The First Multilingual Surface Realisation Shared Task (SR'18): Overview and Evaluation Results. In *Proceedings of the 1st Workshop on Multilingual Surface Realisation (MSR), 56th Annual Meeting of the Association for Computational Linguistics*, pages 1–10, Melbourne, Australia.

Simon Mille, Anja Belz, Bernd Bohnet, and Leo Wanner. 2018b. Underspecified Universal Dependency Structures as Inputs for Multilingual Surface Realisation. In *Proceedings of the 11th International Conference on Natural Language Generation*, pages 199–209. Association for Computational Linguistics.

Ines Montani and Matthew Honnibal. 2018. Prodigy: A new annotation tool for radically efficient machine teaching. *Artificial Intelligence*, to appear.

Amit Moryossef, Yoav Goldberg, Ido Dagan, and Ramat Gan. 2019. Separating Planning from Realization in Neural Data to Text Generation. In *Forthcoming NAACL*.

Jekaterina Novikova, Ondej Dušek, and Verena Rieser. 2017. The E2E Dataset: New Challenges For End-to-End Generation. In *Proceedings of the 18th Annual SIGdial Meeting on Discourse and Dialogue*, August, pages 201–206, Stroudsburg, PA, USA. Association for Computational Linguistics.

Martha Palmer, Daniel Gildea, and Paul Kingsbury. 2005. The Proposition Bank: An Annotated Corpus of Semantic Roles. *Computational Linguistics*, 31(1):71–106.

Kishore Papineni, Salim Roukos, Todd Ward, and Wei-Jing Zhu. 2002. BLEU: A Method for Automatic Evaluation of Machine Translation. In *Proceedings of the 40th Annual Meeting on Association for Computational Linguistics*, ACL '02, pages 311–318, Stroudsburg, PA, USA. Association for Computational Linguistics.

Ratish Puduppully, Li Dong, and Mirella Lapata. 2018. Data-to-Text Generation with Content Selection and Planning. *Aaai*.

Peng Qi, Timothy Dozat, Yuhao Zhang, and Christopher D Manning. 2018. Universal Dependency Parsing from Scratch. In *Proceedings of the (CoNLL) 2018 Shared Task: Multilingual Parsing from Raw Text to Universal Dependencies*, pages 160–170, Brussels, Belgium. Association for Computational Linguistics.

Ehud Reiter and Robert Dale. 2000. *Building Natural Language Generation Systems*. Cambridge University Press, New York, NY, USA.

Anastasia Shimorina. 2018. Human vs Automatic Metrics: on the Importance of Correlation Design.

Ramakrishna Vedantam, C. Lawrence Zitnick, and Devi Parikh. 2015. CIDEr: Consensus-based image description evaluation. *Proceedings of the IEEE Computer Society Conference on Computer Vision and Pattern Recognition*, 07-12-June:4566–4575.

Oriol Vinyals, Meire Fortunato, and Navdeep Jaitly. 2015. Pointer Networks. In *Advances in Neural Information Processing Systems 28*, pages 2692–2700.

Hongning Wang, Yue Lu, and Chengxiang Zhai. 2010. Latent aspect rating analysis on review text data. In *Proceedings of the 16th ACM SIGKDD international conference on Knowledge discovery and data mining - KDD '10*, pages 783–792, Washington, DC, USA. ACM Press.

Sam Wiseman, Stuart Shieber, and Alexander Rush. 2017. Challenges in Data-to-Document Generation. In *Proceedings of the 2017 Conference on Empirical Methods in Natural Language Processing*, pages 2253–2263.

Sam Wiseman, Stuart Shieber, and Alexander Rush. 2018. Learning Neural Templates for Text Generation. In *Proceedings of the 2018 Conference on Empirical Methods in Natural Language Processing*, pages 3174–3187.

Neural Text Style Transfer via Denoising and Reranking

Joseph Lee[*], **Ziang Xie**[*], **Cindy Wang, Max Drach, Dan Jurafsky, Andrew Y. Ng**
Computer Science Department, Stanford University
{joseph.lee,zxie,cindyw,mdrach,ang}@cs.stanford.edu,
jurafsky@stanford.edu

Abstract

We introduce a simple method for text style transfer that frames style transfer as denoising: we synthesize a noisy corpus and treat the source style as a noisy version of the target style. To control for aspects such as preserving meaning while modifying style, we propose a reranking approach in the data synthesis phase. We evaluate our method on three novel style transfer tasks: transferring between British and American varieties, text genres (formal vs. casual), and lyrics from different musical genres. By measuring style transfer quality, meaning preservation, and the fluency of generated outputs, we demonstrate that our method is able both to produce high-quality output while maintaining the flexibility to suggest syntactically rich stylistic edits.

1 Introduction

Following exciting work on style transfer for images (Gatys et al., 2016), neural style transfer for text has gained research interest as an application and testbed for syntactic and semantic understanding of natural language (Li et al., 2018; Shen et al., 2017; Hu et al., 2017; Prabhumoye et al., 2018). Unfortunately, unlike image style transfer, which often requires only a single reference image in the desired style, neural text style transfer typically requires a large parallel corpus of sentences in the source and target style to train a neural machine translation model (Sutskever et al., 2014; Bahdanau et al., 2014).

One approach to mitigate the need for a large parallel corpus is to develop methods to disentangle stylistic attributes from semantic content, for example by using adversarial classifiers (Shen et al., 2017) or by predefining markers associated with stylistic attributes (Li et al., 2018). However, such approaches can reduce fluency and alter

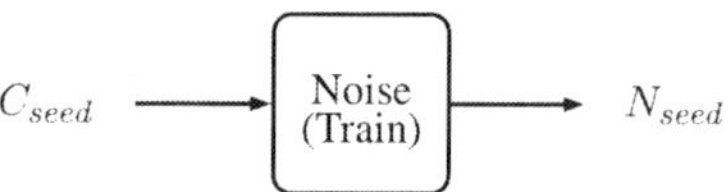

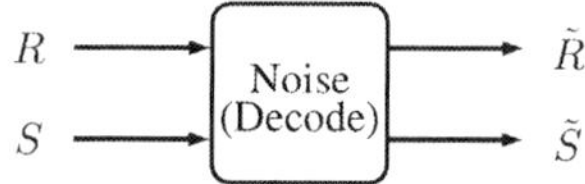

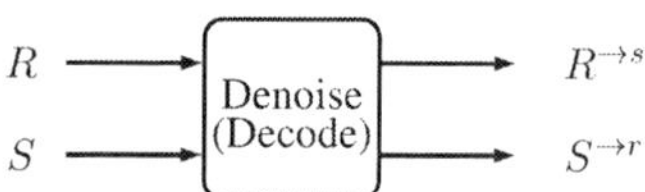

Figure 1: An overview of our method. We assume a seed corpus of parallel (clean, noisy) sentence pairs $(C, N) = \{(C_k, N_k)\}_{k=1}^{M_{\text{seed}}}$, as well as two non-parallel corpora $R = \{R_k\}_{k=1}^{M_R}$ and $S = \{S_k\}_{k=1}^{M_S}$ of different styles. We first use noising to generate synthetic parallel data in both styles, then "denoise" to transfer from one style to the other.

meaning, or make only lexical changes instead of larger, phrase-level edits.

Given the limitations of these techniques, we propose an approach which uses backtranslation (Sennrich et al., 2015a) to synthesize parallel data, starting with nonparallel data in differing styles. We introduce a simple method for unsupervised text style transfer that frames style transfer as a *denoising* problem in which we treat the source style as a noisy version of the target style. By further introducing hypothesis reranking techniques in the data synthesis procedure, our method

---

[*]Equal contribution.

Proceedings of the Workshop on Methods for Optimizing and Evaluating Neural Language Generation (NeuralGen), pages 74–81
Minneapolis, Minnesota, USA, June 6, 2019. ©2019 Association for Computational Linguistics

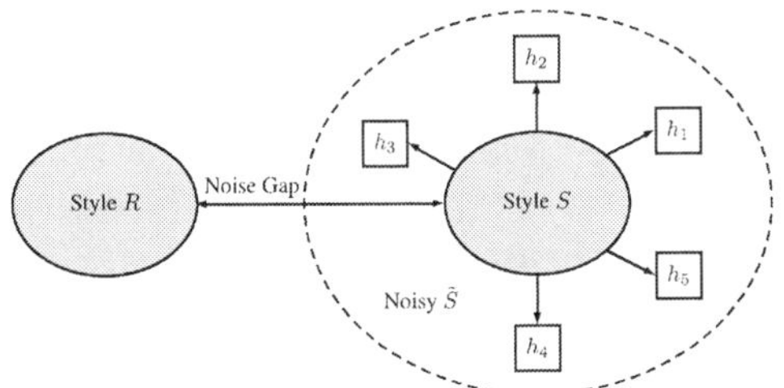

Figure 2: When synthesizing noisy sentences to train the denoising model $\tilde{S} \to S$, we use style reranking to choose the noisy hypothesis h closest to the alternate style R. In this case, h_3 minimizes the "noise gap."

(summarized in Figure 1) allows for rich syntactic modifications while encouraging preservation of meaning.

We evaluate our method on three distinct style transfer tasks, transferring between English varieties (American and British), formal and informal writing (news data and Internet forum data), and lyrics of different musical genres (pop and hip hop). We use three criteria to measure the quality of outputs that have been mapped to the target style: style transfer strength, meaning preservation, and fluency. Despite the simplicity of the method, we demonstrate that it is capable of making syntactically rich suggestions. The proposed reranking technique can also be used to modulate aspects of the style transfer, such as the degree to which the style is applied or the extent to which meaning is changed.

2 Method

We assume a seed corpus of parallel (clean, noisy) sentence pairs $(C, N) = \{(C_k, N_k)\}_{k=1}^{M_{\text{seed}}}$, as well as two non-parallel corpora $R = \{R_k\}_{k=1}^{M_R}$ and $S = \{S_k\}_{k=1}^{M_S}$ of different styles.

2.1 Noising

We first synthesize noisy versions of R and S. We first obtain a seed noise corpus of (clean, noisy) sentence pairs from a language learner forum. Using the seed noise corpus, we train a neural sequence transduction model to learn the mapping from clean to noisy $C \to N$ from our (clean, noisy) sentence pairs. Then, we decode R and S using the noising model to synthesize the corresponding noisy versions, $\tilde{R}$ and $\tilde{S}$.

- **Baseline** As a baseline, we apply the noising method described in Xie et al. (2018). This

method utilizes beam search noising techniques to encourage diversity during the noising process in order to avoid copying of the inputs.

- **Style Reranking** A shortcoming of the baseline noising method is that it mimics the noise in the initial seed corpus, which may not match well with the input style. In order to produce noise that better matches the inputs that will later be fed to the denoising model, we perform reranking to bias the synthesized noisy corpora $\tilde{R}$ and $\tilde{S}$ towards the clean corpora S and R, respectively.

Consider the noise synthesis for S, and denote the noising procedure for a single input as $f_{\text{noise}}(\cdot)$. We generate multiple noise hypotheses, $h_i = f_{\text{noise}}(S_k)$ and select the hypothesis closest to the alternate style R, as ranked by a language model trained on R:

$$h^* = \arg\max_i p_R(h_i)$$

Figure 2 illustrates the intuition that the style reranking will result in noised data "closer" to the expected source inputs.

- **Meaning Reranking** Similar to style reranking, we rerank the hypotheses to encourage meaning preservation by ranking the different noise hypotheses according to the cosine similarity of the sum of word embeddings between the hypothesis and the original source input.

2.2 Denoising

After the synthesized parallel corpus is generated, we train a denoising model between the synthesized noisy corpora and the clean counterparts. To encode style information, we prepend a start token to each noisy sentence corresponding to its style, i.e. $\tilde{R}_k = (\langle \text{style} \rangle, w_1, w_2, \ldots, w_T)$.

Besides providing a simple method to specify the desired target style, this also allows us to combine the noisy-clean corpora from each of the two styles and train a single model using both corpora. This provides two benefits. First, it allows us to learn multiple styles in one model. This allows one model to perform style transfer from both $R \to S$ and $S \to R$. Second, multi-task learning often improves the performance for each of the separate tasks (Luong et al., 2016).

We then join the corpora to obtain the (clean, noisy) sentence pairs,

$$(X, \tilde{X}) = \{(X_k, \tilde{X}_k)\}_{k=1}^{M_{R+S}},$$

from which we will learn our denoising model. Our denoising model learns the probabilistic mapping $P(X|\tilde{X})$, obtaining model parameters θ^* by minimizing the loss function:

$$\mathcal{L}(\theta) = - \sum_{k=1}^{M_{R+S}} \log P(X_k|\tilde{X}_k; \theta)$$

For our experiments we use the Transformer encoder-decoder model (Vaswani et al., 2017) with byte-pair encoding (Sennrich et al., 2015b) with vocabulary size of 30000. We follow the usual training procedure of minibatch gradient descent to minimize negative log-likelihood.

The trained denoising model is then applied to the source style—that we treat as the "noisy" corpus—with the start token of the target style to perform style transfer (Figure 1).

3   Experiments

Task	Dataset	Training	LM
US/UK	NYT/BNC	800K	2.5MM
Forum/News	NYT/Reddit	800K	2.5MM
Music Genres	Hip Hop/Pop	500K	400K

Table 1: Style transfer datasets and number of sentences. *Training* refers to examples used to synthesize noisy sentences and train the denoising model. *LM* refers to examples used to train language models for reranking and evaluation. In addition to training and LM data, 20K examples are held out for each of the dev and test sets.

3.1   Data

We evaluate our methods on three different style transfer tasks between the following corpus pairs: (1) American and British English, (2) formal news writing and informal forum writing, and (3) pop and hip hop lyrics. The first task of transferring between American and British English is primarily intended as a preliminary test for our proposed technique by demonstrating that it can capture lexical changes. The latter two tasks require more sophisticated syntactic edits and form the basis of our later analysis.

A summary of the datasets used for the three tasks is provided in Table 1. We use The New York Times for the American English data, the British National Corpus for the British English data, and the Reddit comments dataset for informal forum data. The pop and hip hop lyrics are gathered from MetroLyrics.[1] For the parallel seed corpus used to train the noising model, we use a dataset of roughly 1MM sentences collected from an English language learner forum (Tajiri et al., 2012).

3.2   Evaluation

We define effective style transfer using the following criteria:

1. **Transfer strength** For a given output sentence, effective style transfer should increase the probability under the target style distribution relative to the probability of observing it under the source style distribution. We thus define transfer strength as the ratio of target-domain to source-domain shift in sentence probability. Let R be the source style inputs and $R^{\to \text{tgt}}$ be the target style outputs. Then,

$$\text{SHIFT}_{\text{src}} = \exp\left[\frac{1}{n}\sum_{k=1}^{n}\log(P(R_k^{\to \text{tgt}}|LM_{\text{src}}))\right.$$
$$\left. -\frac{1}{n}\sum_{k=1}^{n}\log(P(R_k|LM_{\text{src}}))\right]$$

$$\text{SHIFT}_{\text{tgt}} = \exp\left[\frac{1}{n}\sum_{k=1}^{n}\log(P(R_k^{\to \text{tgt}}|LM_{\text{tgt}}))\right.$$
$$\left. -\frac{1}{n}\sum_{k=1}^{n}\log(P(R_k|LM_{\text{tgt}}))\right]$$

$$\text{TRANSFERSTRENGTH}_{\text{src}\to\text{tgt}} \stackrel{\text{def}}{=} \frac{\text{SHIFT}_{\text{tgt}}}{\text{SHIFT}_{\text{src}}}$$

A positive transfer is any ratio greater than one.

2. **Meaning preservation** The target output should also have similar meaning and intent as the source. To measure this, we compute the cosine similarity between embeddings r of the source and target:

$$\text{MEANINGPRESERVATION} \stackrel{\text{def}}{=} \frac{r_{\text{src}}^{\top} r_{\text{tgt}}}{\|r_{\text{src}}\|\|r_{\text{tgt}}\|}$$

---

[1] https://www.kaggle.com/gyani95/380000-lyrics-from-metrolyrics

Method	NYT↔BNC		NYT↔Reddit		Pop↔Hip hop	
	→	←	→	←	→	←
Baseline	1.315	1.227	1.252	1.202	1.097	1.086
Style Rerank	**1.359**	**1.274**	**1.312**	**1.246**	1.110	1.072
Meaning Rerank	1.285	1.222	1.281	1.145	**1.118**	**1.092**

Table 2: The transfer strength for each style transfer task.

Method	NYT↔BNC		NYT↔Reddit		Pop↔Hip hop	
	→	←	→	←	→	←
Baseline	92.22	92.17	97.00	91.56	96.84	97.22
Style Rerank	91.93	91.66	97.25	91.10	96.84	97.18
Meaning Rerank	**94.40**	**93.47**	**98.34**	**94.18**	**97.29**	**97.48**

Table 3: Meaning preservation for each style transfer task. All reported numbers scaled by 10^2 for display.

Method	NYT↔BNC		NYT↔Reddit		Pop↔Hip hop	
	→	←	→	←	→	←
Pre-Transfer	**5.763**	3.891	**4.609**	**5.763**	**2.470**	**1.453**
Baseline	4.016	**4.012**	3.920	5.506	2.112	1.429
Style Rerank	3.877	3.992	3.603	5.194	1.930	1.310
Meaning Rerank	3.874	3.743	3.808	5.395	1.915	1.284

Table 4: Fluency of each style transfer task. All reported numbers scaled by 10^3 for display.

To compute the embeddings r, we use the sentence encoder provided by the InferSent library, which has demonstrated excellent performance on a number of natural language understanding tasks (Conneau et al., 2017).

3. **Fluency** The post-transfer sentence should remain grammatical and fluent. We use the average log probability of the sentence post-transfer with respect to a language model trained on CommonCrawl as our measure of fluency.

Task	Base	Rerank	No Pref
NYT → BNC	6.00	6.25	87.8
BNC → NYT	10.8	6.5	82.8
NYT → Reddit	6.75	9.5	83.8
Reddit → NYT	9.75	18.3	72.0
Pop → Hip Hop	5.25	6.50	88.3
Hip Hop → Pop	7.5	10.3	82.3

Table 5: Human evaluation results for style transfer strength. Entries give percentage of time where annotator preferred base vs. rerank (combined for 2 annotators).

The source and target language models are 4-gram (in the case of music lyrics) or 5-gram (in the case of other datasets) language models trained on a held-out subset of each corpus, estimated with Kneser-Ney smoothing using KenLM (Heafield et al., 2013).

3.3 Pairwise Human Evaluation of Reranking

While language model likelihood is an established measure of fluency or grammaticality, and InferSent has been used as an effective sentence representation on a number of natural language understanding tasks (Conneau et al., 2017), we wish to validate our transfer strength results for our proposed reranking method using human evaluation as well.

For each of the six tasks (3 pairs crossed with 2 directions), we randomly selected 200 sentences, then took the outputs with models trained using style reranking and without style reranking. We then randomized the outputs such that the human evaluators would not be given the label for which output was produced using reranking.

Two annotators then labeled each (randomized) pair with the sentence that seemed to have higher transfer strength. We allowed for a "No preference" option for cases where neither output seemed to have higher transfer strength. We chose pairwise comparisons as it seemed most robust to sometimes minor changes in the sentences. Results are shown in Table 5. We see that while for Reddit $\rightarrow$ NYT there seems to be a clear preference, in most cases stylistic differences tend to be subtle given small differences in transfer strength.

3.4 Results

As shown in Table 2, we observed positive style transfer on all six transfer tasks. For the task of British and American English as well as formal news writing and informal forum writing, applying style reranking during the noising process increased the transfer strength across all four of these tasks. On the other hand, applying meaning reranking during the noising process often decreased the transfer strength. For pop and hip hop lyrics, we do not observe the same pattern; this may be due to the lack of data for the language model, thereby leading to less effective style reranking. In Section 4.1, we also address the possibility of a mismatch with the initial seed corpus.

As noted in Table 3, meaning is also well-preserved. On this metric, the meaning rerank method outperformed the other two models across all six tasks, showing the effectiveness of the reranking method.

In all six style transfer tasks in Table 4, the fluency was highest for the baseline model as compared to the reranked models, although fluency is often higher for the original sentence pairs. We suspect that transfer strength and meaning preservation are largely orthogonal to fluency, and hence encouraging one of the metrics can lead to

dropoffs in the others.

4 Discussion

After experimental evidence that the proposed method produces reasonable stylistic edits, we wished to better understand the effects of our reranking methods as well as the choice of our initial seed corpus.

4.1 Limitations of Noise Corpus

A key factor in the performance of our style transfer models is the noisy data synthesis. Our method relies on an initial seed corpus of (clean, noisy) sentence pairs to bootstrap training. However, such a corpus is not ideal for the style transfer tasks we consider, as there is mismatch in many cases between the style transfer domains (e.g. news, music lyrics, forum posts) and the seed corpus (language learner posts). We observe in Table 2 that more significant transfer appears to occur for the tasks involving news data, and less for music lyrics.

To examine why this might be the case, we trained a 5-gram LM on the clean portion of the initial seed corpus, corresponding to the input of the noise model. We then measured the perplexity of this language model on the different domains. Results are given in Table 7. This may indicate why style transfer with music lyrics proved most difficult, as there is the greatest domain mismatch between the initial seed corpus and those corpora.

4.2 Comparing with Prior Work on Sentiment Transfer

Prior work on text style transfer has often focused on transferring between positive and negative sentiment (Li et al. (2018), Shen et al. (2017)). When we applied our method and evaluation trained on the same Yelp sentiment dataset as Li et al. (2018), using a subset of the Yelp Dataset for training our language model,[2] we obtained positive style transfer results across all three models (Table 8).

However, on further inspection of our decoded outputs, sentiment did not appear to change despite our evaluation metrics suggesting positive style transfer. This apparent contradiction can be explained by our approach treating sentiment as a *content* attribute instead of a *style* attribute.

The problem of sentiment transfer can be construed as changing certain content attributes while

---

[2]https://www.kaggle.com/yelp-dataset/yelp-dataset

Task	Source	Target
UK to US	As the *BMA*'s own study of alternative therapy showed, life is not as simple as that.	As the *F.D.A.'s* own study of alternative therapy showed, life is not as simple as that.
US to UK	The Greenburgh Drug and Alcohol Force and investigators in the Westchester District Attorney's Narcotics Initiative Program Participated in the arrest.	The *Royal Commission on Drug and Attache Force* and investigators in the Westchester District Attorney's Initiative Program Participated in the arrest.
NYT to Reddit	The votes weren't there.	*There weren't any upvotes.*
Reddit to NYT	i guess you need to refer to bnet website then.	*I* guess you need to refer to *the* bnet website then.
Pop to Hip Hop	My money's low	My money's *on the low*
Hip Hop to Pop	Yo, where the hell you been?	Yo, where the hell *are you?*

Table 6: Qualitative examples of style transfer results for different tasks. No parallel data outside of the initial noise corpus was used. Note that the style transfer approach can generate targets with significant syntactic changes from the source. All examples shown are without reranking during data synthesis. BMA refers to the British Medical Association.

NYT	686 (460)	BNC	608 (436)
Reddit	287 (215)	Pop	702 (440)
Hip hop	1239 (802)		

Table 7: Perplexities with (and without) OOVs for different datasets under seed corpus language model.

Method	Yelp Pos $\leftrightarrow$ Neg	
	$\rightarrow$	$\leftarrow$
Baseline	1.182	1.184
Style Rerank	1.189	1.198
Meaning Rerank	1.197	1.191

Table 8: Transfer strength for our method on Yelp sentiment transfer task shows positive style transfer (> 1).

Method	Yelp Pos $\leftrightarrow$ Neg	
	$\rightarrow$	$\leftarrow$
Baseline	96.91	97.87
Style Rerank	97.33	97.74
Meaning Rerank	97.17	98.18
Shen et al. (2017)	96.03	96.32
Li et al. (2018)	90.82	92.36

Table 9: Meaning Preservation for our models as well as CROSSALIGN (Shen et al. (2017)) and DELETE-ANDRETRIEVE (Li et al. (2018)) on Yelp Sentiment Transfer Task. All reported numbers scaled by 10^2 for display.

keeping other style and content attributes constant. Meanwhile, style transfer aims to change style attributes while preserving all content attributes and thus preserving semantic meaning. Modifying style attributes include syntactic changes or word choices which might be more appropriate for the target style, but does not fundamentally change the meaning of the sentence.

A look at the meaning preservation metric across our models and across some models from prior work (Table 9) validates this hypothesis. Models that report higher-quality sentiment transfer such as Li et al. (2018) perform more poorly on the metric of meaning preservation, suggesting that changing a Yelp review from a positive review to a negative one fundamentally changes the content and meaning of the review, not just the style. Our model thus performs poorly on sentiment transfer, since our denoising method is limited to modifying style attributes while preserving all content attributes.

5   Related Work

Our work is related to broader work in training neural machine translation models in low-resource settings, work examining effective methods for applying noise to text, as well as work in style transfer.

Machine translation Much work in style transfer builds off of work in neural machine translation, in particular recent work on machine translation without parallel data using only a dictionary or aligned word embeddings (Lample et al., 2017; Artetxe et al., 2017). These approaches also use backtranslation while introducing token-level corruptions to avoid the problem of copying during an initial autoencoder training phase. They additionally use an initial dictionary or embedding alignments which may be infeasible to collect for many style transfer tasks. Finally, our work also draws from work on zero-shot translation between languages given parallel corpora with a pivot language (Johnson et al., 2017).

Noising and denoising To our knowledge, there has been no prior work formulating style transfer as a denoising task outside of using token corruptions to avoid copying between source and target. Our style transfer method borrows techniques from the field of noising and denoising to correct errors in text. We apply the noising technique in Xie et al. (2018) that requires an initial noise seed corpus instead of dictionaries or aligned embeddings. Similar work for using noise to create a parallel corpus includes Ge et al. (2018).

Style transfer Existing work for style transfer often takes the approach of separating *content* and *style*, for example by encoding a sentence into some latent space (Bowman et al., 2015; Hu et al., 2017; Shen et al., 2017) and then modifying or augmenting that space towards a different style. Hu et al. (2017) base their method on variational autoencoders (Kingma and Welling, 2014), while Shen et al. (2017) instead propose two constrained variants of the autoencoder. Yang et al. (2018) use language models as discriminators instead of a binary classifier as they hypothesize language models provide better training signal for the generator. In the work perhaps most similar to the method we describe here, Prabhumoye et al. (2018) treat style transfer as a backtranslation problem, using a pivot language to first transform the original text to another language, then encoding the translation to a latent space where they use adversarial techniques to preserve content while removing style.

However, such generative models often struggle to produce high-quality outputs. Li et al. (2018) instead approaches the style transfer task by observing that there are often specific phrases that define the attribute or style of the text. Their model segments in each sentence the specific phrases associated with the source style, then use a neural network to generate the target sentence with replacement phrases associated with the target style. While they produce higher quality outputs than previous methods, this method requires manual annotation and may be more limited in capturing rich syntactic differences beyond the annotated phrases.

6 Conclusion

In this paper, we propose a *denoising* method for performing text style transfer by treating the source text as a noisy version of the desired target. Our method can generate rich edits to map inputs to the target style. We additionally propose two reranking methods during the data synthesis phase intended to encourage meaning preservation as well as modulate the strength of style transfer, then examine their effects across three varied datasets. An exciting future direction is to develop other noising methods or datasets in order to consistently encourage more syntactically rich edits.

References

Mikel Artetxe, Gorka Labaka, Eneko Agirre, and Kyunghyun Cho. 2017. Unsupervised neural machine translation. *arXiv preprint arXiv:1710.11041*.

Dzmitry Bahdanau, Kyunghyun Cho, and Yoshua Bengio. 2014. Neural machine translation by jointly learning to align and translate. *arXiv preprint arXiv:1409.0473*.

Samuel R Bowman, Luke Vilnis, Oriol Vinyals, Andrew M Dai, Rafal Jozefowicz, and Samy Bengio. 2015. Generating sentences from a continuous space. *arXiv preprint arXiv:1511.06349*.

Alexis Conneau, Douwe Kiela, Holger Schwenk, Loïc Barrault, and Antoine Bordes. 2017. Supervised learning of universal sentence representations from natural language inference data. In *Proceedings of the 2017 Conference on Empirical Methods in Natural Language Processing*, pages 670–680. Association for Computational Linguistics.

Leon A Gatys, Alexander S Ecker, and Matthias Bethge. 2016. Image style transfer using convolutional neural networks. In *Proceedings of the IEEE*

Conference on Computer Vision and Pattern Recognition, pages 2414–2423.

Tao Ge, Furu Wei, and Ming Zhou. 2018. Fluency boost learning and inference for neural grammatical error correction. *Association for Computational Linguistics*.

K. Heafield, I. Pouzyrevsky, J. H. Clark, and P. Koehn. 2013. Scalable modified Kneser-Ney language model estimation. In *ACL-HLT*, pages 690–696, Sofia, Bulgaria.

Zhiting Hu, Zichao Yang, Xiaodan Liang, Ruslan Salakhutdinov, and Eric P. Xing. 2017. Toward controlled generation of text. In *ICML*.

Melvin Johnson, Mike Schuster, Quoc V. Le, Maxim Krikun, Yonghui Wu, Zhifeng Chen, and Nikhil Thorat. 2017. Googles multilingual neural machine translation system: Enabling zero-shot translation. *arXiv preprint arXiv:1611.04558*.

Diederik P Kingma and Max Welling. 2014. Auto-encoding variational bayes. In *ICLR*.

Guillaume Lample, Ludovic Denoyer, and Marc'Aurelio Ranzato. 2017. Unsupervised machine translation using monolingual corpora only. *arXiv preprint arXiv:1711.00043*.

Juncen Li, Robin Jia, He He, and Percy Liang. 2018. Delete, retrieve, generate: a simple approach to sentiment and style transfer. In *Proceedings of the 2018 Conference of the North American Chapter of the Association for Computational Linguistics: Human Language Technologies, Volume 1 (Long Papers)*, pages 1865–1874. Association for Computational Linguistics.

Minh-Thang Luong, Quoc V Le, Ilya Sutskever, Oriol Vinyals, and Lukasz Kaiser. 2016. Multi-task sequence to sequence learning. In *ICLR*.

Shrimai Prabhumoye, Yulia Tsvetkov, Ruslan Salakhutdinov, and Alan W Black. 2018. Style transfer through back-translation. In *Proceedings of the 56th Annual Meeting of the Association for Computational Linguistics (Volume 1: Long Papers)*, pages 866–876. Association for Computational Linguistics.

Rico Sennrich, Barry Haddow, and Alexandra Birch. 2015a. Improving neural machine translation models with monolingual data. *arXiv preprint arXiv:1511.06709*.

Rico Sennrich, Barry Haddow, and Alexandra Birch. 2015b. Neural machine translation of rare words with subword units. *arXiv preprint arXiv:1508.07909*.

Tianxiao Shen, Tao Lei, Regina Barzilay, and Tommi Jaakkola. 2017. Style transfer from non-parallel text by cross-alignment. In *Advances in Neural Information Processing Systems*, pages 6830–6841.

Ilya Sutskever, Oriol Vinyals, and Quoc V Le. 2014. Sequence to sequence learning with neural networks. In *Advances in neural information processing systems*, pages 3104–3112.

Toshikazu Tajiri, Mamoru Komachi, and Yuji Matsumoto. 2012. Tense and aspect error correction for esl learners using global context. In *Proceedings of the 50th Annual Meeting of the Association for Computational Linguistics: Short Papers-Volume 2*, pages 198–202. Association for Computational Linguistics.

Ashish Vaswani, Noam Shazeer, Niki Parmar, Jakob Uszkoreit, Llion Jones, Aidan N Gomez, Lukasz Kaiser, and Illia Polosukhin. 2017. Attention is all you need. *arXiv preprint arXiv:1706.03762*.

Ziang Xie, Guillaume Genthial, Stanley Xie, Andrew Y. Ng, and Dan Jurafsky. 2018. Noising and denoising natural language: Diverse backtranslation for grammar correction. *NAACL-HLT 2018*.

Zichao Yang, Zhiting Hu, Chris Dyer, Eric P. Xing, and Taylor Berg-Kirkpatrick. 2018. Unsupervised text style transfer using language models as discriminators. In *NIPS*.

Better Automatic Evaluation of Open-Domain Dialogue Systems with Contextualized Embeddings

Sarik Ghazarian
Information Sciences Institute
University of Southern California
sarik@isi.edu

Johnny Tian-Zheng Wei
College of Natural Sciences
University of Massachusetts Amherst
jwei@umass.edu

Aram Galstyan
Information Sciences Institute
University of Southern California
galstyan@isi.edu

Nanyun Peng
Information Sciences Institute
University of Southern California
npeng@isi.edu

Abstract

Despite advances in open-domain dialogue systems, automatic evaluation of such systems is still a challenging problem. Traditional reference-based metrics such as BLEU are ineffective because there could be many valid responses for a given context that share no common words with reference responses. A recent work proposed Referenced metric and Unreferenced metric Blended Evaluation Routine (RUBER) to combine a learning-based metric, which predicts relatedness between a generated response and a given query, with reference-based metric; it showed high correlation with human judgments. In this paper, we explore using contextualized word embeddings to compute more accurate relatedness scores, thus better evaluation metrics. Experiments show that our evaluation metrics outperform RUBER, which is trained on static embeddings.

1 Introduction

Recent advances in open-domain dialogue systems (i.e. chatbots) highlight the difficulties in automatically evaluating them. This kind of evaluation inherits a characteristic challenge of NLG evaluation - given a context, there might be a diverse range of acceptable responses (Gatt and Krahmer, 2018).

Metrics based on n-gram overlaps such as BLEU (Papineni et al., 2002) and ROUGE (Lin, 2004), originally designed for evaluating machine translation and summarization, have been adopted to evaluate dialogue systems (Sordoni et al., 2015; Li et al., 2016; Su et al., 2018). However, Liu et al. (2016) found a weak segment-level correlation between these metrics and human judgments

Dialogue Context
Speaker 1: Hey! What are you doing here?
Speaker 2: I'm just shopping.

Query: What are you shopping for?
Generated Response: Some new clothes.
Reference Response: I want buy gift for my mom!

Table 1: An example of zero BLEU score for an acceptable generated response in multi-turn dialogue system

of response quality. As shown in Table 1, high-quality responses can have low or even no n-gram overlap with a reference response, showing that these metrics are not suitable for dialogue evaluation (Novikova et al., 2017; Lowe et al., 2017).

Due to the lack of strong automatic evaluation metrics, many researchers resort primarily to human evaluation for assessing their dialogue systems performances (Shang et al., 2015; Sordoni et al., 2015; Shao et al., 2017). There are two main problems with human annotation: 1) it is time-consuming and expensive, and 2) it does not facilitate comparisons across research papers. For certain research questions that involve hyper-parameter tuning or architecture searches, the amount of human annotation makes such studies infeasible (Britz et al., 2017; Melis et al., 2018). Therefore, developing reliable automatic evaluation metrics for open-domain dialog systems is imperative.

The Referenced metric and Unreferenced metric Blended Evaluation Routine (RUBER) (Tao et al., 2018) stands out from recent work in automatic dialogue evaluation, relying minimally on human-annotated datasets of response quality for training. RUBER evaluates responses with a blending of scores from two metrics:

Proceedings of the Workshop on Methods for Optimizing and Evaluating Neural Language Generation (NeuralGen), pages 82–89
Minneapolis, Minnesota, USA, June 6, 2019. ©2019 Association for Computational Linguistics

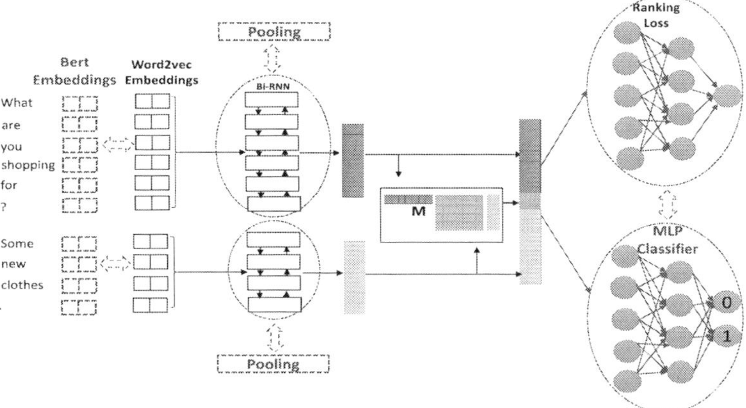

Figure 1: An illustration of changes applied to RUBER's unreferenced metric's architecture. Red dotted double arrows show three main changes. The leftmost section is related to substituting word2vec embeddings with BERT embeddings. The middle section replaces Bi-RNNs with simple pooling strategies to get sentence representations. The rightmost section switches ranking loss function to MLP classifier with cross entropy loss function.

- an *Unreferenced* metric, which computes the relevancy of a response to a given query inspired by Grice (1975)'s theory that the quality of a response is determined by its relatedness and appropriateness, among other properties. This model is trained with negative sampling.
- a *Referenced* metric, which determines the similarities between generated and reference responses using word embeddings.

Both metrics strongly depend on learned word embeddings. We propose to explore the use of contextualized embeddings, specifically BERT embeddings (Devlin et al., 2018), in composing evaluation metrics. Our contributions in this work are as follows:

- We explore the efficiency of contextualized word embeddings on training unreferenced models for open-domain dialog system evaluation.
- We explore different network architectures and objective functions to better utilize contextualized word embeddings, and show their positive effects.

2 Proposed models

We conduct the research under the RUBER metric's referenced and unreferenced framework, where we replace their static word embeddings with pretrained BERT contextualized embeddings and compare the performances. We identify three points of variation with two options each in the unreferenced component of RUBER. The main changes are in the word embeddings, sentence representation, and training objectives that will be explained with details in the following section. Our experiment follows a 2x2x2 factorial design.

2.1 Unreferenced Metric

The unreferenced metric predicts how much a generated response is related to a given query. Figure 1 presents RUBER's unreferenced metric overlaid with our proposed changes in three parts of the architecture. Changes are illustrated by red dotted double arrows and include word embeddings, sentence representation and the loss function.

2.1.1 Word Embeddings

Static and contextualized embeddings are two different types of word embeddings that we explored.

- **Word2vec.** Recent works on learnable evaluation metrics use simple word embeddings such as word2vec and GLoVe as input to their models (Tao et al., 2018; Lowe et al., 2017; Kannan and Vinyals, 2017). Since these static embeddings have a fixed context-independent representation for each word, they cannot represent the rich semantics of words in contexts.
- **BERT.** Contextualized word embeddings are recently shown to be beneficial in many NLP tasks (Devlin et al., 2018; Radford et al., 2018; Peters et al., 2018; Liu et al., 2019). A noticeable contextualized word embeddings, BERT (Devlin et al., 2018), is shown to per-

form competitively among other contextualized embeddings, thus we explore the effect of BERT embeddings on open domain dialogue systems evaluation task. Specifically, we substitute the word2vec embeddings with BERT embeddings in RUBER's unreferenced score as shown in the leftmost section of Figure 1.

2.1.2 Sentence Representation

This section composes a single vector representation for both a query and a response.

- **Bi-RNN.** In the RUBER model, Bidirectional Recurrent Neural Networks (Bi-RNNs) are trained for this purpose.
- **Pooling.** We explore the effect of replacing Bi-RNNs with some simple pooling strategies on top of words BERT embeddings (middle dotted section in Figure 1). The intuition behind this is that BERT embeddings are pre-trained on bidirectional transformers and they include complete information about word's context, therefore, another layer of bi-RNNs could just blow up the number of parameters with no real gains.

2.1.3 MLP Network

Multilayer Perceptron Network (MLP) is the last section of RUBER's unreferenced model that is trained by applying negative sampling technique to add some random responses for each query into training dataset.

- **Ranking loss.** The objective is to maximize the difference between relatedness score predicted for positive and randomly added pairs. We refer to this objective function as a ranking loss function. The sigmoid function used in the last layer of MLP assigns a score to each pair of query and response, which indicates how much the response is related to a given query.
- **Cross entropy loss.** We explore the efficiency of using a simpler loss function such as cross entropy. In fact, we consider unreferenced score prediction as a binary classification problem and replace baseline trained MLP with MLP classifier (right dotted section in Figure 1). Since we do not have a human labeled dataset, we use negative sampling strategy to add randomly selected responses to queries in training dataset. We assign label 1 to original pairs of queries and

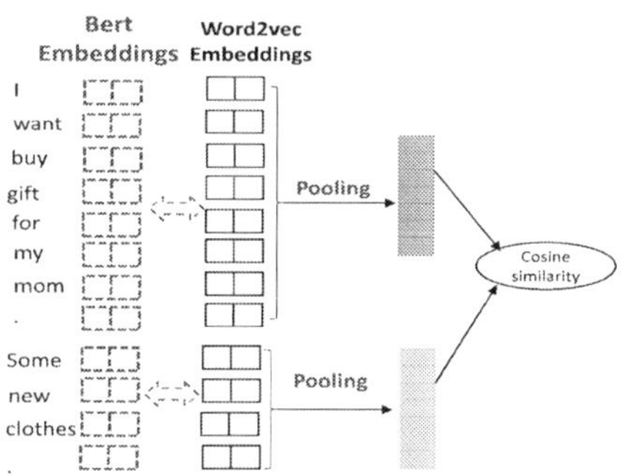

Figure 2: BERT-based referenced metric. Static word2vec embeddings are replaced with BERT embeddings (red dotted section).

responses and 0 to the negative samples. The output of softmax function in the last layer of MLP classifier indicates the relatedness score for each pair of query and response.

2.2 Referenced Metric

The referenced metric computes the similarity between generated and reference responses. RUBER achieves this by applying pooling strategies on static word embeddings to get sentence embeddings for both generated and reference responses. In our metric, we replace the word2vec embeddings with BERT embeddings (red dotted section in Figure 2) to explore the effect of contextualized embeddings on calculating the referenced score. We refer to this metric as BERT-based referenced metric.

3 Dataset

We used the DailyDialog dataset[1] which contains high quality multi-turn conversations about daily life including various topics (Li et al., 2017), to train our dialogue system as well as the evaluation metrics. This dataset includes almost 13k multi-turn dialogues between two parties splitted into 42,000/3,700/3,900 query-response pairs for train/test/validation sets. We divided these sets into two parts, the first part for training dialogue system and the second part for training unreferenced metric.

3.1 Generated responses

We used the first part of train/test/validation sets with overall 20,000/1,900/1,800 query-response

---

[1] http://yanran.li/dailydialog

Query	Response	Human rating
Can I try this one on?	Yes, of course.	5, 5, 5
This is the Bell Captain's Desk. May I help you?	No, it was nothing to leave.	1, 2, 1
Do you have some experiences to share with me? I want to have a try.	Actually, it good to say. Thanks a lot.	3, 2, 2

Table 2: Examples of query-response pairs, each rated by three AMT workers with scores from 1 (not appropriate response) to 5 (completely appropriate response).

pairs to train an attention-based sequence-to-sequence (seq2seq) model (Bahdanau et al., 2014) and generate responses for evaluation. We used OpenNMT (Klein et al., 2017) toolkit to train the model. The encoder and decoder are Bi-LSTMs with 2 layers each containing 500-dimensional hidden units. We used 300-dimensional pretrained word2vec embeddings as our word embeddings. The model was trained by using SGD optimizer with learning rate of 1. We used random sample with temperature control and set temperature value to 0.01 empirically to get grammatical and diverse responses.

3.2 Human Judgments

We collected human annotations on generated responses in order to compute the correlation between human judgments and automatic evaluation metrics. Human annotations were collected from Amazon Mechanical Turk (AMT). AMT workers were provided a set of query-response pairs and asked to rate each pair based on the appropriateness of the response for the given query on a scale of 1-5 (not appropriate to very appropriate). Each survey included 5 query-response pairs with an extra pair for attention checking. We removed all pairs that were rated by workers who failed to correctly answer attention-check tests. Each pair was annotated by 3 individual turkers. Table 2 demonstrates three query-response pairs rated by three AMT workers. In total 300 utterance pairs were rated from contributions of 106 unique workers.

4 Experimental Setup

4.1 Static Embeddings

To compare how the word embeddings affect the evaluation metric, which is the main focus of this paper, we used word2vec as static embeddings trained on about 100 billion words of Google News Corpus. These 300 dimensional word embeddings include almost 3 million words and phrases. We applied these pretrained embed-

dings as input to dialogue generation, referenced and unreferenced metrics.

4.2 Contextualized Embeddings

In order to explore the effects of contextualized embedding on evaluation metrics, we used the BERT base model with 768 vector dimensions pretrained on Books Corpus and English Wikipedia with 3,300M words (Devlin et al., 2018).

4.3 Training Unreferenced model

We used the second part of the DailyDialog dataset composed of 22,000/1,800/2,100 train/test/validation pairs to train and tune the unreferenced model, which is implemented with Tensorflow. For sentence encoder, we used 2 layers of bidirectional gated recurrent unit (Bi-GRU) with 128-dimensional hidden unit. We used three layers for MLP with 256, 512 and 128-dimensional hidden units and tanh as activation function for computing both ranking loss and cross-entropy loss. We used Adam (Kingma and Ba, 2015) optimizer with initial learning rate of 10^{-4} and applied learning rate decay when no improvement was observed on validation data for five consecutive epochs. We applied early stop mechanism and stopped training process after observing 20 epochs with no reduction in loss value.

5 Results

We first present the unreferenced metrics' performances. Then, we present results on the full RUBER's framework - combining unreferenced and referenced metrics. To evaluate the performance of our metrics, we calculated the Pearson and Spearman correlations between learned metric scores and human judgments on 300 query-response pairs collected from AMT. The Pearson coefficient measures a linear correlation between two ordinal variables, while the Spearman coefficient measures any monotonic relationship. The

Embedding	Representation	Objective	Pearson (p-value)	Spearman (p-value)	Cosine Similarity
word2vec	Bi-RNN	Ranking	0.28 $(<6e\text{-}7)$	0.30 $(<8e\text{-}8)$	0.56
		Cross-Entropy	0.22 $(<9e\text{-}5)$	0.25 $(<9e\text{-}6)$	0.53
	Max Pooling	Ranking	0.19 $(<8e\text{-}4)$	0.18 $(<1e\text{-}3)$	0.50
		Cross-Entropy	0.25 $(<2e\text{-}5)$	0.25 $(<2e\text{-}5)$	0.53
	Mean Pooling	Ranking	0.16 $(<5e\text{-}3)$	0.18 $(<2e\text{-}3)$	0.50
		Cross-Entropy	0.04 $(<5e\text{-}1)$	0.06 $(<3e\text{-}1)$	0.47
BERT	Bi-RNN	Ranking	0.38 $(<1e\text{-}2)$	0.31 $(<4e\text{-}8)$	0.60
		Cross-Entropy	0.29 $(<2e\text{-}7)$	0.24 $(<3e\text{-}5)$	0.55
	Max Pooling	Ranking	0.41 $(<1e\text{-}2)$	0.36 $(<7e\text{-}9)$	0.65
		Cross-Entropy	**0.55** $(<1e\text{-}2)$	**0.45** $(<1e\text{-}2)$	**0.70**
	Mean Pooling	Ranking	0.34 $(<2e\text{-}9)$	0.27 $(<2e\text{-}6)$	0.57
		Cross-Entropy	0.32 $(<2e\text{-}8)$	0.29 $(<5e\text{-}7)$	0.55

Table 3: Correlations and similarity values between relatedness scores predicted by different unreferenced models and human judgments. First row is RUBER's unreferenced model.

third metric we used to evaluate our metric is cosine similarity, which computes how much the scores produced by learned metrics are similar to human scores.

5.1 Unreferenced Metrics Results

This section analyzes the performance of unreferenced metrics which are trained based on various word embeddings, sentence representations and objective functions. The results in the upper section of Table 3 are all based on word2vec embeddings while the lower section are based on BERT embeddings. The first row of table 3 corresponds to RUBER's unreferenced model and the five following rows are our exploration of different unreferenced models based on word2vec embeddings, for fair comparison with BERT embedding-based ones. Table 3 demonstrates that unreferenced metrics based on BERT embeddings have higher correlation and similarity with human scores. Contextualized embeddings have been found to carry richer information and the inclusion of these vectors in the unreferenced metric generally leads to better performance (Liu et al., 2019).

Comparing different sentence encoding strategies (Bi-RNN v.s. Pooling) by keeping other variations constant, we observe that pooling of BERT embeddings yields better performance. This would be because of BERT embeddings are pretrained on deep bidirectional transformers and using pooling mechanisms is enough to assign rich representations to sentences. In contrast, the models based on word2vec embeddings benefit from Bi-RNN based sentence encoder. Across settings, max pooling always outperforms mean pooling. Regarding the choice of objective functions, ranking loss generally performs better for models based on word2vec embeddings, while the best model with BERT embeddings is obtained by using cross-entropy loss. We consider this as an interesting observation and leave further investigation for future research.

5.2 Unreferenced + Referenced Metrics Results

This section analyzes the performance of integrating variants of unreferenced metrics into the full RUBER framework which is the combination of unreferenced and referenced metrics. We only considered the best unreferenced models from Table 3. As it is shown in Table 4, across different settings, max combinations of referenced and unereferenced metrics yields the best performance. We see that metrics based on BERT embeddings have higher Pearson and Spearman correlations with human scores than RUBER (the first row of Table 4) which is based on word2vec embeddings.

In comparison with purely unreferenced metrics (Table 3), correlations decreased across the board. This suggests that the addition of the referenced component is not beneficial, contradicting RUBER's findings (Tao et al., 2018). We hypothesize that this could be due to data and/or language differences, and leave further investigation for future work.

Model	Unreferenced			Referenced	Pooling	Pearson	Spearman	Cosine Similarity
	Embedding	Representation	Objective	Embedding				
RUBER	word2vec	Bi-RNN	Ranking	word2vec	min	0.08 ($<$0.16)	0.06 ($<$0.28)	0.51
					max	0.19 ($<$1e-3)	0.23 ($<$4e-5)	0.60
					mean	0.22 ($<$9e-5)	0.21 ($<$3e-4)	0.63
Ours	BERT	max Pooling	Cross-Entropy	BERT	min	0.05 ($<$0.43)	0.09 ($<$0.13)	0.52
					max	**0.49** ($<$1e-2)	**0.44** ($<$1e-2)	0.69
					mean	0.45 ($<$1e-2)	0.34 ($<$1e-2)	0.70

Table 4: Correlation and similarity values between automatic evaluation metrics (combination of Referenced and Unreferenced metrics) and human annotations for 300 query-response pairs annotated by AMT workers. The "Pooling" column shows the combination type of referenced and unreferenced metrics.

6 Related Work

Due to the impressive development of open domain dialogue systems, existence of automatic evaluation metrics can be particularly desirable to easily compare the quality of several models.

6.1 Automatic Heuristic Evaluation Metrics

In some group of language generation tasks such as machine translation and text summarization, n-grams overlapping metrics have a high correlation with human evaluation. BLEU and METEOR are primarily used for evaluating the quality of translated sentence based on computing n-gram precisions and harmonic mean of precision and recall, respectively (Papineni et al., 2002; Banerjee and Lavie, 2005). ROUGE computes F-measure based on the longest common subsequence and is highly applicable for evaluating text summarization (Lin, 2004). The main drawback of mentioned n-gram overlap metrics, which makes them inapplicable in dialogue system evaluation is that they don't consider the semantic similarity between sentences (Liu et al., 2016; Novikova et al., 2017; Lowe et al., 2017). These word overlapping metrics are not compatible with the nature of language generation, which allows a concept to be appeared in different sentences with no common n-grams, while they all share the same meaning.

6.2 Automatic Learnable Evaluation Metrics

Beside the heuristic metrics, researchers recently tried to develop some trainable metrics for automatically checking the quality of generated responses. Lowe et al. (2017) trained a hierarchical neural network model called Automatic Dialogue Evaluation Model (ADEM) to predict the appropriateness score of dialogue responses. For this purpose, they collected a training dataset by asking human about the informativeness score for various responses of a given context. However,

ADEM predicts highly correlated scores with human judgments in both sentence and system level, collecting human annotation by itself is an effortful and laborious task.

Kannan and Vinyals (2017) followed the GAN model's structure and trained a discriminator that tries to discriminate the model's generated response from human responses. Even though they found discriminator can be useful for automatic evaluation systems, they mentioned that it can not completely address the evaluation challenges in dialogue systems.

RUBER is another learnable metric, which considers both relevancy and similarity concepts for evaluation process (Tao et al., 2018). Referenced metric of RUBER measures the similarity between vectors of generated and reference responses computed by pooling word embeddings, while unreferenced metric uses negative sampling to train the relevancy score of generated response to a given query. Despite ADEM score, which is trained on human annotated dataset, RUBER is not limited to any human annotation. In fact, training with negative samples makes RUBER to be more general. It is obvious that both referenced and unreferenced metrics are under the influence of word embeddings information. In this work, we show that contextualized embeddings that include much more information about words and their context can have good effects on the accuracy of evaluation metrics.

6.3 Static and Contextualized Words Embeddings

Recently, there has been significant progress in word embedding methods. Unlike previous static word embeddings like word2vec [2], which maps words to constant embeddings, contextualized embeddings such as ELMo, OpenAI GPT and BERT

---

[2]https://code.google.com/archive/p/word2vec/

consider word embeddings as a function of the word's context in which the word is appeared (McCann et al., 2017; Peters et al., 2018; Radford et al., 2018; Devlin et al., 2018). ELMo learns word vectors from a deep language model pretrained on a large text corpus (Peters et al., 2018). OpenAI GPT uses transformers to learn a language model and also to fine-tune it for specific natural language understanding tasks (Radford et al., 2018). BERT learns words' representations by jointly conditioning on both left and right context in training all levels of deep bidirectional transformers (Devlin et al., 2018). In this paper, we show that beside positive effects of contextualized embeddings on many NLP tasks including question answering, sentiment analysis and semantic similarity, BERT embeddings also have the potential to help evaluate open domain dialogue systems closer to what would human do.

7   Conclusion and Future work

In this paper, we explored applying contextualized word embeddings to automatic evaluation of open-domain dialogue systems. The experiments showed that the unreferenced scores of RUBER metric can be improved by considering contextualized word embeddings which include richer representations of words and their context.

In the future, we plan to extend the work to evaluate multi-turn dialogue systems, as well as adding other aspects, such as creativity and novelty into consideration in our evaluation metrics.

8   Acknowledgments

We thank the anonymous reviewers for their constructive feedback, as well as the members of the PLUS lab for their useful discussion and feedback. This work is supported by Contract W911NF-15-1-0543 with the US Defense Advanced Research Projects Agency (DARPA).

References

Dzmitry Bahdanau, Kyunghyun Cho, and Yoshua Bengio. 2014. Neural machine translation by jointly learning to align and translate. *CoRR*, abs/1409.0473.

Satanjeev Banerjee and Alon Lavie. 2005. METEOR: an automatic metric for MT evaluation with improved correlation with human judgments. In *Proceedings of the Workshop on Intrinsic and Extrinsic Evaluation Measures for Machine Translation and/or Summarization@ACL 2005, Ann Arbor, Michigan, USA, June 29, 2005*, pages 65–72.

Denny Britz, Anna Goldie, Minh-Thang Luong, and Quoc Le. 2017. Massive exploration of neural machine translation architectures. In *Proceedings of the 2017 Conference on Empirical Methods in Natural Language Processing*, pages 1442–1451. Association for Computational Linguistics.

Jacob Devlin, Ming-Wei Chang, Kenton Lee, and Kristina Toutanova. 2018. BERT: pre-training of deep bidirectional transformers for language understanding. *CoRR*, abs/1810.04805.

Albert Gatt and Emiel Krahmer. 2018. Survey of the state of the art in natural language generation: Core tasks, applications and evaluation. *J. Artif. Intell. Res.*, 61:65–170.

H. Paul Grice. 1975. Logic and conversation. In Peter Cole and Jerry L. Morgan, editors, *Speech Acts*, volume 3 of *Syntax and Semantics*, pages 41–58. Academic Press, New York.

Anjuli Kannan and Oriol Vinyals. 2017. Adversarial evaluation of dialogue models. *CoRR*, abs/1701.08198.

Diederik P. Kingma and Jimmy Ba. 2015. Adam: A method for stochastic optimization. In *3rd International Conference on Learning Representations, ICLR 2015, San Diego, CA, USA, May 7-9, 2015, Conference Track Proceedings*.

Guillaume Klein, Yoon Kim, Yuntian Deng, Jean Senellart, and Alexander M. Rush. 2017. OpenNMT: Open-source toolkit for neural machine translation. In *Proc. ACL*.

Jiwei Li, Michel Galley, Chris Brockett, Jianfeng Gao, and Bill Dolan. 2016. A diversity-promoting objective function for neural conversation models. In *NAACL HLT 2016, The 2016 Conference of the North American Chapter of the Association for Computational Linguistics: Human Language Technologies, San Diego California, USA, June 12-17, 2016*, pages 110–119.

Yanran Li, Hui Su, Xiaoyu Shen, Wenjie Li, Ziqiang Cao, and Shuzi Niu. 2017. Dailydialog: A manually labelled multi-turn dialogue dataset. In *Proceedings of the Eighth International Joint Conference on Natural Language Processing, IJCNLP 2017, Taipei, Taiwan, November 27 - December 1, 2017 - Volume 1: Long Papers*, pages 986–995.

Chin-Yew Lin. 2004. Rouge: a package for automatic evaluation of summaries.

Chia-Wei Liu, Ryan Lowe, Iulian Serban, Michael Noseworthy, Laurent Charlin, and Joelle Pineau. 2016. How NOT to evaluate your dialogue system: An empirical study of unsupervised evaluation metrics for dialogue response generation. In *Proceedings of the 2016 Conference on Empirical Methods in Natural Language Processing, EMNLP 2016, Austin, Texas, USA, November 1-4, 2016*, pages 2122–2132. The Association for Computational Linguistics.

Nelson F. Liu, Matt Gardner, Yonatan Belinkov, Matthew Peters, and Noah A. Smith. 2019. Linguistic knowledge and transferability of contextual representations. *CoRR*, abs/1903.08855.

Ryan Lowe, Michael Noseworthy, Iulian Vlad Serban, Nicolas Angelard-Gontier, Yoshua Bengio, and Joelle Pineau. 2017. Towards an automatic turing test: Learning to evaluate dialogue responses. In *Proceedings of the 55th Annual Meeting of the Association for Computational Linguistics, ACL 2017, Vancouver, Canada, July 30 - August 4, Volume 1: Long Papers*, pages 1116–1126. Association for Computational Linguistics.

Bryan McCann, James Bradbury, Caiming Xiong, and Richard Socher. 2017. Learned in translation: Contextualized word vectors. In *Advances in Neural Information Processing Systems 30: Annual Conference on Neural Information Processing Systems 2017, 4-9 December 2017, Long Beach, CA, USA*, pages 6297–6308.

Sheila A. McIlraith and Kilian Q. Weinberger, editors. 2018. *Proceedings of the Thirty-Second AAAI Conference on Artificial Intelligence, (AAAI-18), the 30th innovative Applications of Artificial Intelligence (IAAI-18), and the 8th AAAI Symposium on Educational Advances in Artificial Intelligence (EAAI-18), New Orleans, Louisiana, USA, February 2-7, 2018*. AAAI Press.

Gbor Melis, Chris Dyer, and Phil Blunsom. 2018. On the state of the art of evaluation in neural language models. In *International Conference on Learning Representations*.

Jekaterina Novikova, Ondrej Dusek, Amanda Cercas Curry, and Verena Rieser. 2017. Why we need new evaluation metrics for NLG. In *Proceedings of the 2017 Conference on Empirical Methods in Natural Language Processing, EMNLP 2017, Copenhagen, Denmark, September 9-11, 2017*, pages 2241–2252.

Kishore Papineni, Salim Roukos, Todd Ward, and Wei-Jing Zhu. 2002. Bleu: a method for automatic evaluation of machine translation. In *Proceedings of the 40th Annual Meeting of the Association for Computational Linguistics, July 6-12, 2002, Philadelphia, PA, USA.*, pages 311–318. ACL.

Matthew E. Peters, Mark Neumann, Mohit Iyyer, Matt Gardner, Christopher Clark, Kenton Lee, and Luke Zettlemoyer. 2018. Deep contextualized word representations. In *Proceedings of the 2018 Conference of the North American Chapter of the Association for Computational Linguistics: Human Language Technologies, NAACL-HLT 2018, New Or-*leans, Louisiana, USA, June 1-6, 2018, Volume 1 (Long Papers)*, pages 2227–2237.

Alec Radford, Karthik Narasimhan, Tim Salimans, and Ilya Sutskever. 2018. Improving language understanding by generative pre-training.

Lifeng Shang, Zhengdong Lu, and Hang Li. 2015. Neural responding machine for short-text conversation. In *Proceedings of the 53rd Annual Meeting of the Association for Computational Linguistics and the 7th International Joint Conference on Natural Language Processing of the Asian Federation of Natural Language Processing, ACL 2015, July 26-31, 2015, Beijing, China, Volume 1: Long Papers*, pages 1577–1586.

Yuanlong Shao, Stephan Gouws, Denny Britz, Anna Goldie, Brian Strope, and Ray Kurzweil. 2017. Generating high-quality and informative conversation responses with sequence-to-sequence models. In *Proceedings of the 2017 Conference on Empirical Methods in Natural Language Processing, EMNLP 2017, Copenhagen, Denmark, September 9-11, 2017*, pages 2210–2219.

Alessandro Sordoni, Michel Galley, Michael Auli, Chris Brockett, Yangfeng Ji, Margaret Mitchell, Jian-Yun Nie, Jianfeng Gao, and Bill Dolan. 2015. A neural network approach to context-sensitive generation of conversational responses. In *NAACL HLT 2015, The 2015 Conference of the North American Chapter of the Association for Computational Linguistics: Human Language Technologies, Denver, Colorado, USA, May 31 - June 5, 2015*, pages 196–205. The Association for Computational Linguistics.

Hui Su, Xiaoyu Shen, Pengwei Hu, Wenjie Li, and Yun Chen. 2018. Dialogue generation with GAN. In (McIlraith and Weinberger, 2018), pages 8163–8164.

Chongyang Tao, Lili Mou, Dongyan Zhao, and Rui Yan. 2018. RUBER: an unsupervised method for automatic evaluation of open-domain dialog systems. In (McIlraith and Weinberger, 2018), pages 722–729.

Jointly Measuring Diversity and Quality
in Text Generation Models

Ehsan Montahaei[*]
Sharif University of
Technology / Tehran, Iran
ehsan.montahaei@gmail.com

Danial Alihosseini[*]
Sharif University of
Technology / Tehran, Iran
dalihosseini@ce.sharif.edu

Mahdieh Soleymani Baghshah
Sharif University of
Technology / Tehran, Iran
soleymani@sharif.edu

Abstract

Text generation is an important Natural Language Processing task with various applications. Although several metrics have already been introduced to evaluate the text generation methods, each of them has its own shortcomings. The most widely used metrics such as BLEU only consider the quality of generated sentences and neglect their diversity. For example, repeatedly generation of only one high quality sentence would result in a high BLEU score. On the other hand, the more recent metric introduced to evaluate the diversity of generated texts known as Self-BLEU ignores the quality of generated texts. In this paper, we propose metrics to evaluate both the quality and diversity simultaneously by approximating the distance of the learned generative model and the real data distribution. For this purpose, we first introduce a metric that approximates this distance using n-gram based measures. Then, a feature-based measure which is based on a recent highly deep model trained on a large text corpus called BERT is introduced. Finally, for oracle training mode in which the generators density can also be calculated, we propose to use the distance measures between the corresponding explicit distributions. Eventually, the most popular and recent text generation models are evaluated using both the existing and the proposed metrics and the preferences of the proposed metrics are determined.

1 Introduction

Generative models and especially Generative Adversarial Networks (GANs) have been received much attention in the last few years. However, the evaluation of generated samples by these models is challenging. Although some studies have recently focused on introducing measures like Inception Score and Fréchet Inception Distance (FID) to compare results of different GAN models for image generation, there is not a study to propose proper metrics for evaluation of text generation models. In the last few years, many GAN-based text generation models (Yu et al., 2017; Lin et al., 2017; Che et al., 2017; Guo et al., 2018; Zhang et al., 2017) have been proposed. However, measuring the performance of these models in the corresponding papers is not comprehensive. GANs suffer from the mode collapse problem (Metz et al., 2016) and the GAN-based text generation models may just produce a highly limited set of sentences and therefore just considering the quality of these generated sentences for comparison is not comprehensive.

On the other hand, there are measures like Self-BLEU (Zhang et al., 2017) for evaluating the diversity of generated sentences, but they can not consider the quality of samples at all. Besides, designing an experiment of evaluating diversity by humans is not straightforward and thus it's necessary to have a jointly quality-diversity measuring metric.

In this paper, we intend to propose metrics sensitive to both quality and diversity simultaneously, assigning low scores not only to models generating low-quality samples but also to the ones with low-diversity samples (including the mode collapsed models). To this end, we first propose the MS-Jaccard as an n-gram based measure that considers the quality and diversity of generated samples simultaneously. It attempts to find the similarity of the set of generated samples by a model and the set of real (or test) samples. Then, a feature-based measure is proposed to compare the real data distribution and the generative model distribution in the feature space. Indeed, by borrowing the idea of FID (Heusel et al., 2017) that is a popular feature-based evaluation metric in im-

---

[*] These authors contributed equally to this work.

Proceedings of the Workshop on Methods for Optimizing and Evaluating Neural Language Generation (NeuralGen), pages 90–98
Minneapolis, Minnesota, USA, June 6, 2019. ©2019 Association for Computational Linguistics

age generation tasks and advent of a recent highly deep model named BERT (Devlin et al., 2018) as a reference feature extractor for natural language texts, a metric is proposed for evaluation of natural language generation. Finally, appropriate divergences between the oracle distribution and the (learned) model distribution is introduced for when the probabilistic oracle is considered as synthetic data distribution (and thus the target distribution is available for evaluation).

2 Text Generation Models

The neural models on text generation first used LSTMs and trained them by the Maximum Likelihood Estimation (MLE) via teacher forcing (Hochreiter and Schmidhuber, 1997). These models suffer from the exposure bias problem which is due to the train-test discrepancy. Although some solutions such as scheduled sampling were introduced to overcome the exposure bias problem, it has been shown that they are incompatible with the language nature (Bengio et al., 2015; Huszar, 2015). By introducing GANs (Goodfellow et al., 2014) as successful image generation models, it has gained much attention to propose GAN-based text generation models. However, the discrete nature of text needs the generator with discrete outputs that makes passing the gradient from the discriminator to the generator difficult. SeqGAN (Yu et al., 2017) alleviates this difficulty by a gradient policy approach using a REINFORCE-like method to train the generator as a stochastic policy. This method has some difficulties such as reward sparsity and high variance for large action spaces. Subsequent methods try to pass more informative signal from the discriminator to the generator. RankGAN(Lin et al., 2017) trains the discriminator as a ranker which assigns a higher score to the more realistic sequences (in comparison with other sentences in the current batch). LeakGAN (Guo et al., 2018) takes advantage of the feudal networks and considers the discriminator as a manager and the generator as a worker while the feature layer of the discriminator is fed to the generator as leaked information. MaliGAN (Che et al., 2017) attempts to redefine the generator's objective. It minimizes KL divergence between the generator and the real distribution which is obtained by the discriminator in the optimality assumption of the discriminator. This new objective leads to an importance sampling procedure.

TextGAN (Zhang et al., 2017) also applies a new objective for the generator. It tries to push the generator focus from the last layer of the discriminator to its last feature layer. Real data and generator samples will each have some distribution in the feature layer of the discriminator. The generator's objective is to make them closer by Maximum Mean Discrepancy (MMD) metric.

3 Metrics

In this section, we first indicate the main difficulties of the existing measures for evaluation of text generation models. Then, we introduce metrics that evaluate the capability of the models in generating both right sentences and various ones. The proposed metrics (that are all symmetric) jointly specify to what extent probable sentences in real data are likely in the generative model and also the probable sentences in the model are likely in the real data.

3.1 Shortcomings of the existing metrics

In this section, shortcomings of the metrics that either evaluate the quality or the diversity of generated samples are presented. Moreover, a recent attempt to simultaneously considering these metrics is introduced.

3.1.1 Quality metrics

BLEU: It is the most widely used metric for text generation. Originally BLEU (Papineni et al., 2002) is a metric to evaluate the quality of machine-translated text. In unconditional text generation, all sentences in the test set are considered as the reference set and generated sentences are evaluated by computing their average BLEU score on this reference set. In conditional text generation tasks like machine translation which include a limited reference set (for each condition), computing the similarity of the generated text and the reference set may be sensible. However, the reference set for the unconditional text generation task is whole available sentences and measures like BLEU just consider the validity of generated sentences without measuring what proportion of the reference sentences can be covered by the text generation model. On the other hand, GAN-based text generation models may generate a highly limited set of sentences and sacrifice the diversity (due to the mode collapse problem). Therefore, evaluating these models using BLEU score just shows the validity of their outputs without considering their coverage.

Oracle-NLL: It was introduced by SeqGAN (Yu et al., 2017) and is based on assuming a synthetic oracle distribution. It considers a random distribution as the real distribution (or the oracle) and the training dataset is prepared by sampling from this distribution. The score is defined to be the Negative Log Likelihood (NLL) of the generated samples from the trained model in the oracle distribution. In this measure, the coverage is again neglected and a model that generates only one high quality sentence can reach high performance.

3.1.2 Diversity metric

As mentioned above, BLUE and Oracle-NLL just consider the quality of the generated samples and ignore their diversity. Below, we introduce two metrics measuring the diversity. However, these metrics evaluate only diversity and don't consider the quality of samples at all.

Self-BLEU: In (Zhu et al., 2018), Self-BLEU was introduced to evaluate just variety of sentences. It measures BLEU score for each generated sentence by considering other generated sentences as reference. By averaging these BLEU scores (obtained for generated sentences), a metric that is called Self-BLEU is achieved where its lower values shows more diversity.

Entropy: On the other side, we can use the entropy of probabilistic generative model to measure the diversity where the lower values show lower diversity. As the direct calculation of the entropy is not feasible, a Monte-Carlo estimation of it can be used.

3.1.3 Quality and diversity

Recently (Caccia et al., 2018) mentioned the flaws of only evaluating the quality and found that MLE outperforms the GAN variants for text generation since it dominates GANs in the quality-diversity space. (Caccia et al., 2018) uses the quality-diversity spectrum obtained by changing the temperature parameter that controls entropy of the models' conditional distributions. However, it does not provide a measure to assess both the quality and the diversity without needing to inspect the whole quality-diversity spectrum.

Likelihood: Although the likelihood of a generative model on real (test) data evaluates the ability of the model in generating the test samples, it doesn't measure the quality of the whole set of generated texts by the model. In fact, a model with a low NLL value on test data (or equivalently a model in which the likelihood of the test data is high) may also assign high probability to many other sentences that are not valid or qualified. Specifically for sequence models, the likelihood doesn't assess the free-running mode of models. To be more detailed, most of the probabilistic sequence models, decompose the joint distribution to conditional distributions using the chain rule. These conditional distributions are the probability of each token conditioned on the prior tokens. Thus, in the likelihood evaluation, each of token's probability is conditioned on a prefix that is a real sequence itself and the likelihood is not assessed on the previously generated tokens of the model during evaluation (it is similar to the exposure bias problem of MLE for sequence generation).

Moreover, measuring a model by its likelihood score has another problem. When a model misses one mode of a multi-modal distribution, its score decreases severely; so it is an unfair metric for comparing MLE method with other methods because MLE method uses likelihood as its objective and has mean seeking behavior (Goodfellow, 2017).

3.2 Proposed metrics

In this section, we propose metrics that simultaneously considers the quality and the diversity of the generated samples. To this end, we compare the real distribution of texts with the obtained distribution by the text generation model.

3.2.1 MS-Jaccard

We first propose a metric that finds the similarity of the generative model and the real distribution by comparing text samples generated by them. To this end, n-grams of generated samples and those of real samples are considered as two multi-sets (that also preserve repetition of n-grams) and the similarity of the resulted multi-sets is computed. In simple words, the MS-Jaccard focuses on the similarity of the n-grams frequencies in the two sets and inspired by the well-known Jaccard Index which determines the similarity of two sets as the ratio of the cardinality of their intersection to that of their union.

To define it formally, let S_1 and S_2 be two sets of sentences, G_n be the set of n-grams in $S_1 \cup S_2$, and $C_n(g, S)$ be the normalized counts of the n-gram g in the set S. The similarity between n-grams of two sets S_1 and S_2 is defined as:

$$score_n = \frac{\sum_{g \in G_n} min\{C_n(g, S_1), C_n(g, S_2)\}}{\sum_{g \in G_n} max\{C_n(g, S_1), C_n(g, S_2)\}}.$$

(1)

The geometric mean of the $\{score_n\}_{n=1}^{N}$ will be the MS-Jaccard score called MS-Jaccard-N where the N is the maximum length of n-grams. It is worth noting that the frequencies of the n-grams in each set is normalized with respect to the total number of sentences in the set (to avoid diminishing the score when the size of only one of these sets grows). Thus, the $C_n(g, S)$ will denotes the average frequency per sentence for n-gram g in the set S. If the generated sentences won't have diversity or quality, the n-gram distribution of generated texts will be different from that of the real texts and causing to decrease the MS-Jaccard score consequently. As it is obvious, the MS-Jaccard is a similarity measure and so its higher value will be better.

3.2.2 Fréchet BERT Distance (FBD)

One popular metric for evaluation of image generation models is FID introduced in (Heusel et al., 2017). Each of real and generated images in a feature space (found by Inception network) is modeled by a Gaussian distribution, and the FID is defined as the Fréchet distance between these two Gaussian distributions. We want to introduce a similar measure for the text generation task. To this end, we utilize BERT (Devlin et al., 2018) that provides a proper feature space for texts. We use Fréchet distance in BERT's feature space as a metric that considers quality and variety of generated sentences, and name it Fréchet BERT Distance (FBD). There is a set of pooled features (for classification task) in the BERT network that has a constant size for different input sequence lengths; we used these features for FBD. The Fréchet distance is also known as Wasserstein-2 divergence, and this distance between two Gaussian distribution is as follows:

$$\sqrt{||m_1 - m_2||_2^2 + Tr(C_1 + C_2 - 2(C_1 C_2)^{1/2})},$$

(2)

where m_i and C_i show the mean vector and the covariance matrix of these Gaussians respectively. It should be noted as the FBD is a distance measure, its lower values will be better.

3.2.3 Oracle Based Evaluation

In Oracle-NLL evaluation introduced in (Yu et al., 2017), the measured distance is Kullback–Leibler (KL) divergence of the generative model and the oracle which ignores the variety of generated sentences. On the other hand, the inverse KL (that is relevant to the likelihood of real data in the text generation model) can not guarantee the quality of generated samples by the model. We propose measuring the distance of the probabilistic oracle distribution P (that generates real data) and the probabilistic generative model Q by a symmetric distance as an evaluation metric. A wide range of distances can be utilized for this purpose. One symmetric distance is Bhattacharyya that can be estimated by the Monte-Carlo as below:

$$B(P, Q) =$$

$$\frac{-1}{2}\left(\ln \frac{1}{N} \sum_{i=0}^{N} \sqrt{\frac{q(x_i)}{p(x_i)}} + \ln \frac{1}{M} \sum_{j=0}^{M} \sqrt{\frac{p(x_j)}{q(x_j)}} \right),$$

(3)

where $\{x_i\}$ and $\{x_j\}$ are sets of samples from P and Q distributions respectively. Similar to the FBD, Bhattacharyya is also a distance measure and thus its lower values are better.

4 Evaluation

In this section, we first conduct some experiments to evaluate text generation models using the existing and the proposed measures. Then, we discuss about the appropriateness of the proposed metrics.

4.1 Datasets

We evaluate the models on COCO image captions (Lin et al., 2014), EMNLP2017 WMT News (Bojar et al., 2017), and IMDB (Maas et al., 2011) as the popular datasets for text generation. In addition to these datasets, similar to (Yu et al., 2017; Lin et al., 2017; Guo et al., 2018), we also consider a synthetic oracle produced by a probabilistic text generator that is a random initialized LSTM as a synthetic dataset. The description of the datasets is as follows:

- COCO Captions (Lin et al., 2014): It is a collection of image captions containing around 600,000 captions. Sentences having between 5 and 25 words are selected (resulting in 524,225 sentences) where 5,328 is the vocab size of the resulted dataset. Among the resulted dataset, 40,000 samples are used for training, 20,000 samples for validation, and 20,000 for test.

- EMNLP2017 WMT News (Bojar et al., 2017): It is a collection of news texts for the machine translations task [1]. Among a version of this dataset for English corpus containing 500,000 sentences, sentences having more than 3 words with less than 150 frequency (these words are replaced with UNK) were dropped and sentences that have between 20 and 40 words selected. The vocab size of the resulted dataset is 6,148. Among this dataset, 40,000 samples are used for training, 20,000 samples for validation, and 20,000 for test.

- IMDB Movie Reviews (Maas et al., 2011): It is a collection of IMDB movie reviews for the sentiment analysis task, containing 25,000 labeled and 50,000 unlabeled ones. We have selected the first two sentences of each review and replace words with less that 50 times frequency with UNK and keep sentences from length 5 to 40 with less than 5 UNKs. The final dataset is subsampled to have 20,000 sentences for training data, 10,000 for validation, and 10,000 for test data leading to vocab size of 5,810.

- Oracle synthetic dataset (Yu et al., 2017): A randomly initialized LSTM generator as a real distribution used in oracle training mode; the network implementation is borrowed from the SeqGAN released code[2]. This network's hidden size is 32 and its embedding size is 3,200. Moreover, the vocab size is 5,000 and the length of sequences is 20. The dataset of 100,000 samples are generated according to the above model. Among this dataset, 50,000 samples are used for training, 25,000 for validation, and 25,000 for test.

4.2 Experimental Setup

4.2.1 Text Generation Models

As the recent methods for text generation, we evaluate SeqGAN (Yu et al., 2017), RankGAN (Lin et al., 2017), and MaliGAN (Che et al., 2017). We also consider vanilla Maximum Likelihood Estimation (MLE) language model using LSTM as the baseline method. We used the implementation of the above methods in the Texygen platform (Zhu et al., 2018) and train them in this framework[3]. The models were trained on the similar dataset existing in their released code but collected from the original sites reported in corresponding reference papers.

In order to have a fair comparison, all settings of the models (e.g., same hidden) were kept the same as the Texygen framework. Since setting a fixed number of epochs for terminating training of different methods does not seem such reasonable and resulting in unfair scores, we targeted multiple training termination criteria. In the real-world datasets training, the training termination of the GANs were based on obtaining the best BLEU4 on validation data in addition to setting a max number of iterations for all the models. Besides, the training termination of MLE is based the NLL on the validation data while also setting a max number of iterations as above. In the oracle training mode, the termination were done based on both Oracle-NLL on the validation set and again on a max number of iterations for all models.

4.2.2 Metrics

Among the existing measures, BLEU2 upto BLEU5 (evaluating only quality), Self-BLUE2 upto Self-BLEU5 (evaluating only diversity), and NLL that shows the negative log likelihood of the model on test data are utilized for real datasets. Moreover, due to the low performance of the Python NLTK (Bird et al., 2009) BLEU library[4] when needing to evaluate multiple sentences with a fixed reference set, we have re-implemented it to achieve parallel computation and high performance [5].

Among the proposed measures, MS-Jaccard2 upto MS-Jaccard5 and FBD are assayed on real-world datasets. For synthetic oracle, NLL and Oracle-NLL as the existing measures and the proposed measure for comparing distributions, i.e. Bhattacharyya, are evaluated. It should be noted that, in order to make the metric's directions the same (i.e. their lower values show better performance), the $1-$MS-Jaccard, $1-$BLEU and $-1\times$Entropy is used in some plots.

---

[1] http://statmt.org/wmt17/translation-task.html
[2] https://github.com/LantaoYu/SeqGAN/

[3] https://github.com/geek-ai/Texygen
[4] https://www.nltk.org/_modules/nltk/
[5] https://github.com/Danial-Alh/FastBLEU

Table 1: Performance of models (using different measures) on *COCO Captions* dataset. MSJ, BL, and SBL denote MS-Jaccard, BLEU, and Self-BLEU respectively.

Method	NLL	FBD	MSJ2	MSJ3	MSJ4	MSJ5	BL2	BL3	BL4	BL5	SBL2	SBL3	SBL4	SBL5
Real Data	-	0.460	0.760	0.585	0.430	0.306	0.926	0.794	0.622	0.454	0.864	0.685	0.489	0.329
MLE	**38.416**	1.971	0.655	0.473	0.322	0.210	0.891	0.715	0.507	0.334	**0.849**	**0.644**	**0.425**	**0.268**
SeqGAN	55.610	4.590	0.301	0.229	0.164	0.111	0.904	0.771	**0.578**	**0.380**	0.941	0.842	0.700	0.545
MaliGAN	39.916	**1.474**	**0.671**	**0.495**	**0.345**	**0.231**	0.901	0.736	0.536	0.361	0.859	0.662	0.451	0.288
RankGAN	48.816	3.574	0.440	0.323	0.224	0.147	**0.927**	**0.782**	0.569	0.376	0.913	0.774	0.583	0.402

Table 2: Performance of models (using different measures) on *EMNLP2017 WMT News* dataset. MSJ, BL, and SBL denote MS-Jaccard, BLEU, and Self-BLEU respectively.

Method	NLL	FBD	MSJ2	MSJ3	MSJ4	MSJ5	BL2	BL3	BL4	BL5	SBL2	SBL3	SBL4	SBL5
Real Data	-	0.905	0.691	0.432	0.243	0.129	0.886	0.644	0.380	0.198	0.797	0.512	0.261	0.133
MLE	**143.246**	**4.827**	**0.585**	**0.334**	**0.164**	**0.071**	0.837	0.542	0.264	0.125	**0.777**	**0.452**	**0.196**	**0.095**
SeqGAN	195.867	5.955	0.231	0.138	0.071	0.031	0.476	0.358	0.200	0.105	0.906	0.729	0.507	0.324
MaliGAN	163.931	5.690	0.405	0.249	0.132	0.061	**0.856**	**0.595**	**0.314**	**0.141**	0.847	0.591	0.328	0.155
RankGAN	177.346	5.104	0.261	0.156	0.081	0.036	0.461	0.326	0.183	0.097	0.841	0.605	0.371	0.224

Table 3: Performance of models (using different measures) on *IMDB Movie Reviews* dataset. MSJ, BL, and SBL denote MS-Jaccard, BLEU, and Self-BLEU respectively.

Method	NLL	FBD	MSJ2	MSJ3	MSJ4	MSJ5	BL2	BL3	BL4	BL5	SBL2	SBL3	SBL4	SBL5
Real Data	-	0.683	0.696	0.469	0.296	0.181	0.889	0.691	0.468	0.286	0.853	0.629	0.405	0.241
MLE	**125.223**	**3.538**	**0.601**	**0.375**	**0.214**	**0.115**	0.860	0.620	0.368	0.198	**0.844**	**0.593**	**0.342**	**0.179**
SeqGAN	150.213	4.587	0.377	0.247	0.147	0.082	**0.903**	**0.695**	**0.434**	0.226	0.924	0.763	0.552	0.345
MaliGAN	141.558	4.482	0.446	0.294	0.178	0.103	0.878	0.662	0.424	**0.233**	0.889	0.695	0.480	0.290
RankGAN	151.828	3.958	0.354	0.227	0.132	0.070	0.900	0.693	0.432	0.228	0.909	0.739	0.527	0.331

Table 4: Performance of models (using different measures) on *Oracle* dataset.

Method	NLL	Oracle-NLL	Bhattacharyya
MLE	**141.948**	167.014	**7.105**
SeqGAN	155.353	**163.179**	10.076
MaliGAN	146.260	168.054	8.503
RankGAN	160.424	166.774	12.127

4.3 Results

Results of different methods on COCO Captions, EMNLP2017 WMT News, and IMDB datasets as real-world datasets are shown in Tables 1, 2, and 3, respectively. To provide a target, we have also shown metrics for training data themselves and called the method as *Real* (indeed training data is considered as the generated data by Real and the measures are computed on them). These tables show that MLE has the best performance according to the proposed measures considering both quality and diversity of samples. In fact, GAN-based methods can not generally achieve good performance according to the proposed measures. This result is consistent with the reported results in (Caccia et al., 2018) that compares GANs and MLE for text generation.

Table 4 shows results of different methods on synthetic oracle dataset and MLE again shows the best results according to the proposed metric (that approximates the distance of the real distribution and the generative model distribution).

As mentioned in Section 3.1.3 about (Caccia et al., 2018), the whole spectrum of quality-diversity is considered for evaluation of Natural Language Generation (NLG) methods. In fact, in (Caccia et al., 2018), the temperature sweep is utilized to robustly evaluate text generation methods. More precisely, the generators conditional distribution $G(x_t|x_{1:t-1})$ is defined as $Softmax(o_t/T)$ where o_t denotes the logit at time t. Decreasing T below 1.0 will decrease the entropy of conditional probability and thus reduce the probability of generating low quality samples. On the other hand, increasing this temperature above 1.0 will upraise the entropy of the conditional distribution and thus improve the diversity of the generated samples (Caccia et al., 2018).

We intend to show that the proposed metrics are correlated with the analysis of the whole space of quality-diversity obtained by changing the temperature. In fact, using the proposed metrics we can

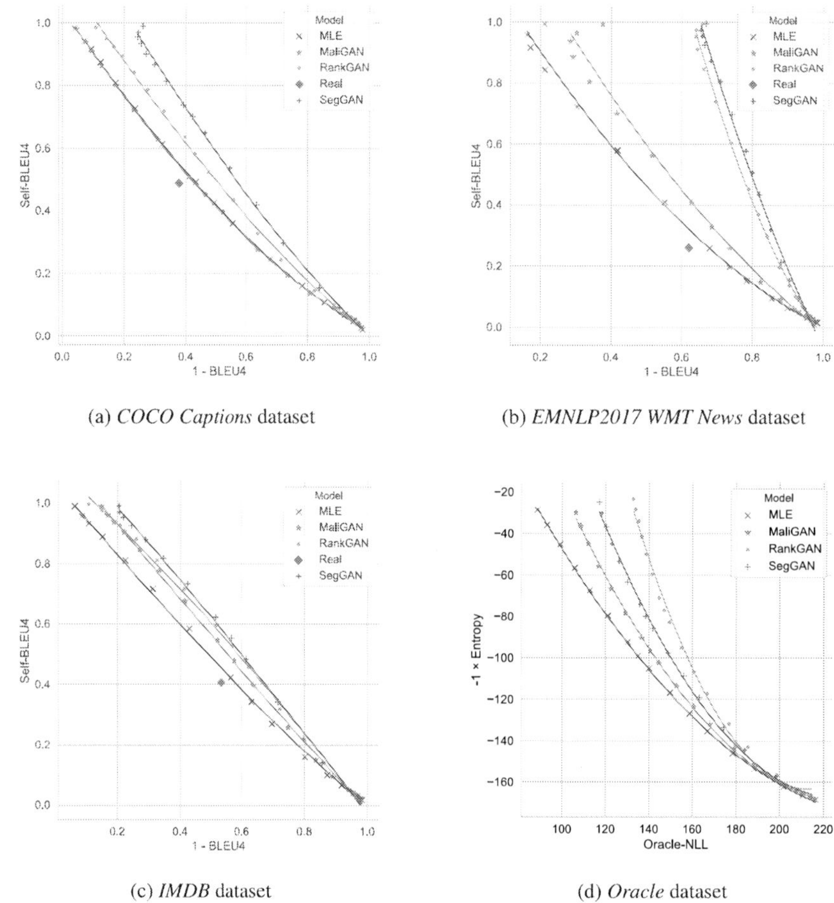

(a) *COCO Captions* dataset   (b) *EMNLP2017 WMT News* dataset

(c) *IMDB* dataset   (d) *Oracle* dataset

Figure 1: Diversity vs. quality measure of various models with temperatures from 1.5^{-3} to 1.5^4 on different datasets. Each point in the plot corresponds to the performance of a model in a special temperature (A second-degree polynomial has been fitted to the points). Lower values in both axes show better ones.

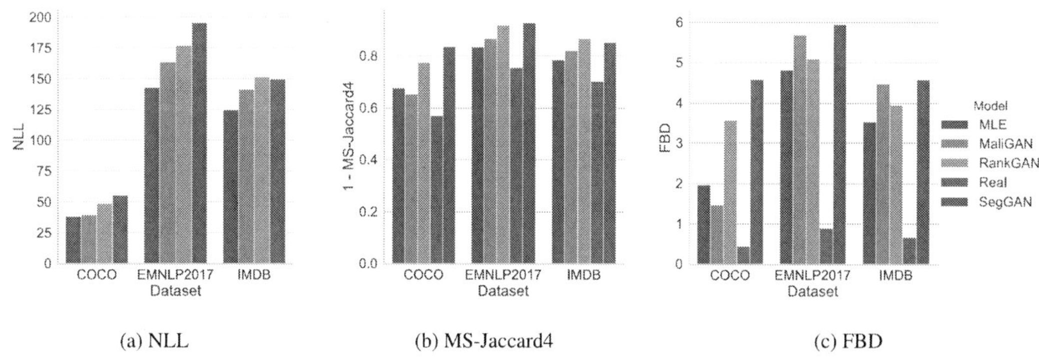

(a) NLL   (b) MS-Jaccard4   (c) FBD

Figure 2: NLL, $1-$MS-Jaccard4, and FBD scores of all the models without applying temperature (i.e. $T = 1$) on different datasets. Lower values show better performance.

usually predict the behavior of the model in whole spectrum without needing to provide this quality-diversity space.

Fig. 1 shows the diversity against quality measures with different values of temperature. Figs. 1a, 1b, and 1c consider Self-BLEU4 as diversity and BLEU4 as quality measure for each of the methods on real-world COCO, EMNLP2017,

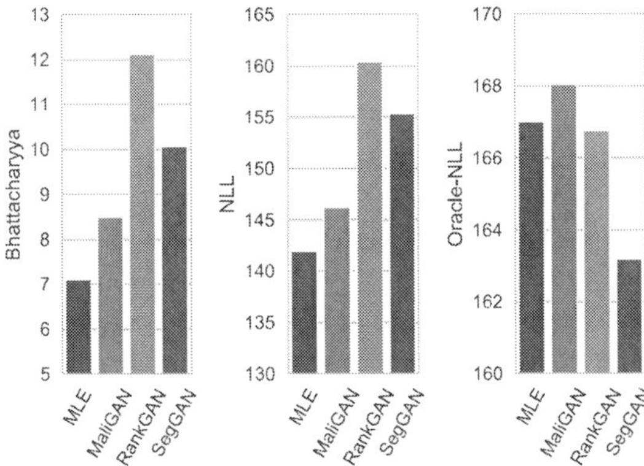

Figure 3: The performance of all models (without applying temperature, i.e. $T = 1$) on the Oracle dataset using different measures. Lower values show better performance.

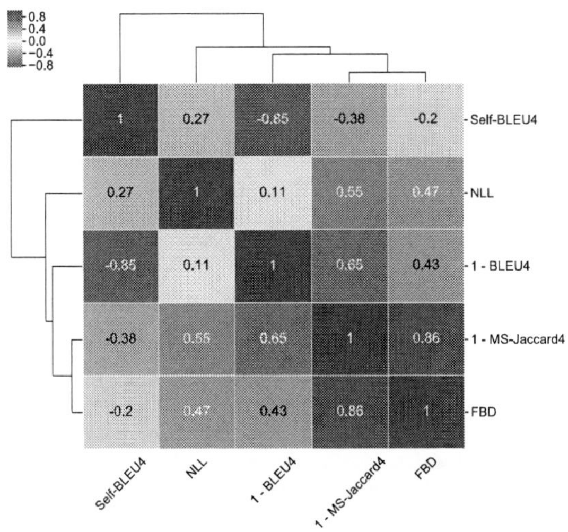

Figure 4: Pearson correlation of all metrics when aggregating results on the real world text datasets and all temperatures.

and IMDB datasets. The metrics are also evaluated on the train data itself which is called Real in the mentioned figures. Moreover, for Oracle dataset, since we have the probabilistic distribution of data, we can compute the likelihood of the generated samples by the model in the real distribution (i.e. Oracle) to find the quality of the generated samples. Therefore, the Oracle-NLL is used as quality measure of the methods on the synthetic dataset in Fig. 1d and Entropy is used as a diversity measure in this figure.

On the other hand, Figs. 2 and 3 present the performance of different methods (with $T = 1$) on non-synthetic and synthetic datasets respectively.

It is worth noting that NLL, Entropy, and Bhattacharyya of Real could not be computed, since we do not have a model for real data and just considering training data as its samples. According to Fig. 2b, the ordering of the methods obtained by MS-Jaccard4 on these datasets is almost always consistent with the ordering of the methods according to their dominance in Figs. 1a to 1c. For example, in Fig. 1b that shows results on EMNLP2017 dataset, the best method which dominates others is MLE, the second best is MaliGAN, the third one is RankGAN, and SeqGAN is the last one that under-performs all other methods. Consistently, the proposed MS-Jaccard4 measure shown in Fig. 2b provides the same ordering. Moreover, the ordering of the methods according to FBD metric in Fig. 2c on different datasets is almost always consistent with their ordering obtained by analyzing the whole spectrum in Figs. 1a to 1c. For the oracle dataset 3, the proposed Bhattacharyya distance of the distributions introduced in Section 3.2.3 is consistent with the ordering obtained in Fig. 1d.

Finally, we display the Pearson correlation of different metrics on real datasets in Fig. 4. According to this figure, the proposed metrics for real-world datasets, i.e. $1-$MS-Jaccard and FBD, are highly correlated. Besides, among the measures, these are the most correlated ones to NLL.

5 Conclusion

In this paper, we first discussed shortcomings of the existing measures for evaluating text generation models. Then, we proposed some measures to more effectively specify the capability of models in generating both qualified and diverse texts. The MS-Jaccard as an n-gram based metric was firstly introduced that is capable of measuring both the quality and coverage of methods in text generation. Then, a feature-based metric FBD which is based on the BERT model was introduced. Moreover, for oracle training mode in which the generators density can also be calculated, we proposed to use (estimation of) divergences like Bhattacharyya defined on probability distributions as a metric to compute the distance of the generative model and the oracle. Finally, the performance of different text generation models were evaluated, the obtained results were analyzed and showed that the proposed metrics have high correlations and are almost consistent with the dominance ordering of models in quality-diversity spectrum.

References

Samy Bengio, Oriol Vinyals, Navdeep Jaitly, and Noam Shazeer. 2015. Scheduled sampling for sequence prediction with recurrent neural networks. In *Advances in Neural Information Processing Systems 28: Annual Conference on Neural Information Processing Systems 2015, December 7-12, 2015, Montreal, Quebec, Canada*, pages 1171–1179.

Steven Bird, Ewan Klein, and Edward Loper. 2009. *Natural Language Processing with Python*. O'Reilly.

Ondrej Bojar, Rajen Chatterjee, Christian Federmann, Yvette Graham, Barry Haddow, Shujian Huang, Matthias Huck, Philipp Koehn, Qun Liu, Varvara Logacheva, Christof Monz, Matteo Negri, Matt Post, Raphael Rubino, Lucia Specia, and Marco Turchi. 2017. Findings of the 2017 conference on machine translation (WMT17). In *Proceedings of the Second Conference on Machine Translation, WMT 2017, Copenhagen, Denmark, September 7-8, 2017*, pages 169–214. Association for Computational Linguistics.

Massimo Caccia, Lucas Caccia, William Fedus, Hugo Larochelle, Joelle Pineau, and Laurent Charlin. 2018. Language gans falling short. *CoRR*, abs/1811.02549.

Tong Che, Yanran Li, Ruixiang Zhang, R. Devon Hjelm, Wenjie Li, Yangqiu Song, and Yoshua Bengio. 2017. Maximum-likelihood augmented discrete generative adversarial networks. *CoRR*, abs/1702.07983.

Jacob Devlin, Ming-Wei Chang, Kenton Lee, and Kristina Toutanova. 2018. Bert: Pre-training of deep bidirectional transformers for language understanding. *arXiv preprint arXiv:1810.04805*.

Ian J. Goodfellow. 2017. NIPS 2016 tutorial: Generative adversarial networks. *CoRR*, abs/1701.00160.

Ian J. Goodfellow, Jean Pouget-Abadie, Mehdi Mirza, Bing Xu, David Warde-Farley, Sherjil Ozair, Aaron C. Courville, and Yoshua Bengio. 2014. Generative adversarial networks. *CoRR*, abs/1406.2661.

Jiaxian Guo, Sidi Lu, Han Cai, Weinan Zhang, Yong Yu, and Jun Wang. 2018. Long text generation via adversarial training with leaked information. In *Proceedings of the Thirty-Second AAAI Conference on Artificial Intelligence, New Orleans, Louisiana, USA, February 2-7, 2018*. AAAI Press.

Martin Heusel, Hubert Ramsauer, Thomas Unterthiner, Bernhard Nessler, and Sepp Hochreiter. 2017. Gans trained by a two time-scale update rule converge to a local nash equilibrium. In *Advances in Neural Information Processing Systems*, pages 6626–6637.

Sepp Hochreiter and Jürgen Schmidhuber. 1997. Long short-term memory. *Neural Computation*, 9(8):1735–1780.

Ferenc Huszar. 2015. How (not) to train your generative model: Scheduled sampling, likelihood, adversary? *CoRR*, abs/1511.05101.

Kevin Lin, Dianqi Li, Xiaodong He, Ming-Ting Sun, and Zhengyou Zhang. 2017. Adversarial ranking for language generation. In *Advances in Neural Information Processing Systems 30: Annual Conference on Neural Information Processing Systems 2017, 4-9 December 2017, Long Beach, CA, USA*, pages 3158–3168.

Tsung-Yi Lin, Michael Maire, Serge J. Belongie, James Hays, Pietro Perona, Deva Ramanan, Piotr Dollár, and C. Lawrence Zitnick. 2014. Microsoft COCO: common objects in context. In *Computer Vision - ECCV 2014 - 13th European Conference, Zurich, Switzerland, September 6-12, 2014, Proceedings, Part V*, volume 8693 of *Lecture Notes in Computer Science*, pages 740–755. Springer.

Andrew L. Maas, Raymond E. Daly, Peter T. Pham, Dan Huang, Andrew Y. Ng, and Christopher Potts. 2011. Learning word vectors for sentiment analysis. In *The 49th Annual Meeting of the Association for Computational Linguistics: Human Language Technologies, Proceedings of the Conference, 19-24 June, 2011, Portland, Oregon, USA*, pages 142–150. The Association for Computer Linguistics.

Luke Metz, Ben Poole, David Pfau, and Jascha Sohl-Dickstein. 2016. Unrolled generative adversarial networks. *CoRR*, abs/1611.02163.

Kishore Papineni, Salim Roukos, Todd Ward, and Wei-Jing Zhu. 2002. Bleu: a method for automatic evaluation of machine translation. In *Proceedings of the 40th Annual Meeting of the Association for Computational Linguistics, July 6-12, 2002, Philadelphia, PA, USA.*, pages 311–318. ACL.

Lantao Yu, Weinan Zhang, Jun Wang, and Yong Yu. 2017. Seqgan: Sequence generative adversarial nets with policy gradient. In *Proceedings of the Thirty-First AAAI Conference on Artificial Intelligence, February 4-9, 2017, San Francisco, California, USA.*, pages 2852–2858. AAAI Press.

Yizhe Zhang, Zhe Gan, Kai Fan, Zhi Chen, Ricardo Henao, Dinghan Shen, and Lawrence Carin. 2017. Adversarial feature matching for text generation. In *Proceedings of the 34th International Conference on Machine Learning, ICML 2017, Sydney, NSW, Australia, 6-11 August 2017*, volume 70 of *Proceedings of Machine Learning Research*, pages 4006–4015. PMLR.

Yaoming Zhu, Sidi Lu, Lei Zheng, Jiaxian Guo, Weinan Zhang, Jun Wang, and Yong Yu. 2018. Texygen: A benchmarking platform for text generation models. *SIGIR*.